Desktop Publishing
with PageMaker

For the Macintosh

Tony Bove
Cheryl Rhodes

John Wiley & Sons, Inc.

New York • Chichester • Brisbane • Toronto • Singapore

Publisher: Stephen Kippur
Editor: Therese A. Zak
Managing Editor: Andrew B. Hoffer

88T003367

Figures 1-1, 1-2, and 1-3 on pp. 4, 5, and 6 are courtesy of Apple Computer, Inc.

Library of Congress Cataloging in Publication Data

Bove, Tony
  Desktop Publishing with PageMaker

ISBN 0-471-62618-X
ISBN 047185994x (cover)
Printed in the United States of America

87 88 10 9 8 7 6 5 4 3 2 1

Trademarks

Related Titles of Interest From John Wiley & Sons

ASSEMBLY LANGUAGE PROGRAMMING FOR THE 68000 FAMILY, Skinner

EXCEL: A POWER USER'S GUIDE, Hodgkins

JAZZ AT WORK, Venit & Burns

MACINTOSH LOGO, Haigh & Radford

SCIENTIFIC PROGRAMMING WITH MAC PASCAL, Crandall

DESKTOP PUBLISHING WITH PAGEMAKER: IBM PC AT, PS/2, AND COMPATIBLES, Bove & Rhodes

VENTURA PUBLISHER FOR THE IBM PC: MASTERING DESKTOP PUBLISHING, Jantz

Acknowledgements

We would like to thank the following people for their support:

Carolyn Bakamis, Paul Brainerd, Colleen Byrum, Karen Howe, Jeremy Jaech, Mike Solomon, and Julie Larson (Aldus), Keri Walker and Martha Steffen (Apple), Lenny Schafer and ImageSet (San Francisco, CA), Laurie McLean (McLean PR), Marty Taucher (Microsoft), Steve Edelman, John Duhring, and Tom Reilly (SuperMac Technology), Bill Gladstone (Waterside Productions), Sanjay and Krishna Copy (San Francisco, CA), PageWorks (Cambridge, MA) Troy Soult, and Paul Winternitz.

Dedicated to our parents and families.

Contents

Preface

This book provides a step-by-step approach to setting up templates for typical office documents, technical manuals, marketing literature, books, newsletters, and magazines. It assumes only a basic knowledge of word processing, so that anyone with a need to publish documents (but without the training in page makeup or production) can use the book to produce these documents.

Each chapter introduces a different type of publication. We also introduce the most basic concepts of design and typography. The intent is not to bog you down in details, but to show you some of the tried and true elements of good design. In some cases we use examples of real publications, and in others we use simulated publications.

Here's a breakdown of the chapters and what you can expect to find in them:

Chapter One: Preparing for Desktop Publishing

The first chapter provides a brief description of the desktop publishing process, including word processing, graphics creation, text and graphics scanning, page makeup, laser printing, and typesetting. This chapter also explains in detail why certain word processing and graphics programs are better than others for working in conjunction with PageMaker. It also recommends spelling checkers and thesauri, various utility programs, and other programs that generate or manage information to be published (mailing lists and other data bases, spreadsheets, business charts and graphs). The chapter concludes with descriptions of the similarities and differences between the various laser printers, scanners, typesetters, and other output devices that work with PageMaker.

Chapter Two: A Newsletter

This chapter takes you step by step through the process of producing a four-page newsletter, from starting PageMaker and designing a template from scratch (or starting with an already-designed template), to producing and printing an intelligent-looking newsletter. The instructions are suitable for starting up any design and production effort and serve as a basis for understanding techniques used in subsequent chapters. It can also serve as an impatient user's tutorial, since it covers nearly everything PageMaker can do.

Some highlights are step-by-step instructions on creating a newsletter title, using graphics with text, scaling and cropping graphics, sizing and resizing text, changing type styles, placing formatted and unformatted text files, changing column widths, changing the entire layout, and setting up automatic page numbers.

Chapter Three: Business Reports and Manuals

In this chapter, you learn how to put together a company annual report featuring spreadsheets, charts and graphs, the company logo on the cover, and a designed interior. Special design effects include head and subhead treatments, adjusting word spacing to fix any widows or orphans, wrapping text around images, and working with halftones and scanned images. Spreadsheets and graphs are enhanced with boxes and drop shadow effects.

The chapter then applies what you have learned so far to produce a typical technical manual and book. It also explains how to set up master style sheets for corporate users, so that all documents will have the same corporate look (using the same graphic elements, logo, etc.). Using master pages and stylesheets allows your group to work efficiently, sharing master page designs and graphic elements.

Chapter Four: Advanced Design

This chapter offers techniques for customizing pages and adding design touches and special effects. You learn how to mix column layouts, wrap text around graphics, spread headlines and titles, control word spacing and letterspacing, do manual as well as automatic kerning, and use special effects such as enlarged initial capitals, reverse type, boxes, rules, and borders.

The examples include a book about whales (see Bibliography) that was designed and produced with PageMaker and many other examples of advanced magazine, newsletter, manual, and book pages. You will also learn how to prepare electronic pages with separate color overlays for handling spot color and four-color separations.

Chapter Five: Tips and Techniques

This chapter is a summary of the tips and techniques that can shorten your production time and keep you from constantly referring to manuals (although the Aldus manuals are quite good — you should read them!). You could use this chapter as an impatient user's summary, together with the laminated *PageMaker Quick Reference Guide* from Aldus.

Appendixes

The appendixes include instructions on using word processing programs and painting and drawing programs with PageMaker, a list of special characters that can be produced, and hints on transferring files between PCs and Macintoshes. Appendix E is a bibliography, and the book concludes with an index.

How We Produced This Book

This book has been fun to produce, thanks to PageMaker. The entire book was written and edited on several Macintosh computers (512K and 512KE Macintoshes, a Macintosh Plus, SE and II), placed onto Page-Maker pages, and printed first on an Apple LaserWriter and then on an Allied Linotype Linotronic 100 typesetter (both PostScript devices).

Our examples were prepared by taking electronic snapshots of the screen (using Command Shift 3), then editing the images with MacPaint, before placing the images onto PageMaker pages, where we used PageMaker's automatic scaling feature (Aldus calls it "magic stretch") to select a size optimized for our final printer. We used Microsoft Word (both on Macintosh computers and PC AT computers), MacWrite, and WriteNow for the Macintosh to prepare text files, and Word to produce the index for this book. Figure captions were first created as footnotes in the Word text files, then all footnotes were copied to a separate figure caption text file for ease of placement onto PageMaker pages. After placing all the Word and WriteNow text files onto PageMaker pages, we exported the Word and WriteNow files to include last-minute changes (made in PageMaker) and PageMaker page breaks, as well as index entries and the table of contents entries. Word generated the index and table of contents from the text files, and we placed the index and table of contents onto PageMaker pages.

This book is an example of what can be accomplished, in a relatively short time and with little cost, using a desktop publishing system and PageMaker.

Aldus Manutius, the "patron saint" of publishing, would be proud of Aldus Corporation for its efforts to advance the state of the art.

Tony Bove and Cheryl Rhodes
Woodside, California

Introduction

Talk of nothing but business, and dispatch that business quickly.
— Aldus Manutius (placard on the door of the
Aldine Press, Venice, established about 1490).

What do Northwestern Mutual Life Insurance, 3Com Corporation, the U.S. Congress, Hesston Corporation, Lawrence Livermore Laboratory, RTE Deltec Corporation, and the Queen Elizabeth II have in common? These organizations currently use PageMaker to produce publications. Hundreds of small- and medium-sized commercial publishers use Page-Maker (which is to be expected), but it is significant that companies that are not commercial publishers are doing desktop publishing.

Many people are involved with publishing, whether or not they see themselves as publishers. If you are producing sales literature, marketing brochures, flyers, newsletters, advertisements, operating manuals, or other business communications, you may be able to save time and money — and have a great deal of control over the production process — if you use a desktop publishing system. A page makeup program such as Aldus's PageMaker plays the central role in any desktop publishing system.

For example, Northwestern Mutual switched from conventional methods of production to PageMaker for an in-house technical newsletter and cut the production time in half; the company also found PageMaker useful for producing advertising flyers and transparencies for speeches.

3Com Corporation, Lawrence Livermore Laboratory, and Hesston Corporation all use PageMaker to produce large manuals. Livermore Lab also uses PageMaker to produce research reports and papers for publication in scientific journals, and Hesston uses PageMaker to produce parts catalogs, department forms, and other instructional material.

The Queen Elizabeth II uses PageMaker to produce a daily world news bulletin. The news pages are put together into a PageMaker publication file in London, then transmitted by satellite to the luxury liner where a laser printer is used to print 1,200 copies for the ship's passengers.

Newspapers such as *The State Journal* (Charleston, West Virginia), *Behind the Times* (Corinth, Vermont), and *Roll Call* (weekly newspaper for the U.S. Congress), and magazines such as *Publish!, Personal Publishing, Chartering Magazine, American Demographics* and *Balloon Life* use PageMaker because the desktop publishing equipment shortens the production cycle and saves money.

Graphics experts and consultants can now focus on the design task and perform that work much more quickly and inexpensively with desktop publishing equipment, or let their clients do their own production work. Small publishers have the ability to produce commercial publications that have the same quality look and feel as publications from the large publishers. Corporations can cut down on the cost of designing forms, brochures, and marketing literature, and technical publications departments can produce manuals and data sheets very quickly.

The desktop publishing phenomenon started when laser printers, offering near-typeset-quality text and graphics printing, were introduced to work with personal computers. As a result, inexpensive publishing tools became available, which made it easier for people to do publishing production tasks without resorting to typesetting services and graphic design houses.

Desktop publishing tools grew to become useful for commercial and corporate publishing when they were made compatible with typesetters and higher-resolution devices (such as film recorders and plate makers). The industrywide acceptance of a common language of typesetting, called PostScript (developed by Adobe Systems and used in printers first by Apple, and then by Digital Equipment Corporation, Texas Instruments, Wang, IBM, and other companies) made it possible for desktop publishing software to produce typeset-quality text and high-quality photographs.

A page makeup program plays a central role in a desktop publishing system and is used as a finishing tool for preparing text and graphics for presentation and publication. You would use a word processing program and a graphics program to create the text and graphics, then a page makeup program to bring the elements together on a page. The page makeup program lets you adjust the design of the page at the same time that you are placing the elements, and this electronic pasteup offers many benefits over conventional manual pasteup and design methods. Because the electronic elements can be easily moved, cut, copied, resized, edited, and repasted on the page, your elements do not get lost, there are no cut marks where an exacto knife has slipped, and you do not have to wait for images or type to be reproduced at a new size, or for new typesetting to replace a misspelled word found in a typeset galley.

PageMaker is the quintessential desktop publishing program because it simulates the procedures that artists and designers use in conventional page makeup. Text and graphic images are pasted onto an electronic page and cropped with an electronic "knife." Master page elements are created and duplicated automatically for all or some of the pages. Blocks of text can be moved on the page to fit around graphics. Columns of text are linked so that changes made to a column cause a ripple of reformatting to occur. You can experiment with minor editing changes to shorten or lengthen a block of text, or change the size of the text block itself.

With this paradigm in action on the screen, designers, artists, and graphics-oriented people can feel the power of the computer and relate immediately to its use in desktop publishing. The metaphor of text threading is very close to the physical task of threading typeset galleys through a layout. Designers and graphic artists have no trouble under-standing how PageMaker works; the precision of its rulers and various page displays make it very easy to line things up (without need for a T-square and a fluorescent light table).

The paradigm works with beginners as well, providing a real-world model for the activity of mixing text and graphics on pages. Coupled with a Macintosh computer, which provides a graphical interface and handles file and disk management as well as program execution, PageMaker fits neatly into the desktop environment and is therefore easy to learn. The "menus" from which you select options look just like the "menus" in other

Macintosh applications, although menu titles (and commands and options) may differ from one application to another.

The Macintosh version of PageMaker has been used for many applications, such as magazines and books, even though it was really designed for newsletters. We used it to produce a magazine *(Desktop Publishing, now called Publish!)*. Other magazine publishers worked around its limitations to use PageMaker for production. Writers and editors used it for 300-page books and manuals, even though the early versions had a limitation of 16 pages per publication file. Designers used it to produce tabloids and oversized brochures and flyers, even though the program supported only A4, 8 1/2- by 11-inch, and 8 1/2- by 14-inch pages on the LaserWriter. For a page wider than 8 1/2 inches, PageMaker's tiling techniques allow the printing of tabloid size pages in sections, and you could then paste the pieces together to match up the elements. If you use a typesetter such as the Linotronic 100 or 300 imagesetter, or a printer such as the DataProducts LZR 2665, all of which support a larger paper size (11 by 17 inches), then you can print the tabloid page in one piece without tiling.

The latest versions of PageMaker (for the Macintosh and the PC) are revised in accordance with customer feedback. The features added to PageMaker were in response to the claim that PageMaker did not have enough typographic refinements for producing commercial-quality publications.

Aldus added automatic pair kerning (as supported by the different font manufacturers) and manual kerning, as well as automatic letter and word spacing (for justified text only). (If you run version 2.0 of PageMaker on a 512K Macintosh that has not been upgraded to a 512KE, your screen won't be able to display accurate letter and word spacing, nor will kerning display correctly, but the file will print correctly, with the values you specified for these settings.) PageMaker now offers paragraph spacing, typographic fixed spaces, leader tabs, additional line styles, the ability to size and resize columns at will, and hand-scrolling of an image within the space reserved for it on the page. The program also offers automatic hyphenation based on a 110,000-word dictionary from Houghton Mifflin as well as an up to 1,300-word supplementary dictionary, prompted hyphenation (the program displays words not found in the dictionaries and lets you hyphenate them, and if desired add them to the supplementary dictionary), and manual hyphenation (discretionary hyphens).

Aldus also added Export filters for Microsoft Word and T/Maker's WriteNow to PageMaker 2.0a, and more filters are being developed by Aldus and other vendors, to export other formats. You can even convert PageMaker publications created with version 1.2 to use them with version 2.0. Publications created with the 1.0a (PC) version of PageMaker can also be converted and used with version 2.0a of PageMaker for the Macintosh. Perhaps most valuable is the automatic mini-save of your file that PageMaker performs whenever you turn the page, or click the icon for the current page. In the event of a power failure, it is not likely that much work will be lost. Saving a publication file is also considerably faster than using version 1.2.

With these features, Aldus improved PageMaker so much that it is now an excellent tool for producing commercial publications as well as newsletters and marketing literature. The program is now capable of producing so many different publications that entire books about using PageMaker (like this one) are needed.

Will desktop publishing foster a renaissance in the printed word and image? Some believe that poorly designed results from desktop publishing will prove that publishing should be left to the experts who have design skills. However, the enthusiasm for desktop publishing is infectious, and people can learn design skills by reading books, consulting with experts, and taking design courses.

In an era when automation is making information workers more productive, the ability to self-publish is a valuable asset for the smallest communications service company to the largest corporation, from the individual writer to working partnerships and clinics. If you can present the information in a professional style and publish it for your customers without incurring variable costs or costly delays, you are using desktop publishing for what it was intended: to make you more productive in your business.

1 | Preparing for Desktop Publishing

To produce a publication, even a very small one, you invariably have to go through the major steps of (1) designing the publication, (2) creating the text, photographs, and graphics, (3) making up the pages by combining the text, photos, and graphics with design elements, and (4) using a prepress shop or print shop to prepare film negatives, from which plates for the pages are made. The plates are then used with a printing press.

The goal of desktop publishing is to automate as many of the repetitive tasks in the production cycle as possible. A major advantage of desktop publishing is greater flexibility in design and layout, with changes not only possible, but easy to accommodate, right up to printing time. Page design can be easily performed on personal computers, and sample pages printed with laser printers. Comments and editing changes are more easily incorporated when the manuscript is stored in electronic form. Line art can be precise and revisable in electronic form, and electronic page makeup is faster and more revisable than manual paste-up.

Text and graphics should be in electronic form as early in the process as possible, either by *creating* them electronically with a personal computer [or mainframe, portable computer, etc., and storing them in files on disks (the most popular storage method), tapes, etc.], or by *converting* the information into electronic form — retyping, redrawing, or using a scanner, to capture the text and graphics in an electronic file. You can scan pages of typewritten text and hand-drawn line art very easily with a desktop scanner that costs under $4000 (and perhaps as low as $400).

Perhaps the greatest benefit of storing the elements in electronic form, however, is that the text can be sent to a typesetting machine without retyping, and graphics can be included with the text without manual paste-up. The PageMaker screen closely displays the same image you can expect on paper, so carefully check the screen for any errors, before printing. Once you have finished making all the changes you want, entire pages can roll out of the typesetting machine or laser printer, with no need for further mechanical processes (wax, glue, etc.) to be used as camera copy for volume printing.

If you're new to publishing or production work, you may be surprised to find that there are so many steps to climb before you reach the finished, published work. At the top of the stairs is the volume printing process — the method by which you will print mass quantities of the publication.

Even if you need only 10 copies, you must start with an idea of what the final printing process will entail. Will you use a copier or laser printer to produce 10 or 20 copies? Will you need over 200 but less than 500 copies? Over 1000? Over 10,000? You must answer this basic question first, then plan the publication's production effort.

For example, a newsletter or business report may require a clean, polished look, but since it is inexpensively printed in small quantities (under 500), it does not require the extra expense of production on a 1000 dots-per-inch (dpi) typesetter — a laser printer could do the job. For these applications, you can use almost any desktop laser printer (at 300 dpi) and not worry about compatibility with a typesetter.

On the other hand, a book, magazine, piece of marketing literature (such as a page advertisement, flyer, or brochure), or instruction manual might require typeset-quality text and photographic-quality images. For such production efforts, compatibility with a typesetter could be critical. The surest way to maintain compatibility between your laser printer and higher-resolution typesetters is to use a PostScript-compatible laser printer. PostScript is the most popular page description language used in both printers and typesetters as well as in high-resolution film recorders and display systems.

For some of you, a desktop publishing system needs to have both the speed of laser printing and flexibility and compatibility with typesetters. PageMaker offers the best of both worlds because it supports PostScript typesetters and laser printers. You can proof your file on a laser printer, then provide your file on disk (or via modem) to a typesetting service bureau to produce final typeset pages.

Consider also the type of system you will use: Are all the pieces available now; is retraining necessary; and can you purchase enough systems to handle the project? Will the same computer be used for writing, editing, creating graphics, and composing pages? How much time should you leave for volume printing? All of these factors will contribute to deciding a timetable for production efforts.

Learning the System

If you and your production staff have no experience with Macintosh computers, you should set aside time to become familiar with them. To run PageMaker 2.0 on the preferred Macintosh setup, choose an Apple Macintosh Plus (shown in Figure 1-1), SE (Figure 1-2) or II (Figure 1-3) with a hard disk drive. PageMaker also works on the older Macintosh 512K and 512K Enhanced (also called 512KE), but these systems must be configured properly. Running PageMaker 2.0 on a Macintosh 512K requires a hard disk drive with at least 1.5MB of space available, but the biggest problem is the older 64K ROMs in Mac 512Ks, which use fixed character widths (actually screen character widths) instead of the fractional character widths (actually printer character widths) used in the newer 128K ROMs. The character width tables stored in the ROMs determine kerning and letter spacing values. Thus a Macintosh 512K will not be able to properly control kerning and letter spacing. Upgrade your 512K Macintosh to a 512K Enhanced or use a newer model Macintosh, if you need maximum control over the space between characters (kerning) and words (letter spacing).

PageMaker runs on a Macintosh 512K Enhanced or a Macintosh Plus with only two 800K floppy disk drives, but if you are serious about publishing, you'll want to add a hard disk to your system. When should

Figure 1-1. The Macintosh Plus.

you add a hard disk? If you plan to mix text and many bit-mapped images, or produce multiple-page publications, and especially if you plan to incorporate 8 1/2- by 11-inch scanned bit-mapped images, you gain faster program interaction and additional work space by adding a hard disk to your system. If you want immediate access to all of your files, a 20MB hard disk might be enough, but a 40MB hard disk would be better if you

Figure 1-2. The Macintosh SE with an internal hard disk.

work with many images. If you plan to use PageMaker in a dedicated network and share a hard disk with other users, you will want to use a much larger hard disk. A distributed or background network might be a better choice, with 20MB or 40MB hard disk drives for each user.

We used a Macintosh Plus, an SE, a II, and a 512K Enhanced to write and produce this book. (Our Apple dealer upgraded our 512K Macintosh to a Macintosh 512KE with new ROMs, new keyboard, and a new 800K internal drive.) To produce the final camera-ready pages of the book, we proofed the pages on the Apple LaserWriter Plus, and typeset the final pages on the Linotype Company's Linotronic 100 typesetter.

If you are familiar with the Macintosh Finder and System (operating system), you already know how to format disks, copy or delete disk files,

Figure 1-3. The Macintosh II with an internal hard disk.

add or remove printers and other devices, print files, and run programs. The Macintosh Finder lets you use the operating system without typing specific commands. You can format disks, copy or delete files, add or remove printer control software, print files, and run programs — in short, you can do everything the operating system lets you do, but without having to learn commands. You operate a Macintosh by pulling down menus with a mouse and choosing commands, options, and file names.

We recommend you visit a computer store and run the Guided Tour disk (created by Macromind and Apple) supplied with the Macintosh SE if you have never before used a Macintosh. If you have used a PC or compatible with MS-DOS or PC-DOS, the difference between using the Macintosh with its graphical interface and the PC with its text-based interface is striking. You may have so much fun using a Macintosh that you might not consider operating a Macintosh work. It may even prove to be a more efficient way to work. Once you learn the basics, you can quickly learn any new program you encounter because you can apply what you know. The Macintosh user interface provides basic actions that are the same from one well-designed program to another.

The system software controls any devices (printers, scanners, disk drives, etc.) connected to your computer. The system is constantly being updated (to fix bugs, add enhancements, and improve speed), and updates are available from your Apple dealer. (Future updates planned for the system will let you start more than one application in separate windows.)

Some applications programs also include the latest version of the System and Finder files. For example, PageMaker 2.0a is supplied with System version 4.1. PageMaker does not require use of System 4.1; it also works with earlier versions of the System. Your System (and Finder) software could be one of several versions if it has never been updated. If you are using the Macintosh 512K, you should use version 3.2 of the System instead of System 4.1, as PageMaker is very slow with 4.1 on a 512K Macintosh. However, if you are using a Macintosh Plus, SE, or II, you should use System 4.1 and Finder 5.5.

You can install new system software whenever you wish to, but you should first make a copy of the old system for use with some older programs that may not yet be updated to work with the new system, and to preserve whatever fonts and desk accessories (DAs) you may have installed to customize your system. After you have created the backup copy of the old system, you can install a new system, then use the new DA/ Font Mover (Figure 1-4) to copy your fonts and DAs to the new system.

When you run PageMaker (or any other program) by double-clicking its icon, the application occupies a window on the display (Figure 1-5). The Apple menu always appears in the menu bar, at the top left corner of your screen, and contains DAs and control switches which you should be familiar with, because they should work from within all your applications. The rest of the titles in the menu bar are specific to each application

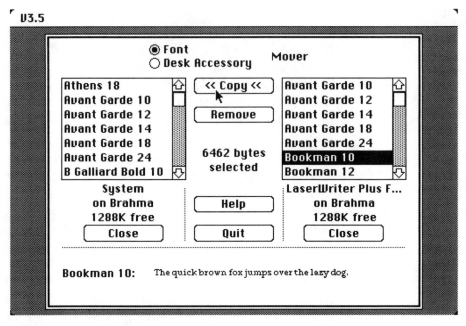

Figure 1-4. The Macintosh comes with the Font/DA Mover utility that lets you install fonts and desk accessories in your System file.

program you use (these menus can be different for each program).

To use PageMaker and other Macintosh applications, you must become familiar with the mouse. All of PageMaker's functions can be used with a single-button mouse or trackball and keyboard. (In addition, the Macintosh SE and Macintosh II have special connectors that allow other pointing devices to be used, instead of a mouse and keyboard.)

There are basically six actions to perform with a mouse (or other pointing device):

Point. When you move the mouse, a pointer moves across the display that has either a wristwatch (the hands on the watch move in newer versions of the ROMs and System) when the Macintosh is busy or an arrow (called the pointer), or when positioned over text you can edit, the arrow changes to an I-beam. Some application programs give you toolboxes to change the pointer into a crosshair (or something similar), to draw lines, or polygons, or other pointers for other tools supplied by that

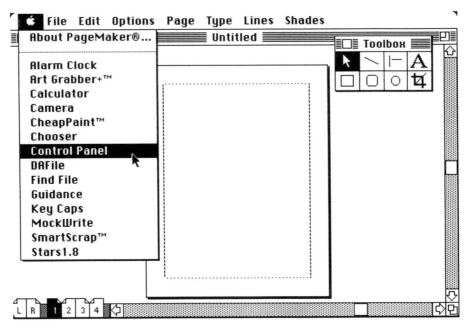

Figure 1-5. A Macintosh application starts as a window with a menu bar containing drop-down menus (including the system menu shown with the Apple logo).

program. The pointer shapes are used by other programs that offer similar tools.

You point by moving the tip of the pointer to the desired area on the display. Use the Control Panel desk accessory (Figure 1-6) in the Apple system menu to set the mouse tracking speed. Newer versions of the system software offer more choices of speed settings than the older versions offered.

Click. You click something by quickly pressing and immediately releasing the mouse button. You click to select an icon, text, or a button (such as OK), which is then highlighted (it turns black when selected).

Double-click. You double-click something by quickly pressing and immediately releasing the mouse button twice. Use the Control Panel in the Apple menu to set the double click speed.

Drag. You drag something (such as a graphic object, block of text, or icon) by pointing the mouse, holding down the mouse button, and moving

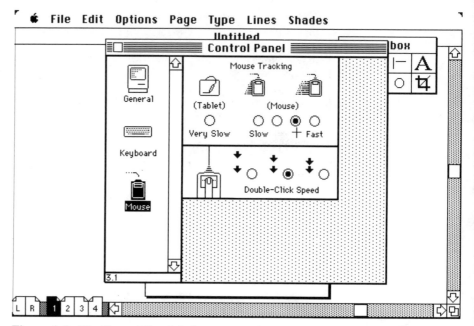

Figure 1-6. The Control Panel desk accessory lets you set the mouse tracking speed as well as other settings for the system.

the mouse so that the pointer (or object) moves to a new position, then releasing the button.

Select. To select a menu option or command, drag down a menu (which drops down to show you the options or commands) until the command or option you want is highlighted (selected), then release the mouse button. To select text, shift-click or double-click a word or drag across one or more words or paragraphs.

Flow (or Place). This is a PageMaker variation of Click, in which you point and click a text placement icon, which "pours" the text down the column.

Drag-Place. You drag-place an icon for a graphic object or block of text by pointing the mouse to a starting position (top left corner), then holding down the mouse button while moving the mouse so that the pointer (or object) moves to a new position (the bottom right corner of a box that displays as you drag with the mouse button depressed), then

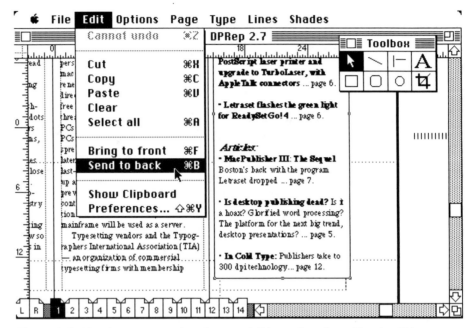

Figure 1-7. The Selected box (handles are visible on the selected box) will be sent behind the text by the Send to back command when the mouse button is released.

releasing the button. The box disappears and the text or image fills the defined area after you release the mouse button.

PageMaker employs familiar Macintosh drop-down menus, and subsequent dialog boxes after you select a command or option. When you position the pointer on a menu title in the menu bar and hold down the mouse button, a menu drops down; release the mouse button and the menu disappears. Drag the mouse down the menu to the desired command (it turns black when selected), and let go of the mouse button to activate the command. Some commands (such as Send to back and Paste) are immediately applied to any selected object or text (Figure 1-7), while other commands (such as Print and Type specs) first present a dialog box. In the dialog boxes you can select items (called options) by clicking boxes or buttons displayed on the screen, and sometimes there are scroll bars (Figure 1-8) for scrolling items in a small window. To operate the scroll bar click in the gray area above or below the white box, click the up or

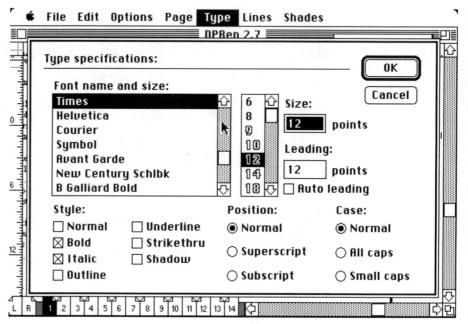

Figure 1-8. Select Type specs from the Type menu for this dialog box, type in numbers to specify the leading, and scroll to select a point size and font name.

down arrow, or drag the white box up or down. Dialog boxes often have text boxes for typing numbers or text, and every dialog box includes an OK or Cancel button.

In addition to the top box that displays the current folder or disk, dialog boxes also contain a list of file names and folders (analogous to MS-DOS directory names) stored in that folder or disk. A folder is represented by a folder icon, and, like a directory, is an area of the disk that contains files and more folders (which contain more files and folders, etc.). You won't run out of folders, and you can easily nest folders within folders, create new folders, and copy files into or out of folders, to keep your lists of files short and well-organized. Use folders to hold related files, and to organize your files in a way that is best for you. You can easily change the organization (from the desktop) at any time.

To select a file from any dialog box, click its name in the dialog box (Figure 1-9) and click Open, or double-click its name. If you do not see

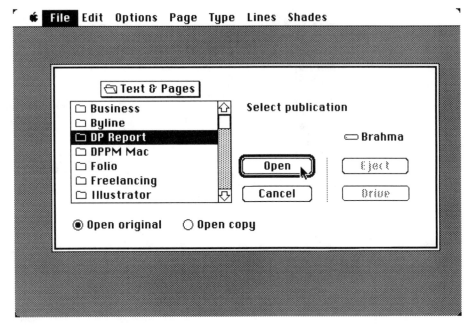

Figure 1-9. A dialog box with file names and a selected folder, which contains more files, about to be opened using the Open button.

the file you want, and there are folders in the list, double-click a folder name to be presented with the list of files within that folder. The dialog box displays all of the files and folders that are in the current folder (Figure 1-10), but files or folders within a folder are hidden until you open that folder.

To search other areas of the disk, click the mouse button and pull down on the current folder (as you would pull down a menu) to see other files and folders elsewhere on your disk, or if the Drive button is not gray, you can click it to see files on another drive. If the Drive button is gray, you can insert a disk and PageMaker will display its files and folders. If you wish to remove a floppy disk to insert another, click the Eject button (however, you can't eject a hard disk), then insert another disk.

Pagemaker does not display the names of all the files on your disk; it displays only files it recognizes and can read as publications, documents, or images. If your file is formatted differently than PageMaker expects,

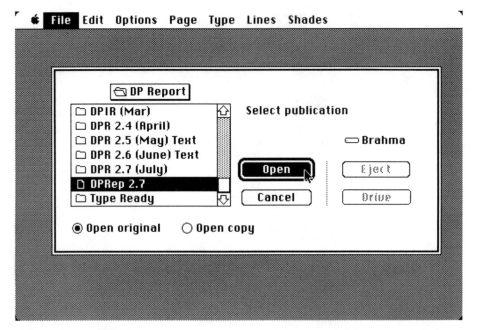

Figure 1-10. The dialog box in Figure 1-9, after opening the selected folder. This folder is now the current folder, and its files and folders are displayed. Close this (and any current) folder to see other files and folders on the disk.

you will not see it listed. Use the program that created the file to save it in a format that Pagemaker recognizes. Here is a brief explanation of file types PageMaker 2.0a currently recognizes (a more detailed description appears later in this chapter and in the supplied PageMaker manuals).

PageMaker reads any text file saved with a Text only option, and several formatted word processor files, including those created with Apple's MacWrite, Microsoft's Word 1.05 and version 3.0, and Microsoft Works, and T/Maker's WriteNow for Macintosh. PageMaker reads some, but not all of the word processor's formatting commands, so read the PageMaker manual sections on preparing documents from other applications to find out what formatting PageMaker uses. Any formatted file can be placed with PageMaker's Text only option to ignore the word processor's formatting and reformat the file before placing it in Page-Maker, or to reformat the file after placing it on the PageMaker page.

PageMaker reads graphics files created with several different painting programs, provided the painting program can save the file in the MacPaint format (nearly all paint programs save a MacPaint format file). Virtually all drawing programs save a PICT or EPS file which PageMaker reads directly, and PageMaker also recognizes graphics from programs that save files in TIFF (Tag Image File Format — for best results with scanned images) or EPS (encapsulated PostScript) format.

The Apple menu in the top left corner of the display contains desk accessories and control functions. Separate from the menu bar is the window presented by an application. You can move, close, or resize a window at any time. To move a window (such as the toolbox window), move the pointer into the window's menu bar and drag the window to a new position. To close a window, click the close box at the top left corner of the window. To resize a window, drag the box in its bottom right corner to the desired size.

You can perform many different operations in different programs, but the operations you will use most often are the Cut, Copy, and Paste commands (found in the Edit menu of most Macintosh applications). You can use these commands to transfer text and graphics within an application, and even from one application to another. You can use this feature to transfer, for example, business graphics or a spreadsheet from a program such as Microsoft Excel or from the Scrapbook to a PageMaker page.

We will not attempt to provide a complete description of operating a Macintosh, since a complete description is available in the manuals shipped with your computer. The *PageMaker User Manual* and tutorials from Aldus will also explain how to operate PageMaker on your Macintosh, even if you have never used a computer. If you have never operated a Macintosh, you might want to first spend a few hours to get familiar with its operation before you begin learning PageMaker. Plan to spend a day to a week learning to operate the Macintosh, and about a day after that learning the basics of PageMaker. At best, you can learn to use PageMaker and the Macintosh in just a couple of hours, and then build on the basic skills as you explore the more advanced features of PageMaker.

As you get more comfortable using PageMaker and the Macintosh, you will discover that there are many shortcuts and other tricks you can use to speed up operations and produce exactly the result you want. To ensure your comfort, the edit menu contains an Undo command. It can only undo the very last operation you did (i.e., use it right away, before doing anything else), if you are not sure about something you just did, and if you then decide that it was correct after all, immediately pull down the edit menu again, before doing anything else, and you will notice that the Undo command has been replaced by a Redo command, so you can repeat the operation. There is also a Revert command in the File menu that reverts back to the last saved version of your publication if you have a problem you don't know how to fix, or if you feel very lost. Every dialog box has a Cancel button, so your files should always be safe from harm. Even when the power fails, PageMaker 2.0 can recover the file without losing much, if anything, but you should still cultivate good computer operation habits (such as, always back-up your important work to a floppy disk for safekeeping).

You may learn to operate your computer without reading the manuals, but you should set time aside to read them to get the most from your computer and applications software investment. Allow time to read the manuals and learn to use the desk accessories contained in the Apple menu (an Alarm Clock, Calculator, Control panel, Chooser, Keycaps, Notepad, and Scrapbook) and perhaps other applications used with PageMaker, such as painting and drawing programs, word processing programs, communications programs, and devices (scanners, graphics tablets, printers, and modems).

PageMaker includes a desk accessory called Guidance that you use the Font/DA mover to add to the Apple Menu. It was used by Aldus to create a series of interactive help screens for PageMaker so that on-line help is available from within PageMaker, with three types of buttons you can expand to see more information on a particular topic.

Point to the *replacement* button, and your pointer changes to a crosshair shape, and you can expand that point to reveal text and/or graphics (your pointer changes to a square when positioned over such "live" text, and if you click anywhere with the square pointer, the "live" area is compressed and hidden).

Point to the second type of button, called a *reference* button, and the pointer changes to a white arrow. Clicking the reference button will instantly move you to another part of the help notes for a cross-reference, and you can click the double caret (an arrowhead shaped box above the single arrow in the top right of your screen, in the scrollbar) to backtrack.

The pointer changes to an asterisk when you point to a *note* button. Hold down the mouse button over a note button to display temporarily a note that disappears when you release the mouse button.

Project Planning

The best tool you can use to schedule everything is a project planner. You can use paper and pencil or a software package such as MacProject (Apple Computer, Inc.) or Micro Planner Plus (Microplanning Software International). A basic critical path chart or schedule showing task completion dates would be useful. You may prefer to plan your project using a drawing program, such as MacDraw (Apple Computer), a spread sheet program, or an outlining program, such as MORE (Living Videotext) for outlining, presentations, and so on, or a hypertextlike product such as Guide (Owl International, Inc.), which lets you create "live" areas in a document that appear on screen as buttons you click to activate (the button changes your pointer shape). Depending on which of three types of buttons you set it to be, the button expands text that was hidden and compresses it again, or it accesses a cross-reference in another part of the document (or in another document, and lets you backtrack when you have followed as far as you wish), or it displays a note in a pop-up window while you hold down the mouse button. Guide was used to create the Guidance help screens included with PageMaker 2.0.

No matter what application you use for planning a project, think of the publishing process as these steps:
• Develop an idea into a written and edited manuscript.
• Create and gather together illustrations and photos.
• Design the overall look and the individual pages.
• Produce the master pages for printing.

Personal computers can be used in all of these steps, and PageMaker plays an important role in the third step (design) as well as being responsible for the last step (production).

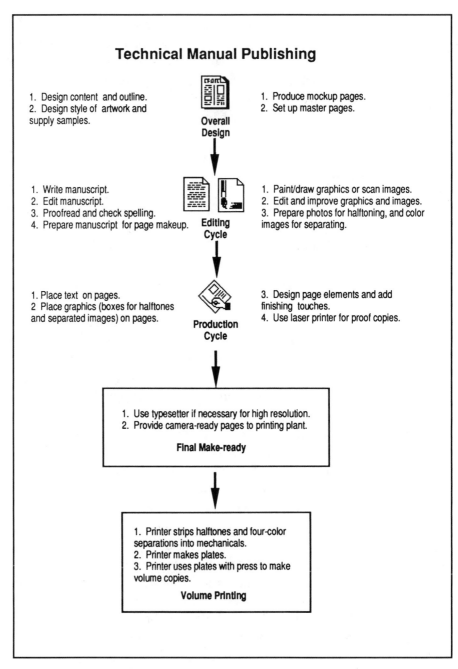

Figure 1-11. Project plan for producing a technical manual.

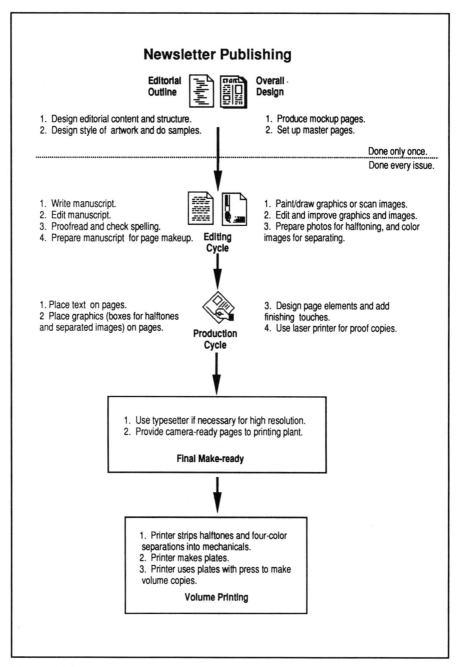

Figure 1-12. Project plan for producing a newsletter.

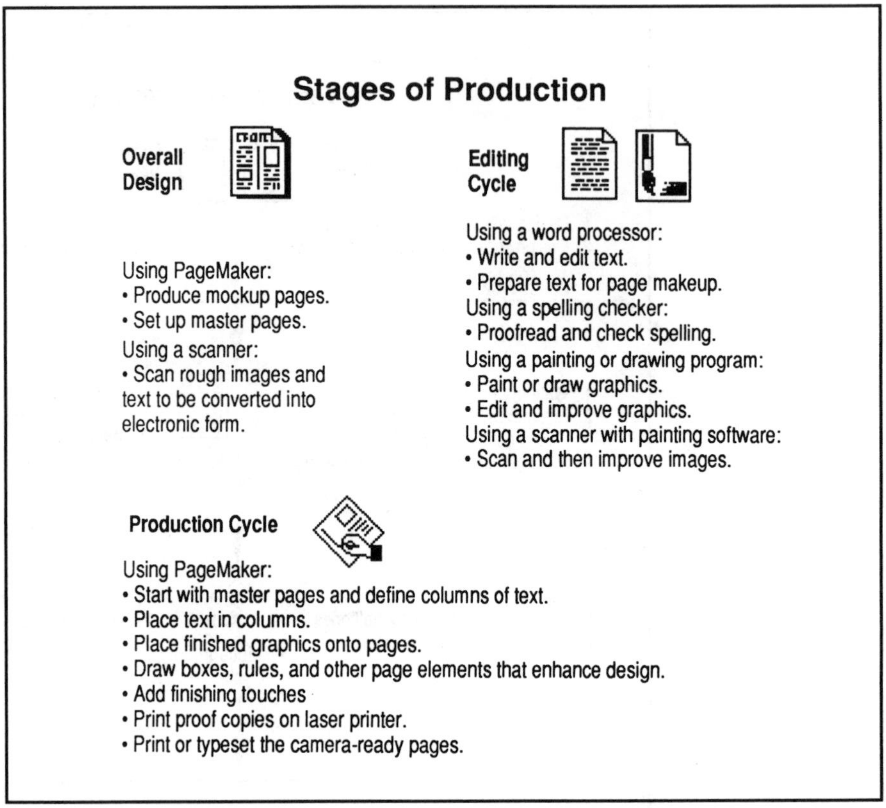

Figure 1-13. Stages of desktop publishing production.

Figure 1-11 shows a project plan for producing a technical manual, and Figure 1-12 shows a plan for producing a newsletter. In both cases, page design occurs early in the project so that the writers and artists have an idea of how the final publication will look.

Page Design

Page design can't be finalized until the designer knows the length of the manuscript and has information about the illustrations and photos. The *manuscript* stage for text and *rough* stage for illustrations and photos

(Figure 1-13) are the starting places for production. From there, manuscripts and roughs are turned into *formatted text* and *final artwork*, which are then combined in PageMaker to make *camera-ready pages*.

However, a designer can start early by using PageMaker to plan the overall look of the publication. With an estimate of the number of pages, he or she can decide the page size, image area, page orientation, and perhaps even the number of columns per page. You can print "thumbnail" sketches of the pages, using gray boxes to represent text, black boxes to represent images, and white boxes for line art. You can experiment with titles and headlines, logos and rough graphics (scanned or created on the computer), and even produce full-size sample pages, before placing manuscript text and final graphics and images. PageMaker has line-drawing, box-drawing, and circle-drawing tools, with 17 line styles (as well as reverse/none for each) and many patterns, as well as the ability to use graphics from a variety of programs.

Writing and Editing a Manuscript

Nearly every popular word processor for the Mac and PC can create text for use with PageMaker. You can use PageMaker to type and edit words on the page, but you should use a word processing program if you are writing more than a page of text, or if you are writing text that will be used with different programs or in other publications.

Word processing programs are designed for writing and editing text, with formatting controls (how to present the text on the page) added almost as an afterthought. Sometimes it is very difficult to do special effects with word processors, such as using a different font for page numbers, or drawing boxes around text and vertical lines (called "column rules") between columns. Macintosh word processing programs allow you to use all of the fonts installed in your system (use the Font/DA Mover to add and delete fonts), and some programs allow you to mix graphics with your text, but most word processing programs do not offer all of the formatting options of a page makeup program such as PageMaker.

Page makeup programs, on the other hand, specialize in formatting, even if they have word processing functions. PageMaker will let you edit text, but it does not offer complete word processing. In some cases, PageMaker can export text from the PageMaker publication for use with your word processing program. PageMaker is designed as a finishing tool, so it accepts text from a variety of word processors and gives you complete control over the page layout.

We recommend that you use the word processor you are already familiar with to prepare your text. If you have never before used a word processor, you may not need to purchase one — you can find public domain (free or Shareware) desk accessories (DAs) such as MockWrite on electronic bulletin boards (and e-mail services such as CompuServe), or DAs are available from user groups. DAs are usually limited in features, but are very easy to install, learn, and use. For applications that require more features, Microsoft offers Word for the Macintosh (as well as Word for the PC), compatible with the Macintosh version of Page-Maker. Microsoft Word on the Macintosh is also compatible with the PC version of PageMaker, through Word's conversion utility. DCA format-ted files from the PC can also be placed in PageMaker 2.0a on the Macintosh.

Other word processing programs are also compatible with PageMaker. PageMaker reads files from some programs directly, retaining some formatting, and files from other word processing programs must be saved in text-only (ASCII) format. Word processors compatible with Page-Maker are MacWrite (Apple Computer, Inc.), Word 1.05 and 3.0 (Micro-soft Corp.), Works (Microsoft Corp.), and WriteNow For Macintosh (T/Maker, Inc.). All of these programs can produce preformatted text for PageMaker — text that already has some of the characteristics (font, type style and size, tab settings, indents, and paragraph endings) needed for eventual appearance on the final pages. If, however, your word processor can produce simple ASCII (American Standard Code for Information Interchange) files, also known as "text only" files, which is a standard among all personal computers, you can use the text with PageMaker.

You don't have to know anything about PageMaker to write and edit text for PageMaker pages. Editors and writers may be using different computers in different offices — or even different countries — and still prepare text for someone who is using PageMaker. Large manuscripts can be sent from one computer to another over the telephone or through network connections, and PC disks are easy to exchange.

Writers and editors can prepare text for printing from the word processors without regard to PageMaker. Margins, footnotes, page numbers, headers, and footers created by word processors are not used by PageMaker, so your settings for these functions can be changed at will, without any consequence to your PageMaker production effort.

Proofreading a Manuscript

Once in electronic form, a large manuscript can be checked for spelling in just a few minutes. Once typed, the words never have to be retyped, and editing changes can be added or deleted in an instant.

Some word processors have built-in spelling checkers, such as Word 3.1 (Microsoft), and WriteNow for Macintosh (T/Maker). Others will work with DAs such as MacLightning 2.0 or Merriam Webster Dictionary for Macintosh (Deneba Software Co), or Liberty Spell II (DataPak Software Inc.), or a desk accessory for Microsoft Works, WorkPlus Spell (Lundeen & Associates). DAs let you check your spelling without quitting your word processing program. Other spelling programs, such as Spellswell 1.3 (Greene, Johnson Inc.) don't work from within the word processing application as the desk accessories do: instead you save your file and quit your word processor to check spelling.

You should use a spelling checker on the final draft of a manuscript, before using it with PageMaker, simply because errors that are not caught make a publication look less professional. Another reason to check the manuscript first is that changes made to the text on a PageMaker page may not be transferable back to the text file. Even if you can export the text back to a word processor formatted file, exporting the file may not transfer all the formatting changes you made in PageMaker, in which case changes must be made in both files, or your text file will not match the text on the PageMaker page.

Some proofreading programs and spell checking programs include a thesaurus or special (Medical, Dental, Legal, etc.) dictionary, and there are style checking programs available such as Doug Clapp's Word Tools (Aegis Development). If you prefer to proofread printed manuscripts, use a word processor that shows different fonts on the screen, and format and print the manuscript using a mono-spaced sans serif font in a large size, such as 12-point Courier, with extra leading (or double spaced) for easy reading and room for corrections between the lines.

Formatting a Manuscript

Although you can change fonts (styles and sizes) as well as faces for the text in PageMaker, you can save time by selecting font styles and sizes in the word processor (PageMaker supports all fonts installed in your system — check the PageMaker manuals for details) while you write and edit the text. The text is then formatted for placing onto a PageMaker page, and you can place text on all pages without stopping to select fonts (however, you cannot place text all at once on multiple pages). PageMaker also uses the right margin setting from your word processor file. When the column width in the PageMaker publication is wider than the right margin setting of your word processor file, the text will not automatically flow wider to fit the column, even if the Snap to guides option is on. You can easily widen the text block if you want to (use the text tool to click an insertion point in the text block, type Command A to select all of the file, and then set the right margin indent to 0 (zero) in the Paragraph dialog box displayed when you select Paragraph from the Type menu), after first placing the text.

An example of where this compatibility is useful is outlined in Chapter 2. While making up the fourth page of a newsletter, a questionnaire is formatted in Microsoft Word (Figure 1-14), complete with Zapf Dingbats boxes. The formatting done in Word is carried over into PageMaker.

Remember, PageMaker does not use the footnotes, page numbers, headers, footers, or special formatting features created by word processors. The following features *are* used:

• Fonts (typefaces, styles, and sizes), line spacing (leading), and upper- and lowercase letters. Special character conversions happen automatically (or to disable this feature you must simply hold down the Option key as you select Place from the file menu to place the file), so that instead of retaining keyboard-style single and double quotes (', "), PageMaker substitutes proper open and close typographic quotes ('' ""). Double hyphens (- -) are converted to an em dash (—) and a line of hyphens becomes a thin rule comprising a row of em dashes.

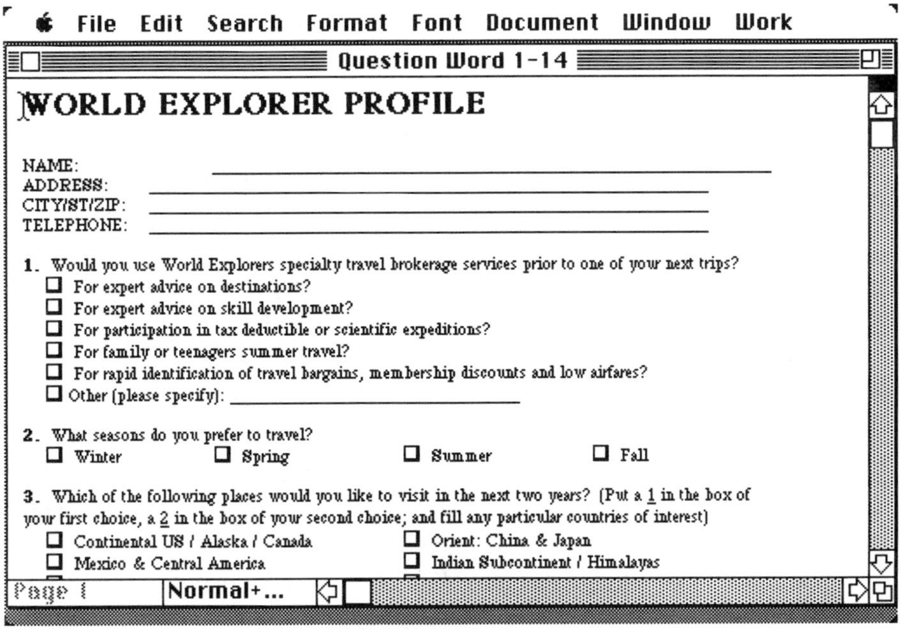

Figure 1-14. Microsoft Word on the Macintosh displays Zapf Dingbats symbols and other font choices that are used by PageMaker.

• The left margin is the basis for indents. If the word processor has a separate setting for the left indent, then it is used by PageMaker, otherwise the text is flowed flush left. PageMaker breaks lines to fit its columns, but if the word processed text has a narrower right margin than the PageMaker column, the word processor set right margin setting is used. The text does not snap to PageMaker's right margin column guide, when the Snap to guide option is turned on (as it did in earlier versions of PageMaker). Use the pointer tool to select the text and drag its right margin to be wider to fit the column. To remove a right margin indent carried over from the word processing setting, click an insertion point in the text block with the text tool, choose Select all from the Edit menu (Command A), then select Paragraph from the Type menu, and set the right margin indent to 0 (zero).
• Left and right indents are measured from the corresponding edges of the PageMaker column. If your text file has a 1-inch indent from the leftor right margin, PageMaker measures 1 inch from the left or right edge of the

column when placing your text file. Hanging indents, bulleted hanging indents, nested indents, and bulleted nested hanging indents are also imported by PageMaker.

• The first line indents of a paragraph are recognized as either regular, indented to the right, or a hanging indent to the left of the left margin. However, if the indent is wider than the PageMaker column, PageMaker ignores it.

• Carriage returns (produced by pressing the Enter or Return key in most word processors) are recognized as paragraph endings and as a forced end of a short line.

• Tabs are recognized and used to align text or numbers in tables. You can use PageMaker to change tab settings to fit the column width, but set tabs for the final PageMaker column width. You can specify the position, alignment, and leader pattern (such as a dot or dash leader to fill the tab space) using PageMaker, or set them in the word processor beforehand (except for Word's bar tabs, which PageMaker converts to left-aligned tabs with no vertical bar). End each tabbed line (such as each line of a table) with a carriage return.

PageMaker will remember the font you've chosen, even if you later open the file on a system without the same fonts installed. PageMaker retains the style, but substitutes its default font (Times 12 point) and remembers and uses the actual font, size, and style when you switch to a system that can print it.

Many writers and typists have the habit of using two spaces following each sentence. Typeset copy should not have two spaces, so one formatting step should be to replace all instances of two consecutive spaces with one space.

Here's another tip: Remove captions, footnotes, graphics, and other independent elements that will be positioned separately from the text of the manuscript. We routinely store the headline or title, images, captions and footnotes in separate files, and the body of the manuscript (including subheadings) in another file. We do this to save time when placing text on pages. If you leave the images in your text file, the file will be larger and slower to place than a text file without images. Also, PageMaker does not wrap text around the images, even if your word processor can do so.

PageMaker places each image on a line by itself following the line of text it was on in the word processing file, and breaks the text into two blocks, one above and one below the image. If you have two images on one line in the word processor file, the images will be placed on separate lines in PageMaker, usually with a line of text separating them. You end up with too many blocks to keep threaded, which makes page layout much more difficult and time consuming than it should be. A better solution is to save a library of images using DAs such as Glue, SmartScrap (both from Solutions Inc.), or PictureBase (Symmetry), or store graphics in separate files, and in the same folder as your publication file.

Here's another tip: Break up very large text files into smaller files of less than 64K, and PageMaker will place them quickly (also be sure the fast save option is not used to save Word 3.0 files before placing them, or PageMaker will require an excessive amount of time). Some word processors also have trouble with text files that are larger than 64K. PageMaker can safely place files well over 2MB in size, but you will get an alert message if you try to cut a block of text more than 64K, saying you can't undo the operation. (This problem can be solved without losing any text, but PageMaker will always work fastest with files smaller than 64K.)

There are many instances where you may have preformatted text, but prefer to use PageMaker's formatting and would rather place plain ASCII text using the Text only option. For example, you may want to use PageMaker default settings and override the word processor font and other settings. Or you may have records from a data base that are in a text format (use your word processing program to save the file using the Text only option, if your word processor can read the data base file). ASCII files are called text-only files by many Macintosh word processing programs, and almost every word processing program on every type of personal computer can create a text-only or ASCII file for use with PageMaker. (If your word processor can't save an ASCII file, you can probably find a service or filter program that will convert your file. Aldus and other companies are creating new filters that will allow the importing of text, with formatting in some cases also to be imported. Filters that are currently provided by Aldus include filters for importing formatted text from applications that create DCA files, as well as the PC word processing programs WordPerfect, XyWrite III, and WordStar 3.3.)

Tabs and carriage returns are recognized in text-only files, as well as spaces; but no formatting settings from the word processor are used. If the file is transmitted from another computer, with line feed characters at the end of each line, you will see strange boxes in your text at the start of each line. Use a program that strips line-feeds during the file transfer to save time, or you will have to delete each box that appears. If your file has too many line breaks in the middles of lines after placing, it is because the word processor inserted a carriage return at the end of each line. Either delete the extra carriage returns in PageMaker, or cut the file from the PageMaker page, and go back and save a new copy of the file with carriage returns only at the ends of paragraphs (and at the ends of rows in tables) with your word processor, and then place the new file. You can bring tables and paragraphs of text into PageMaker using the Text only option (to Place without formatting), and still retain paragraph endings and table column positions (as long as each table row ends with a carriage return).

PageMaker's paragraph default settings apply to text-only files, unless you first change the default values (with the pointer tool and no text selected). If you then place your text, the new settings are applied. You can choose new settings before placing the text, and ignore any existing formatting in the text file, by placing the file using the Text only option.

PageMaker lets you set two levels of default. *Application defaults* are set by running PageMaker, then selecting your choices from the menus, before you open a publication file. Each new publication you then create will have the new application default settings applied. The publication can also have *publication defaults* assigned by selecting your choices from the menus, while that publication is open with no text or images selected.

Publication default settings are saved with the publication file, and are applied (to overrule the application default settings) each time you open the file. You can change the default application and publication settings for page setup, type specs, preferences, rulers, paragraphs, indents, tabs, word and letter spacing, guide settings, lines and shades, and so on (see pages 100–102 of the PageMaker User Manual for a complete list of the default settings, and their initial default values). If you don't change the default settings, you will have the default font Times Roman at 12 points with automatic leading, automatic hyphenation, pair-kerning for all text larger than 12 points, no left or right margin or first line of paragraph indents, no spacing between paragraphs, and flush-left alignment of text in columns with ragged-right margins. (The above default settings are applied to a text file placed with the Text only option. However, if you place the text file with the Retain format option, the settings from your word processor are used to format the text, overruling PageMaker's default settings for the above.)

Since PageMaker exports some, but not all text changes you make on the page back to the word processor files, any changes made during page makeup should be made to the original text using the word processor, so that the two versions (text file and publication file) coincide. You can export the file, or any selected text, from PageMaker back to your word processor using PageMaker's export filters. If there is no export filter for your word processing program, you can export the file with the Text only option, preserving type specs, tabs and indents used by PageMaker. Export filters are available for Microsoft Word and T/Maker's WriteNow, with more to come. For details on how PageMaker deals with text files from popular word processors, see Appendix A.

If you use Microsoft Word 3.0, be sure to turn off the Fast save option before you save the file. If you leave the Fast save option on when you save the Word file, PageMaker will be very slow to place it. Use Word's Save as command to turn off the fast save feature.

Special Characters

You can type special characters in PageMaker 2.0, including trademarks, registered trademark and copyright notices, section and paragraph marks, bullets, and various nonbreaking spaces. Special characters also include a page number marker for automatic page numbering, open and close quotes, and em and en dashes. If you can't type them using your word processor, you can leave place holders (a character or note to the production person) and type the characters using PageMaker.

Some characters are automatically placed by PageMaker on the page. For example, PageMaker automatically changes a double quote (") with a preceding space into an open quote ("), and a double quote with a following space into a closed quote ("). The program also changes a single quote (') in the same manner, so that contractions, possessives, and quotes-within-quotes have the properly slanted symbols (', '). PageMaker changes a double hyphen (- -) into an em dash (—), and a series of hyphens into half as many em dashes (creating a solid line). These special character conversions happen automatically (or to disable this feature you must simply hold down the Option key as you select Place from the file menu to place the file), so that instead of retaining keyboard-style single and double quotes (', "), PageMaker substitutes typographic open and close quotes ('' "").

Although PageMaker automatically handles conversion of single and double quotes and em dashes using a routine described in the manuals, you should always proofread the text after conversion to check for ambiguous cases where the conversion can be wrong, such as the case where an extra space follows a word that should have had a close double quote, but instead has an open quote substituted by PageMaker. (It did not know the extra space was an error in your typing, but you can type real typographic quotes and other symbols in PageMaker, and continue to edit text on the PageMaker page to fix any other errors. However, you should always proofread, spell check, and edit the text carefully with your word processing program before placing it onto the page to minimize editing changes in PageMaker. Your word processor can perform global search/ replace operations and other functions that PageMaker cannot.)

Since PageMaker makes all of the above changes, and special characters and punctuation symbols are not available in most word processors anyway, most writers and editors do not need to think about them. You can use typical word processors and the ASCII character subset available on all PC keyboards, and save the special characters for the formatting and page makeup steps.

Creating and Editing Graphics

There are two kinds of graphic images: *paint-type*, also called bit-map, and *draw-type*, also called object-oriented. Painted images consist of dots corresponding to screen pixels and are limited in resolution to the display used to create them. Drawn images consist of a series of drawing commands that describe the image, and are usually not limited in resolution except by the printer or typesetter.

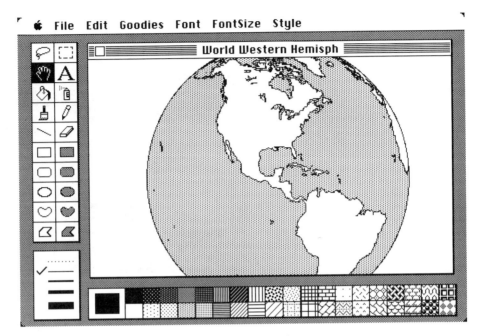

Figure 1-15. MacPaint can create paint-type graphics.

Painting programs (Figure 1-15) are popular with freehand artists and most amateur artists because they are easy to learn and very flexible — you can touch-up the dots to improve images and paint intricate patterns and shapes. Painting programs usually offer a selection of file formats, and almost all offer the MacPaint format.

Drawing programs (Figure 1-16) are popular with commercial artists, designers, architects, and engineers because they offer precision tools, perfect geometric shapes, and movable (and cloneable) graphic objects. Drawing programs usually offer a selection of file formats, and almost all offer the PICT format and/or EPSF (encapsulated PostScript format).

Both painting and drawing programs are popular with desktop publishers, who use drawing programs to create logos, line drawings, business charts and graphs, and schematics and painting programs to create intricate designs and freehand art.

The highest resolution can be achieved with EPSF files and drawing programs, because they produce resolution-independent images (de-

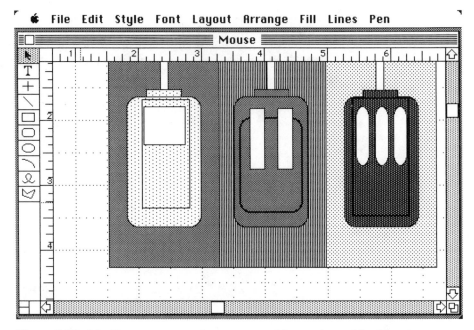

Figure 1-16. MacDraw can create draw-type graphics; each graphic object is separately movable, but is treated as one object in PageMaker.

scribed not by the dots — called pixels — used in painting programs, but by a list of drawing commands).

Paint-type Graphics

PageMaker places graphics saved in MacPaint, PICT, EPSF, or TIFF files. Almost all programs for painting and drawing can save a MacPaint file. MacPaint format images are stored as bit-maps, created from pixels that depend on the resolution you view them at. For example, the built-in Macintosh screen has 72 pixels or dots per inch (dpi), and the LaserWriter has 300 dpi. Because the resolution of the screen and printer do not exactly match, an image may appear distorted (muddy) when resized on the screen, but it will print correctly. If you resize the image to be clear on the screen, it may not be printed correctly.

Since it is difficult to resize bit-map images by hand to proportions that will print properly, especially when different printers can print at different resolutions, PageMaker has a built-in scaling feature. PageMaker displays a series of nested boxes at the best proportions for your printer when you hold down the Command key as you resize images. Once you release the mouse button, the image snaps to the size of the last displayed box, which should print without distortion at your printer's resolution. The choice of sizes will depend on what printer resolution you have chosen in the Page setup menu. If you want the images in your publication to be sized at the best sizes for your printer, first select your printer by choosing the printer type in the Print dialog box, then begin placing images.

If you place some images using the Command key to get optimum size choices, and then you change the printer resolution by changing the printer type in the Print dialog box, and print the file, you may not have the same sizing choices for images you then place at the new resolution. For example, you get more choices at 1270 dpi than at 300 dpi. To enlarge or reduce an image at an optimum size for your printer and to retain its height and width proportions as you resize, hold down both the Command and Shift keys. If you hold down only the Command key when you resize an image, the proportions may change, but you will have more choices of sizes that print without distortion than if you also retain proportions as you resize.

Also, unlike the PC version of PageMaker, the Mac version of Page-Maker does not automatically assign a target printer to your publication file. PageMaker assumes your printer resolution is 300 dpi (the default value, unless you change it in the printer's APD file) until you print the publication file for the first time to a printer with a different resolution, such as a Linotronic 100 (at 1270 dpi) or a Linotronic 300 (at 2540 dpi). PageMaker does not know which printer resolution your printer uses until it has printed the file to that printer once.

To setup your files to print at the desired final resolution when you don't have a printer available at that resolution, you can use any word processor to edit an APD (Adobe Printer Description) file to change the resolution setting for the printer type that is available. For example, if a LaserWriter is available, but your final printer will be a Linotronic typesetter available at a service bureau, (you could even plan to transmit the final publication file via modem and telephone to a service bureau's Linotronic typesetter), you can use your word processor to change the resolution in the LaserWriter APD file in your System folder to be 635 or 1270, then save the file using the word processor's Text only option (use the Save as option to save the modified LaserWriter APD with a new name, such as LaserWriter635, to preserve the original LaserWriter APD file without changes), and select the new APD file from the list of Printer APDs available, using the Change printer option in the Print dialog box, to print the file using the modified LaserWriter APD.

You can move, resize, and crop the image and PageMaker will apply those changes to the original when printing, but not change the original. You can't edit the pixels in PageMaker, nor can you erase parts of an image (use your paint program for cleanup before placing the graphic), but you can crop an image to show only a portion of it. You can also use PageMaker's drawing and text tools to modify the image, but you should use your painting program to duplicate the changes if you want the changes to be made to the original image as well, because PageMaker does not export images.

You can resize paint-type graphics in PageMaker using PageMaker's ability to match the printer's resolution, or you can distort the image as you resize it. If at any time you don't like the printed result after enlarging or reducing the image, you can restore it to its original proportions by selecting the image and then holding the Shift key down as you click it.

Excellent printed results are possible with paint-type graphics, especially if they consist of line art, which can be resized into almost any proportion and size and still look good. Images with tight, regular patterns are not displayed well (they look muddy), but if you use PageMaker's special resizing feature, which limits you to sizes that will print best at your printer's resolution, you can get excellent results. The limitation may force you to use a slightly larger- or smaller-sized image than the reduced one you wanted, but you can use PageMaker's cropping tool to further reduce and edit the placed image. Unlike an exacto knife, scissors, or razor blade, PageMaker's cropping tool can be used to adjust the size of cropped art to be larger or smaller. Or, select an image with the cropping tool and hold down the mouse button in the center of the image to get the grabber hand pointer, and then move the mouse to reposition the image to center it in the cropped window, while retaining the position and size of the window.

Programs that create color graphics usually don't match the standard color systems used in printing plants, and so are not very useful for commercial publishing. Laser printers don't print in color yet, and if you print a graphic that is composed in color on a black-and-white printer, the color areas are replaced with patterns that may not look exactly as you intended.

You can steer clear of problems by composing graphics in black-and-white and by selecting patterns and shades rather than colors for filled areas. PageMaker will accept color images (Aldus is preparing Page-Maker for color laser printers and color separation machines), but you will probably not use this equipment for a while (and by that time, we'll have updated this book). For details on how PageMaker deals with graphics files from popular painting programs, see Appendix B.

Draw-type Graphics

PageMaker places graphics files saved in the PICT format. PageMaker also accepts files using the Encapsulated PostScript format (EPSF). Almost all drawing programs can save a PICT file, and many drawing programs can save an EPSF file. (Or, if you are a PostScript programmer, you can create a PostScript program that saves an EPSF file.) If your drawing program does not save a PICT file, you can probably use the Glue (Solutions, Inc.) desk accessory to print the file to a disk in the PICT format from within your drawing program. (You can even use Glue within PageMaker, to copy entire PageMaker publication pages in the PICT format, paste the pages into the Scrapbook, and then place the pages, as PICT graphics, into another PageMaker publication!)

Drawing programs give you precise tools for drawing geometric shapes. Usually, the drawing tools emulate drafting tools such as a compass, a T-square, a precise ruler, and a grid, and there are extra tools for quickly drawing perfect squares, circles, and geometric shapes. Amateur graphic artists and professional artists may find the tools harder to learn than the painting tools, but they produce precise shapes and perfectly proportioned squares and circles. In addition, the programs save graphics in a format that is independent of the resolution of the display and drawing device, so that when you print the graphics, PageMaker uses the highest possible resolution of the printing device.

Draw-type graphics, described with a command language rather than expressed as a series of dots, can be resized freely (there are no limitations as with paint-type graphics) and even stretched or compressed with very little or no distortion. If you want to create a graphic that must be a certain size on the final page, create it with a drawing program, since the graphic can then be resized to precisely the measurements you want, not just the measurements that PageMaker builds in for printing paint-type graphics.

In many cases you can transfer text used in the graphics to PageMaker with excellent results; in other cases you may want to delete the text from the image first in the drawing program, and then replace it with PageMaker's text tool after positioning the image on the page to get the best results (kerning, word and letter spacing, etc.). For example, font size can be retained when scaling a MacDraw (PICT) image to be smaller with the MacDraw program, before placing it on the PageMaker page. Resizing a PICT image to be smaller on the PageMaker page reduces the fonts as well as the rest of the image. Each PICT file is treated as a single object by PageMaker, but MacDraw can treat a PICT file image's component parts separately or as a group. For details on how PageMaker treats graphics files from popular drawing programs, see Appendix B.

Business Charts and Graphs

Programs that generate charts and graphs (bar and pie charts, x–y graphs, scatter plots, or combinations of these forms) usually save the result in a graphic file compatible with one of the graphics programs already mentioned, such as Macintosh PICT files that can be used with PageMaker.

Usually no graphics experience is required to use these products, since their function is to generate graphics automatically for business-minded people who are not skilled in graphics. Programs for spread sheets can save charts and graphs as draw-type graphics that can be scaled to any size without distortion. All of the rules governing use of draw-type graphics apply to business graphics that are saved in EPSF and PICT formats.

Image and Text Scanning

Most publishing operations require use of existing information, but how can you put existing text and graphics into the computer? Expensive text and image digitizers are currently used by large publishers and the government, but inexpensive desktop models are also available that can handle much of a desktop publisher's needs.

The technology of scanning text — called optical character recognition (OCR)—has not caught up with the technology of typesetting, and today's desktop scanners only have high accuracy rates with typewritten text or text printed in the 10- or 12-point Courier font on a laser printer. (Kerned and justified type has varied word and letter spacing, which results in more reading errors by a desktop scanner than does monospaced type.) Today's desktop scanners can scan text and store it in simple ASCII format, which can then be edited with a word processor.

Text scanning works best with clean, crisp originals that were printed using a Courier Selectric-style typing element or Courier daisy wheel with carbon-film ribbons, either clean and clear copies, or the originals. If characters are broken, or you use a bad photocopy, the software can't automatically recognize the character. The text scanning process is fastest when you use a clean original and place it flat on a glass platen so that the lines of text are parallel to the top of the platen. The OCR software will read slanted text (resulting from the paper being placed askew on the platen) but will take longer than the usual scanning speed. Flatbed scanners are most often used for OCR, because sheetfed scanners are harder to feed paper into without skewing the page.

Many desktop scanners can save images with 16, 64, or 256 different shades of gray, but many personal computers are not well-equipped to handle the immense file storage space required to save these images in digital form. PageMaker can accept these images stored in the Tag Image File Format (TIFF), which is supported by most desktop scanner manufacturers, and provides a method of compressing the image data into a file of a manageable size. There are two kinds of TIFF; bi-level is used to describe images consisting of scanned line drawings, and is tied to the resolution of your scanner, and gray scale TIFF, best for images with many shades of gray or color, such as continuous tone images, and best used with high resolution printers, such as Linotronic 100 typesetters (1270 dpi). Gray scale TIFF can print an image scanned at 150 dpi with 200 shades of gray, equivalent to a 90-line screen photographic halftone, or with 70 shades of gray, equivalent to a 150-line screen). Scanner manufacturers such as Datacopy, DEST, Abaton, MicroTek, Hewlett-Packard, and Thunderware offer painting programs with their scanners so that you can improve a scanned image. Such a scanned image is usually a MacPaint image, but the size of the file may be very large. If it is larger than 64K, the scanned image is displayed with a screen representation, and the higher-resolution image file is linked to the PageMaker publication and used to print the image (the screen representation of the image is therefore at a lower-resolution than the printed image). PageMaker can print scanned images at actual size or at reduced or expanded sizes with excellent results if you use the automatic resizing feature (holding down the Command key while resizing), otherwise, the images can be distorted like any other MacPaint file. Most scanner manufacturers offer programs to save the image in TIFF or MacPaint format, in which case you should use TIFF.

A desktop scanner scanning typewritten pages is faster than the fastest typist, and can continue at top speed all day long. However, there is no substitute for writing and editing by computer if you are looking for the most efficient method. No matter how quickly inexpensive text scanners develop, they will probably not match the efficiency of creating the data electronically in the first place.

Scanners are most useful for scanning pages of text from outside sources to be processed or filed by computer, and for scanning line art and sketches to be improved with drawing software. Laser printers at 300 dpi are not capable of reproducing an image with the same quality as a photographic halftone, so most desktop publishers are using page makeup for everything else and leaving a black-filled box (perhaps with a key line) on the page where a halftone will be dropped in before sending the publication off to the printing press. The cost savings are still tremendous, even if you use a graphics service for the halftones.

However, there are many publications that can use scanned images, especially scanned line art. Real estate listings can be updated frequently by scanning the photos of new houses immediately and preparing the listings with PageMaker. Personnel reports can be prepared that have scanned photos of employees. Architectural studies can be typeset with scanned drawings of building plans along with scanned photos of the landscape. Scanned images are finding their way into art and design magazines as well as newspapers, newsletters, and business reports. A gray scale TIFF image scanned at the highest possible resolution, and typeset at up to 2540 dpi is equivalent to 60-, 90- and 120-line screened halftones. In subsequent chapters we show the use of scanned images in publications as final artwork and as temporary placeholders for designing text and page elements around halftones to be dropped in later.

When you place a scanned image (larger than 64K) on a PageMaker page, PageMaker creates a lower-resolution version for displaying the page and establishes a link to the original, higher-resolution version, so that the program can use the higher-resolution version when printing. PageMaker uses the lower-resolution image for display purposes in order to increase the speed of the program, and to conserve disk space.

For PageMaker's link to work automatically when printing, you should store the original image file in the same folder as your publication file, before you place it on the publication page. You can use your painting program to continue to edit the image after placing it, and PageMaker will print the publication using the edited image instead of the image shown on your screen. If you don't like the printed result, you can continue to edit the image with your painting program, then print the PageMaker publication without ever changing the placed image, and the final version of the image will be printed in the publication.

Laser Printers and Typesetters

We are finally ready to discuss the motivating force behind desktop publishing: inexpensive laser printers and the ability to transfer pages to higher-resolution typesetters.

You start your publishing effort with scanning and word processing, but the quality of your results is directly related to what you can produce with a printer or typesetter. Laser printers have grown in popularity because they offer fonts and image printing at high resolutions compared to conventional dot-matrix and letter-quality printers. Laser printers offer near-typeset quality with a resolution of 300 by 300 (or 400 by 400) dots per square inch (referred to as 300 dpi, or 400 dpi). Laser printers are also capable of emulating daisy wheel and dot matrix printers at much better resolution and print quality, although some printers offer only partial-page graphics at 300 dpi resolution.

The Apple LaserWriter is the recognized leader in desktop publishing applications because it was the first to use the PostScript page description language developed by Adobe Systems and now used in laser printers from IBM, Texas Instruments, Digital Equipment Corporation, and many other manufacturers. PostScript laser printers are compatible with each other and with higher-resolution laser typesetters from Allied Linotype and Compugraphic. For example, a PostScript-type laser printer such as the Apple LaserWriter or LaserWriter Plus (both 300 dpi) is entirely compatible with the Allied Linotype Linotronic class of PostScript-type typesetters, including the Linotronic 100 (1270 dpi, about $35,000) and 300 (2540 dpi, and $70,000).

Typesetters are still out of most business's price range because the machines are expensive and not suitable for the fast printing chores related to business computing. Typesetters produce output of such high quality that most businesses would only want to use one for final typesetting. The paper used with the typesetter has to be developed by a chemical-based processor, so you need a ventilated room (preferably a darkroom) for the processor.

For desktop publishers who need both the speed and flexibility of laser printers and the high resolution of typesetters, PostScript typesetters are available as output devices in copy centers and typesetting services. You can prepare text for them directly or use a PostScript laser printer to proof your pages inexpensively before using the typesetter.

To use a printer with the Macintosh, there must be software on disk and available to the system that communicates with and controls that specific type of printer. This software is called a *printer driver*. Apple supplies the LaserWriter printer driver on the installation disk that ships with the LaserWriter. You place that driver file in your system folder.

PageMaker also uses APD (Adobe Printer Description) files to use with the driver, and Aldus supplies a special file called Aldus Prep that you store in the System folder or in a folder with the PageMaker program. Any PostScript printer can have an APD modified or written to use it with the Macintosh and PageMaker. Nearly all of the major laser printers available on the market support PostScript, including page printers from IBM, Digital Equipment Corporation, Hewlett-Packard (with an upgrade), AST Research, QMS, Qume, Texas Instruments, and others. Most laser printers can print to only standard paper sizes (8 1/2 by 14 inches or smaller), and they do not provide edge-to-edge toner coverage. The Dataproducts LZR-2665 and some others can print tabloid-size pages (11 by 17 inches).

PageMaker controls specific printer features, such as collating, the use of input paper trays, page orientation, and different resolution factors with certain printers (such as Apple LaserWriters and Linotronic typesetters).

When you add new PostScript font files to your system folder, be sure to add the screen versions supplied with the fonts, using the Font/DA Mover supplied with Macintosh System utilities. Screen fonts display representations of the actual PostScript fonts, which are substituted by PageMaker when printing. Non-PostScript bit-map fonts display on the screen exactly as they print with font substitution turned off; they may be useful for decorative purposes, but will look more jagged at the edges than higher-resolution PostScript fonts. (If font substitution is turned on, a built-in PostScript printer font — usually Times for serif, and Helvetica for sans serif fonts — will be substituted for the bit-map font by the printer.) New fonts are easy to install in your Macintosh system using the Font/DA Mover program, and you can use a font downloader program to install new fonts in your printer. PageMaker can print with PostScript fonts on any PostScript printer connected to the AppleTalk network, or with bit-map fonts to any ImageWriter connected directly to the printer port or on AppleTalk. To choose an AppleTalk printer, use the Chooser desk accessory supplied with every Macintosh system, and select the printer by its network name. You can even select a printer in another AppleTalk zone (collection of networks) that is linked to your network. However, if you use downloadable fonts that are not already available in the printer's memory, it may take longer to print.

Since PostScript devices can vary in resolution, resizing bit-mapped images can cause unwanted patterns at different resolutions (for example, a LaserWriter prints at 300 dpi, and the Linotype 100 at 1270 dpi). For example, if you use a different resolution for final output than you used for printing proof pages, you should first print one page on the final output device, then resize the images with the Command key held down to use built-in sizes and avoid unwanted moirè patterns. Aftef printing a page, PageMaker remembers the resolution of the printer when resizing images.

Figure 1-17. The SuperMac display card and large screen monitor for the Macintosh SE displays a complete PageMaker spread (2 pages), with readable (not greeked) 10-point type. If you perform screen-intensive tasks such as page makeup or drawing, a larger screen can offer a fast payback in comfort and increased productivity.

Line length could be a problem if you compose your publication for an ImageWriter and then switch to a LaserWriter for printing (the ends of lines may be cut off because the LaserWriter page width is smaller than the ImageWriter page width). You should check all of the pages for undesirable changes if you switch from an ImageWriter to a PostScript printer such as the LaserWriter, or first define a smaller page size that the LaserWriter can print, before placing your text and graphic elements.

When you print a publication from PageMaker, you can use a spooler program such as SuperLaserSpool (from SuperMac Technology), which handles printing for you so that control comes back to your computer quickly. You can control the spooling program to check status, interrupt, reorder, or cancel printing operations at any time, without leaving PageMaker, and without your tying up your computer while waiting for your file to print.

You can also cause PageMaker to create a "print file" of the pages rather than print the pages by holding down the Option key while clicking Print in the Print dialog box (in the File menu), then transmit that print file to another computer over a modem and telephone line or transfer it by disk. The receiving computer does not have to run PageMaker to send the file to the printer, but it must have the same target printer. You can copy the print file directly to the printer using Glue, or a PostScript dump program. (See Appendix D for more information on file transfers.)

Complete Systems

The rest of the hardware and software you need depends on your application. Most writers and newsletter publishers need enough disk storage to accommodate a year's worth of text (a 20- or 40-megabyte hard disk is usually appropriate). To run PageMaker, you need a Macintosh computer (preferably a Macintosh 512KE, a Plus, an SE, or a II) with a monochrome (black-and-white) monitor, or a color monitor (see Figure 1-17). Higher-resolution full-page black-and-white and color (for the Mac II) monitors are also available, and the larger screen size is a good investment if you plan to do full-time page makeup.

Desktop Design

Many of you who are not designers by trade should prepare yourself by reading books on design and production. We list a few good books in the Bibliography. There is no substitute for a good designer, but it is possible for desktop publishers to learn good design techniques and put them to use without paying top dollar for a professional designer. Your research will help you know what it is you are judging when a top designer provides thumbnail sketches, comps, and finished artwork for your approval.

The purpose of this book is to show you how to use PageMaker to produce general types of publications, but it also has a subordinate mission to teach a few design skills. All of the desktop publishing software in the world can't save a badly designed publication. The best approach is to practice using PageMaker, then read some good design books and seek advice from a professional designer. Finally, use this book to refresh your memory on how to use PageMaker.

2 | A Newsletter

This chapter introduces PageMaker and provides a few layout and production tricks that can save you time and money. Although you may not be interested in producing a newsletter, the format for one is very straightforward for demonstrating PageMaker's features. This book and the Aldus manuals were produced with PageMaker, which is perhaps the best way to show off the program's features for book design and production. We recommend that you keep the *PageMaker Quick Reference Guide* from Aldus at hand as you complete the examples in this book, to become familiar with PageMaker in the shortest possible time.

This book is not a crash course in design, because there are many excellent books that provide such information. (See the Bibliography for a sampling.) This book will describe, using examples, many of the basic production techniques, typesetting and printing terms, and design considerations.

Start with a simple design effort, to acquaint yourself with the limitations of PageMaker as well as the conventional constraints of typical printing presses. Before starting any publishing project, find out how the presses work. The number of copies you want to print (size of press run), the page size (which is partially dependent on your choice of stock) and number of pages, and the use of color can all be factors in determining which printing presses and binding machines are appropriate to use for your job. We suggest you read *Pocket Pal* (see Bibliography) or some other reference to learn printing and production procedures and terms, and then provide a written description of your job (include samples of work that uses the type of paper, or size, or binding, folding or gluing, etc. similar to the result you want) to several printers or a print broker, who can help you determine the mechanical specifications and offer price quotes for the paper, ink, printing, binding, and other services. Using PageMaker could quickly reduce your production costs enough to pay for upgraded printing, such as additional use of color or a better grade of paper, or other services. Always start with an idea of how big the publication will be (number of pages and size of each page) before you design your pages. In this chapter we use as an example a typical 8 1/2- by 11-inch four-page newsletter (Figure 2-1), and we'll use PageMaker's default settings for the image area.

Starting up PageMaker

PageMaker is supplied on two 800K disks ready to be installed on your Macintosh computer. The installation is a simple process of copying the necessary files and folders (after you first copy the PageMaker master disks for safekeeping), and you can later delete any extra files you don't need, such as the tutorial folder.

Installation details depend on which computer you are using, and whether or not you are using a hard disk. The computers to use for the best WYSIWYG (what you see is what you get) — the best match between the screen's display and the printed page — are the Macintosh Plus, SE, or Macintosh II, with a hard disk drive. PageMaker also works on the older Macintosh 512K and 512K Enhanced (also called 512KE), when they are configured properly.

Running PageMaker 2.0 on a Macintosh 512K *requires* a hard disk drive with at least 1.5MB of space available, but the biggest problem is the older 64K ROMs installed in Mac 512Ks, which use fixed character widths (actually screen character widths) instead of the fractional character widths (actually printer character widths) used in the newer 128K

WORLD
Explorers News

Volume 1 Number 6 / JUNE 1987

Learning From Marco Polo

There is no sea innavigable, no land uninhabitable.
— Robert Thorne, merchant and geographer (1527)

Too far East is West. — English proverb

We open this issue with an excerpt from the first printed travel guide of Western Society on how to travel to the Near and Far East. This guide was written 70 years after Marco Polo embarked on his historic visit to China. The following text is from a handbook written in 1340 by Francesco Balducci Pegolotti, agent for the Bardi banking family in Florence:

In the first place, you must let your beard grow long and not shave. And at Tana you should furnish yourself with a dragoman. And you must not try to save money in the matter of dragomen by taking a bad one instead of a good one. For the additional wages of the good one will not cost you so much as you will save by having him. And besides the dragoman it will be well to take at least two good men servants who are acquainted with the Cumanian tongue. And if the merchant likes to take a woman with him from Tana, he can do so; if he does not like to take one there is no obligation, only if he does take one he will be kept much more comfortably than if he does not take one. Howbeit, if he do take one, it will be well if she be acquainted with the Cumanian tongue as well as the men...

Whatever silver the merchants may carry with them as far as Cathay the lord of Cathay will take from them and put into his treasury. And to merchants who thus bring silver they give that paper money of theirs in

exchange. This is of yellow paper, stamped with the seal of the lord aforesaid. And this money is called; and with this money you can readily buy silk and other merchandise that you have a desire to buy. And all the people of the country are bound to receive it. And yet you shall not pay a higher price for your goods because your money is of paper...

(And don't forget that if you treat the custom-house officers with respect, and make them something of a present in goods or money, as well as their clerks and dragomen, they will behave with great civility, and always be ready to appraise your wares below their real value.)

Figure 2-1. Sample newsletter page.

ROMs installed in 512K Enhanced, Plus, SE, and newer Macintosh computers. The character width tables stored in the ROMs (and whichever version of the system software you use) determine kerning and letter spacing values, and so a Macintosh 512K will not be able to control kerning and letter spacing on the screen properly. Upgrade your 512K Macintosh to a 512K Enhanced or use a newer model Macintosh, if you need maximum control over the space between characters (kerning) and words (letter spacing). To avoid problems if you run PageMaker 2.0 on a 512K Macintosh, use System 3.2 instead of the later version of the System folder supplied with PageMaker 2.0. (Also, if you have a 512K Macintosh with a General Computer Hyperdrive hard disk, turn off RAM cacheing before you run PageMaker.)

PageMaker runs on a Macintosh 512K Enhanced or a Mac Plus with only two 800K floppy disk drives, but that setup is a lot slower and more inconvenient than adding a hard disk to your system. If you are serious about publishing, a 20MB hard disk might be enough, but a 40MB hard disk is better, especially if you plan to use PageMaker in a network and share a larger hard disk, or you may instead prefer to use PageMaker in a network with 20MB or 40MB hard disk drives for each user.

If you plan to use PageMaker without a hard disk, you will need two 800K floppy drives, and you won't need to install PageMaker 2.0. You should, however, make copies of the two supplied disks (and put them in a safe place), and use the copies as working disks. You can delete any files you don't need (such as the tutorials) from your working copies of the Startup and Program disks, but don't erase or alter the two supplied disks. Also, to create large publications (which must be less than 800K in size) you must save your publications on a separate publication floppy disk, as there is not much space on the Program and Startup disks for your publications.

To install PageMaker, you should be familiar with the Macintosh Finder and System (operating system), and already know how to format disks, copy or delete disk files, add or remove printers and other devices, print files, and run programs. PageMaker 2.0 is supplied with the latest version of the System folder, and it also works with System version 3.2. If you are using the Macintosh 512K, you should use version 3.2 instead of the new System folder. However, if you are using a Macintosh Plus, SE, or II, you should use the new System 4.1 and Finder 5.5 shipped with PageMaker 2.0a.

You can install new system software whenever you wish to, but you should always first save a copy of the old system. If you choose to upgrade your hard disk to the new System folder, first make a backup copy of the older System folder on an 800K floppy disk (for use with some older programs that may not yet be updated to work with the new system, and to preserve whatever fonts and desk accessories (DAs) you may have installed to customize your system), then make a backup copy of the new System folder on another disk before copying the new System folder to your hard disk. Store the backups in a safe place — they may be needed if your hard disk is damaged or if Aldus supplies an update — but use the Font DA/Mover to copy the old System folder's fonts (for accurate fonts, use only fonts supplied with System 3.2 or greater) and desk accessories for use with the new System. Check your computer's manuals and the installation section of the PageMaker manual for details (the procedure is simple).

PageMaker 2.0

After you have installed PageMaker, you will be ready to begin creating publications. To start PageMaker, simply double-click the program's icon and choose Open from the File menu, or double-click a publication's icon. (Chapter 1 explained how to click, double-click, drag, and do other mouse moves.)

Read Me Now

Before you produce a publication, you should first decide what printer (laser, dot-matrix, typesetter, and so on) you will use for the final version of the publication. PageMaker 2.0 includes Adobe Printer Description (APD) files for an Apple ImageWriter, LaserWriter, LaserWriter Plus, DataProducts LZR 2665, or other PostScript laser printers, and Linotronic typesetters. If your printer is not one of the supplied, contact Aldus or Adobe for help obtaining or modifying an APD for your printer.

You should find out what fonts are installed in the printer, load the screen versions of those fonts into your System folder using the Font/DA Mover, and print the file once, before you begin placing any text or images in your publication. If you plan to use a service bureau with a LaserWriter Plus or a Linotronic for the final pages, it can supply the screen versions of the fonts you need, including screen versions of any downloadable fonts you plan to use. Also, especially if you plan to use downloadable

Figure 2-2. The File menu holds the Printer selection.

fonts, you should decide whether to use the Apple-supplied Laser Prep (also included with PageMaker), or the Aldus Prep supplied with Page-Maker. The Aldus Prep gives you the best results, because it was designed to work with PageMaker. It prints faster, and allows more downloadable fonts than Apple's Laser Prep. Use Apple's Laser Prep if your spooler software requires it.

To choose a printer, select the Print command from the File menu (Figure 2-2) and select Change to choose a printer from the list shown in the printer specific options dialog box (Figure 2-3). Even if you don't have a printer connected to your system, or you intend to first laser print and then typeset your pages, you should select the printer you will use for final page printing (or modify the resolution setting in the chosen printer's APD file to match the final printer's resolution). Then print the file once to notify PageMaker of the new resolution (otherwise PageMaker uses its default 300 dpi printer resolution), to minimize changes to the layout of

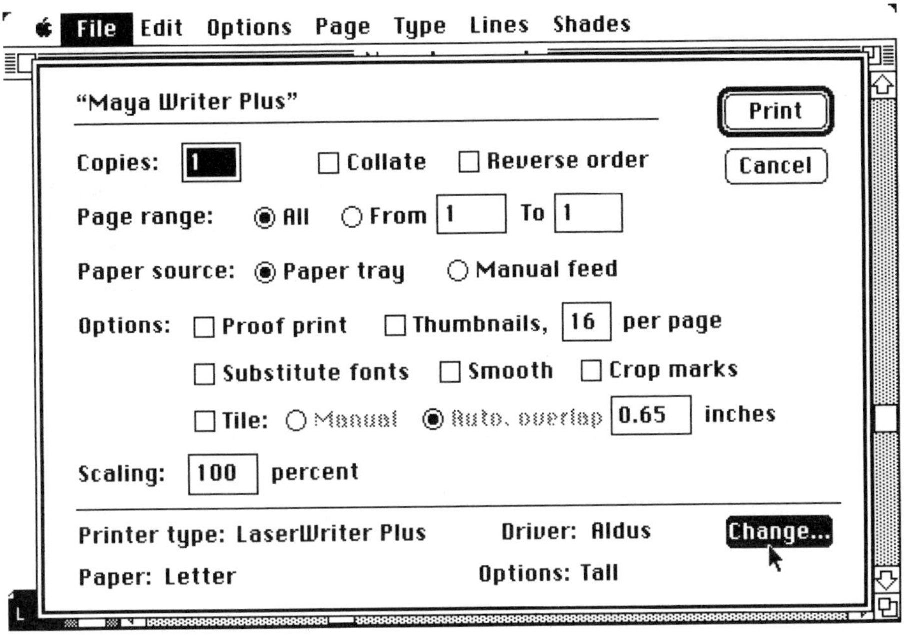

Figure 2-3. The Print dialog box.

your publication. No matter which printer you use, line length and leading of text you place in the publication file will not change, but PageMaker does not know which printer you have chosen until you print to it once. (Many desktop publishing service bureaus and copy shops offer a self-service laser printer and Mac system at which you can rent time to do your own final printing.) PageMaker displays a dialog box with a choice of paper sizes, printer types, drivers, and page orientation (Figure 2-4).

When you start a new publication, you need to define the page size or accept the default settings, as we will do for the newsletter example. You can bypass this decision entirely by first choosing a *template* and loading it into PageMaker using the Open command in the File menu (a template is a predesigned publication file that is empty of text and graphics, but ready for use in page makeup.) Or, you can open a copy of a file and leave the original file unchanged.

We assume you have no template to work with, but with PageMaker, creating publications from scratch is easy. Start by selecting New (from the File menu). PageMaker displays the dialog box in Figure 2-5. Click

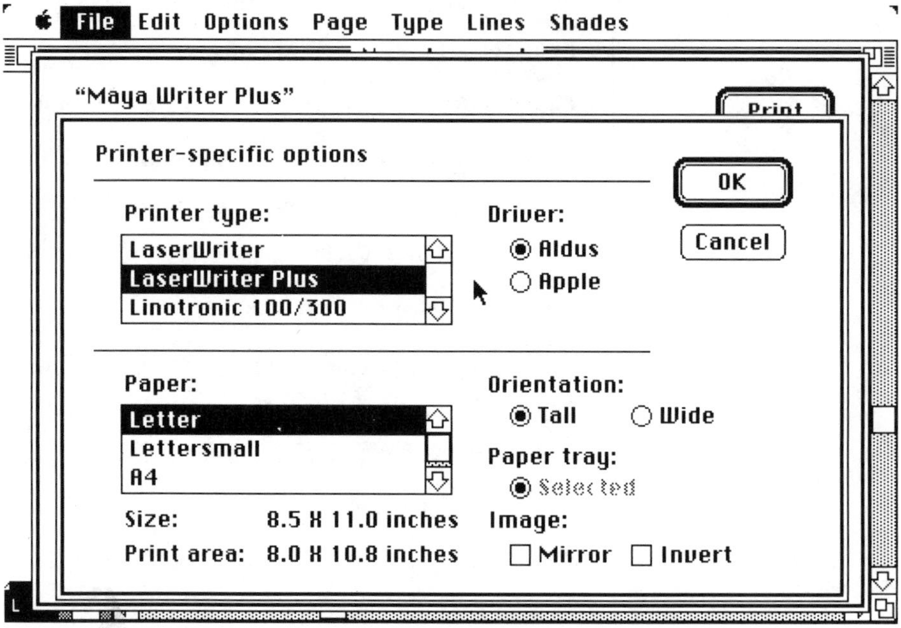

Figure 2-4. Subsequent dialog box to change the target printer.

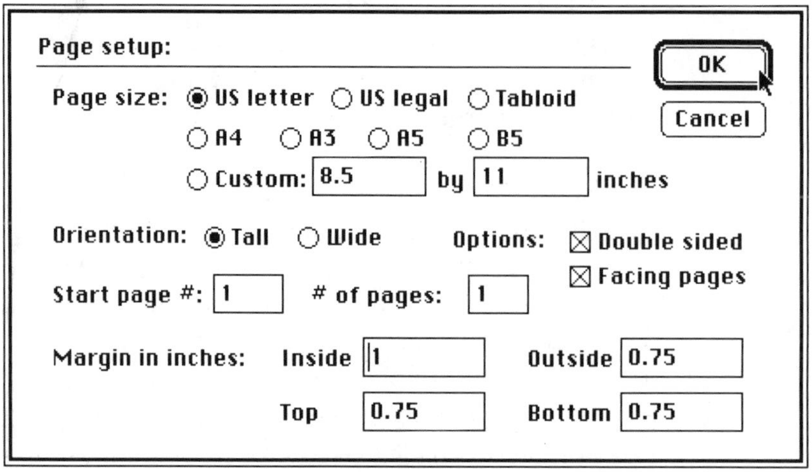

Figure 2-5. Dialog box for page setup to define image area.

the OK button and accept PageMaker's default settings for the page size. If you set up a custom page size, be sure it fits within the Printer's image area. If you decide to change the page size or other page settings (Page setup in the File menu) after you have placed text or graphics, your layout could be affected, so review the pages carefully to make additional changes before printing the publication. If you are not sure you want to make a change that could affect your layout, close the file and open a copy of the publication file, and then change the Page setup and review the changed pages in the copy of the publication file.

Designing the Layout

Next, select the Column guides command from the Options menu, and type 2 for the number of columns, and 0.25 for the amount of space to use for the gap between columns (1/4 inch). Figure 2-6 shows the dialog boxes

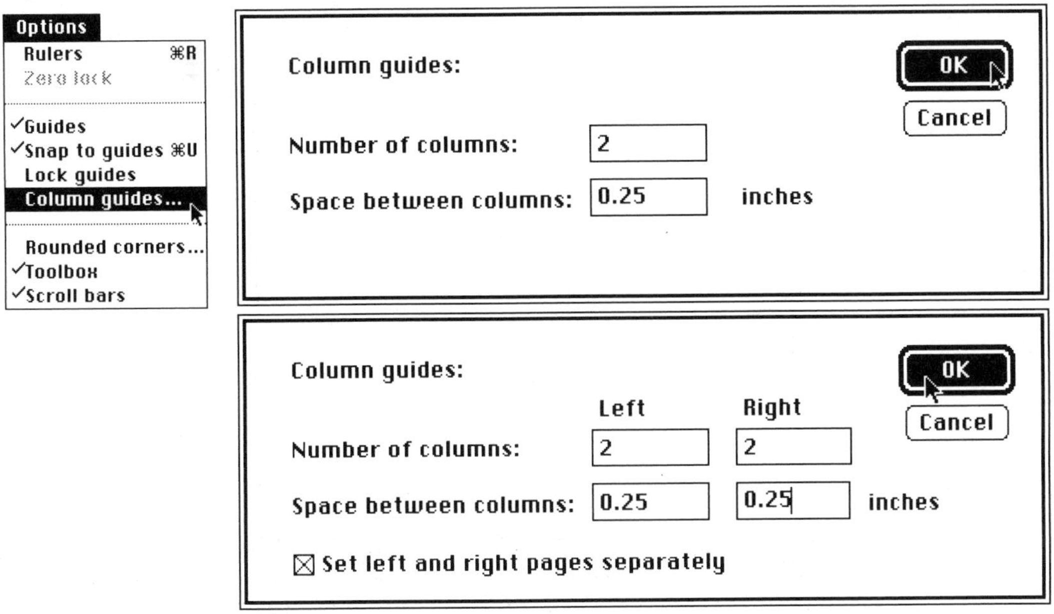

Figure 2-6. Dialog box for Column guides.

for Column guides (you are given the choice of setting left and right pages separately), and Figure 2-7 shows what the page looks like after choosing two columns with a 0.25-inch column gap. If you prefer to work with picas rather than inches, first choose Preferences from the Edit menu to change measurements from inches to picas, before selecting the Column guides command from the Options menu.

At the bottom left corner of the display, PageMaker shows two page markers next to the marker for the first page. They represent left and right "master pages" that describe the default settings of all left and right pages, including any graphic or text elements that should be repeated on every left or right page, or both. For example, you might put page footers on the master pages to repeat them on each page (including a page number that changes for each page). Include on the master pages only those text and graphic items that you want to repeat on *every* left or right (or both) page of the publication file.

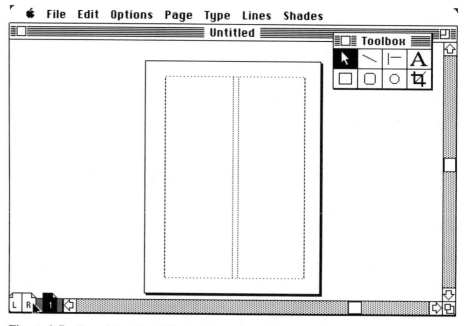

Figure 2-7. First page of publication file after setting column guides.

Back in the page setup menu (Figure 2-5) you could have selected a single page orientation by clicking off the marked box next to Double sided, which sets up only one master page and assumes the publication does not have double-sided pages. Most publications use double-sided page styles starting with a title page as a right-hand page, followed by two-page spreads. When you set a starting page number in the Page Setup menu, or change the starting page number, PageMaker will adjust the pages to match the numbering. For example, if your publication starts on page 1, a right-hand page (also called recto), and you later change the starting page number in the Page setup dialog box to 4, a left-hand page (also called verso), PageMaker automatically changes the pages and page icons.

For the newsletter example, in which every page has two columns, it is efficient to set the two-column format on the master pages, so that all new pages will start with a two-column format. You aren't locked into this

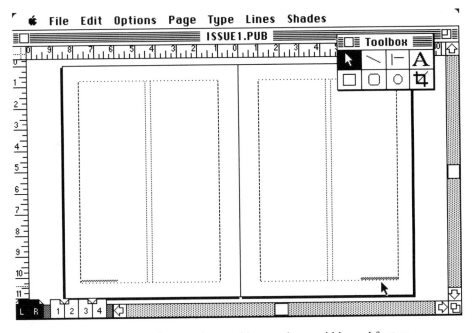

Figure 2-8. Master pages for newsletter with set column widths and footers.

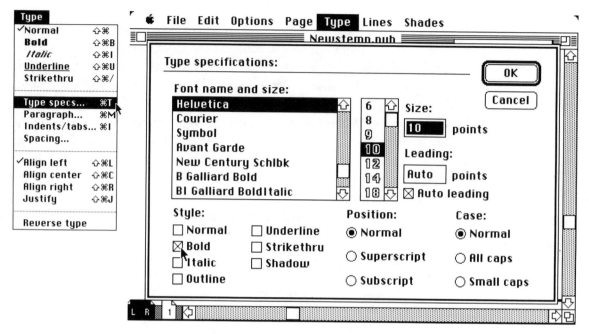

Figure 2-9. Type specifications menu with specs for the footer text.

format — on each page you can move or change the columns (and turn off the display of master page elements) or keep the format set in the master page. The Column guides dialog box always shows the number of columns on the current page.

Figure 2-8 shows the left and right master pages for the newsletter example, with a two-column format and footers on each page. You can place the footers and an automatic page number marker that increments on each page. First choose Actual size from the Page menu, and click once in the right scroll bar below the scroll box, and once to the left of the bottom scroll box, so that the bottom left corner of the left master page is in view. Or, use this shortcut to move quickly to any point on the page: choose Fit in window from the Page menu (or the shortcut, Command W), and use the arrow tool (click on it in the toolbox to select it), then hold down the Option and Command keys, and click the mouse button at the position on the page you want to zoom into. Next, choose the text tool,

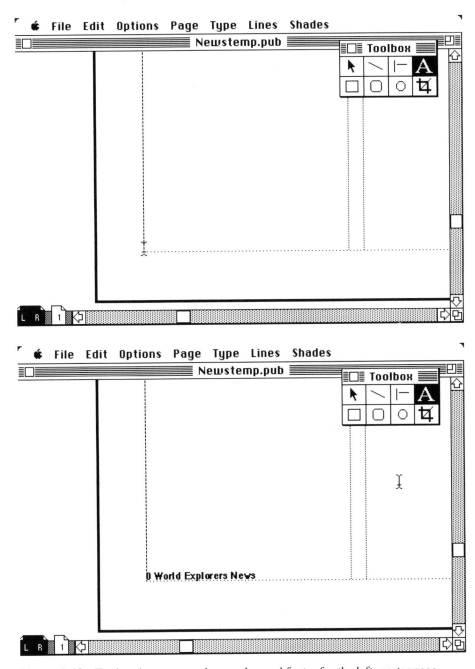

Figure 2-10. Typing the page number marker and footer for the left master page.

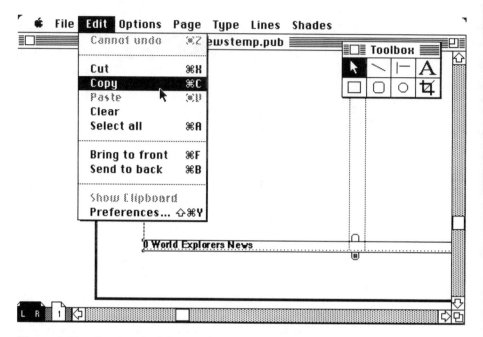

Figure 2-11. Copying the left-page footer into the Clipboard.

click an insertion point at the left margin, and choose the Type specs option from the Type menu (Figure 2-9). Select Helvetica as the font, 10 points in size, and click the box next to Bold, then click the OK button. You can now type the text of the footer (if you are not using the text tool, switch back to it before typing your text).

Start with the automatic page number marker: Hold down Command, Option, and P (altogether, and in that order). PageMaker displays a 0 (zero) to mark the place of a page number that it will add at print time, which is tied to the starting page number you specify in the Page setup menu. Next, add an em space (Command Shift and M) and the text of the footer as shown in Figure 2-10. After typing the footer, choose the pointer tool, and click anywhere in the middle of the footer's text. Two parallel lines (with buttons called handles in their middle and at either end of the lines) should appear above and below the footer. Now choose Copy from the Edit menu (Figure 2-11) to copy the footer to the Clipboard. Click to

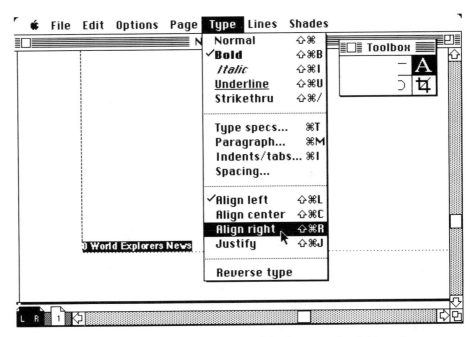

Figure 2-12. After using Paste to put a copy of the footer on the right master page, use Align right to align the footer to the right margin.

the right of the bottom scroll box to view the right master page, and choose Paste from the Edit menu. A copy of the footer should appear, and you can drag the entire footer into position on the bottom right edge of the page. However, since the footer is left-justified, choose the Align right command from the Type menu (Figure 2-12). To finish the job, click on the text tool and an insertion point just to the right of the page number marker in the footer, drag left to select just the marker, choose Cut from the Edit menu. Then click another insertion point at the end of the footer against the right margin, use the backspace key to cut the "s" in "News" (to be sure of deleting all extra spaces that followed the "s"), retype the "s" and an em space. Finally, choose Paste from the Edit menu to paste the page number marker. You will soon get used to selecting an item, copying or cutting it to the Clipboard, and then using Paste, even if you have never done this before. Other Macintosh applications programs (such as painting and drawing) use this same technique.

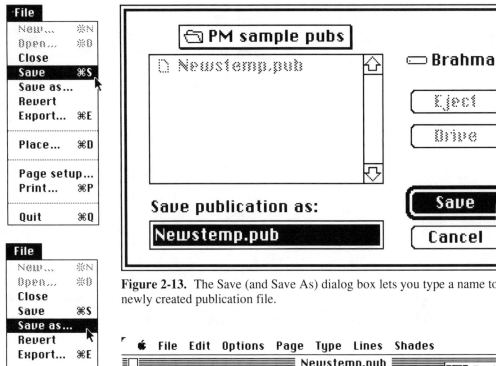

Figure 2-13. The Save (and Save As) dialog box lets you type a name to save a newly created publication file.

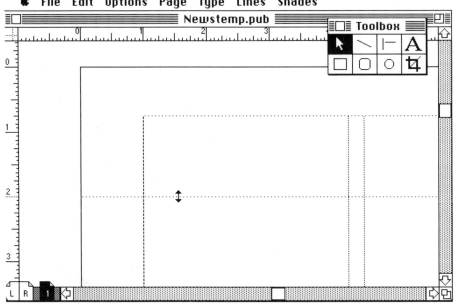

Figure 2-14. Adding a guide to help place text and graphic elements accurately.

It is time to save your publication file (you should save often). If you started from scratch with the New command, choose the Save command from the File menu (Figure 2-13) to save your template as a file, and then choose the Save as command to save a working copy so that you can use the same design for new publications without having to redefine the master page. Name your file **NEWSTEMP** or something similar (and press Return or click Save), so that the next time you start page makeup of a newsletter, you can simply click-on this template file from the desktop to start PageMaker with these settings.

If you started with a template, you should choose the Save as command, and type a different name than the name of the template, so that you can preserve the original and also have a custom version. This operation should soon become second nature to you: starting off with a template for a publication, saving it as a new file to further customize and add elements to it, and leaving behind an empty template for future use.

Designing the Title Page

The style of a newsletter is characterized by its title page, which can say more about your publication than a carefully worded statement. We chose a very simple design for this example so that we could move quickly through PageMaker's features. To move to page 1, click the page 1 icon in the lower left corner.

It will help your design task to display rulers — select Rulers from the Options menu. It automatically uses inches, as in Figure 2-14, but you can change the unit of measurement to centimeters or picas with points by selecting Preferences from the Edit menu. For our examples we leave the ruler in inches.

You may also want to use guides on the page, because you can attach text and graphics blocks to them without requiring the dexterity to position a mouse exactly (the Snap to guides command in the Options menu controls this feature — it is on until you turn it off by selecting it; to turn it back on, select it again). Ruler guides can be positioned anywhere on the page, locked into position, unlocked, moved and deleted; and with the Snap to guides on, placement of elements is easier and alignment is guaranteed. Ruler guides (most accurately calibrated at Actual size) should be used whenever you want to align anything. The

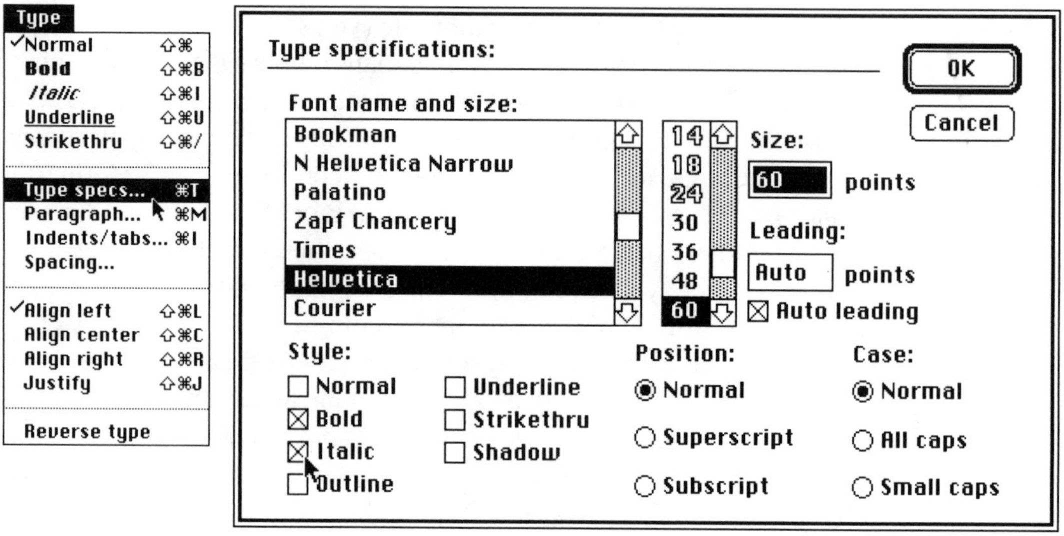

Figure 2-15. The Type specs dialog box.

combination of the 200% size page view (the most accurate view for lining up items on a page) and the extensive use of ruler guides will ensure your publication has all its elements aligned exactly.

To position a ruler guide, first change from the full-page view to Actual size (in the Page Menu, or Command 1), or to 200% size (Command 2) for complete accuracy, and scroll over to the top right corner of the page. Click anywhere in the top ruler and drag the ruler guide down to the desired position on the page. Then click anywhere in the left (vertical) ruler, and drag a ruler guide across the page into position. Use the dotted lines in both the horizontal and vertical rulers for alignment of all page elements. Figure 2-14 shows a guide placed 2 inches below the top of the page (exactly on the 2-inch mark) to show where to type the first line of the newsletter title.

Some designers start with the finished newsletter logo and title, others start with imaginary text blocks and a blank space for a graphic logo and title. You can choose any starting method with PageMaker, but if you're in a hurry, start with a simple title and graphic as we show in the next

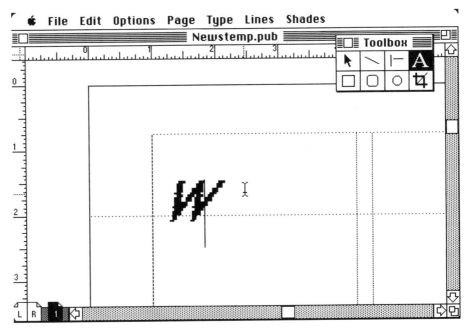

Figure 2-16. Typing the newsletter's title with the text tool.

example, or just draw a box with the box tool as a place holder for such a title, and place all of the articles first. You can then go back and adjust the title or add graphics.

To add a simple title, first select the type style and font with the Type specs command in the Type menu (Figure 2-15). We picked the Helvetica font at 60 points with automatic leading, and both the Bold and Italic styles. Click the text tool, then type the title as shown in Figure 2-16. Type **WORLD** and select the Type specs command again, to change the point size to 36 points. Click OK, and press Return to start a new line, then type the rest of the title — **Explorers News**. Although the text wraps around within the column width, you can change the text block's width by switching to the pointer tool and dragging the bottom right corner of the block of text to be wider, as shown in Figure 2-17.

For easier viewing of the title, switch to the Fit in window display option in the Options menu. (Or, as a shortcut, hold down the Command

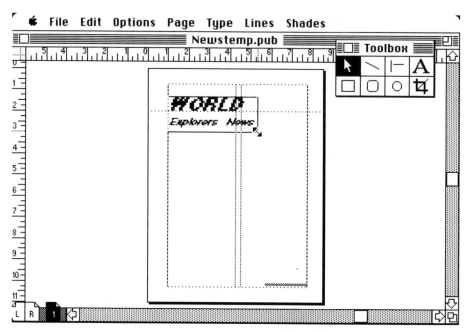

Figure 2-17. Changing the column width of the newsletter's title by dragging the bottom right corner with the pointer tool.

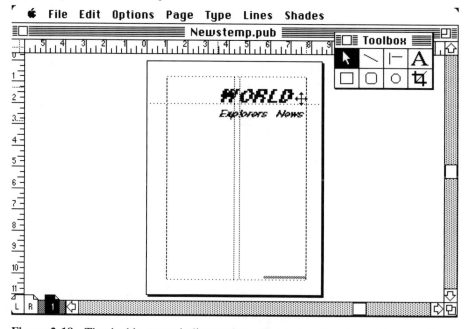

Figure 2-18. The double-arrow indicates that you can drag the element to move it.

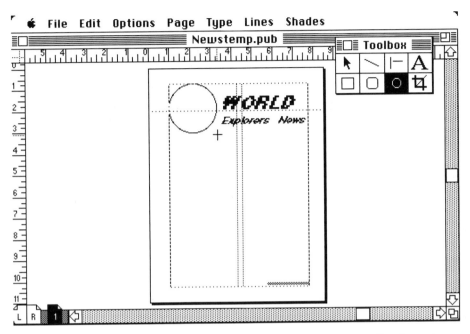

Figure 2-19 Draw a perfect circle with the circle drawing tool by holding down the Shift key while drawing.

key and type W, to go to the Fit in Window view from any page view. As you learn PageMaker you will discover many such shortcuts. Use the pull down menus until you learn the keyboard shortcuts, which are displayed in the menus. You can even pull down the menu to see what the keyboard equivalent is for a specific command you use often, such as Copy (in the Edit menu) or Type specs (in the Type menu), then drag your mouse to the top of the menu to put the menu away without selecting anything, and use the Command C, or Command T shortcut, for faster results than using the menu alone to select the command. As you learn PageMaker, you'll begin to remember the shortcuts for the commands you most often use, and you won't need to use their menus, unless you prefer to use menus.

To move the title into position (using the pointer tool), press and hold down the mouse button over the title until the double-arrow symbol appears (Figure 2-18). Without letting up on the mouse button, drag the title into the proper position on the right side of the page (the word

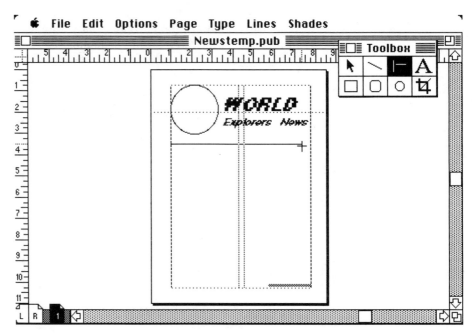

Figure 2-20. Title, circle graphic, and horizontal rule on the title page.

Figure 2-21. Line width and styles menu.

"World" resting on the guide line). You now have space to draw a circle to represent the globe symbol. Select the circle drawing tool from the toolbox, and move the crosshairs cursor to the top left corner of the page, then hold down the Shift key and drag downward and to the right to create a perfect circle as shown in Figure 2-19 (if you don't hold down the Shift key, the shape will be an oval).

Figure 2-20 shows the newsletter title with a horizontal rule being drawn at the 3 1/2 inch mark, using the perpendicular-line tool, selected from the toolbox. With the perpendicular line tool, press down on the mouse button to create an insertion point under the title at the left margin and drag to the right margin. You can pick the line width and style in the Lines menu (Figure 2-21).

Placing Graphics

When you are designing the title page and using a symbol in the title, you should place the symbol (or a rough version, if it is not finished) onto the

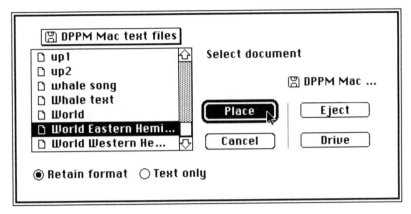

Figure 2-22. The Place command's dialog box.

page so that you can see the entire layout with the image. The graphic
should be in a file format acceptable to PageMaker, described in Chapter
1. If the graphic can be copied to the Clipboard, then you can use the Paste
command to place it on the page; however, for the best results, use
PageMaker's Place command to place the graphic directly from the file
onto the page. If your graphic is not yet available, use PageMaker's
toolbox to create a simple representation of the graphic's outline for now.

Choose the Place command from the File menu, and the Place dialog
box appears (Figure 2-22). You can scroll the list of file names if you move
the box in the scroll bar or click the arrows. The box in Figure 2-22 is at
the bottom of the scroll bar. The folders can be clicked open to see the files
inside them, and you can move back out by pulling down on the current
folder displayed at the top of the list of files. Figure 2-22 shows the files
on a floppy disk, and a file has been selected to place on the PageMaker
page. We used a MacPaint file containing a 72 dpi image of a world globe.
You can place any file containing a graphic image, such as the supplied
MacPaint, PICT, or EPS files from Aldus, or the Scrapbook images
supplied with your Macintosh.

Select the image file and click the Place button (or double-click the file
name). The selected file is in the MacPaint format, so the pointer turns into
the paint pointer icon (a paintbrush). Move the icon to the upper left corner
of the left-hand (first) column, and click to place the image. Use the same
method to place a draw-type document (PICT, or object-oriented graphic,

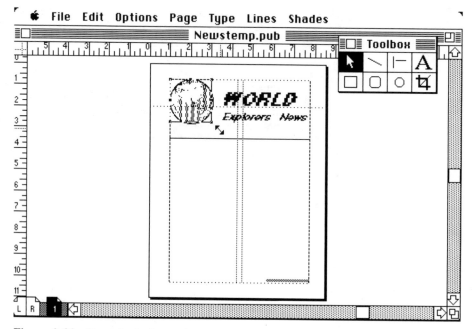

Figure 2-23. To scale the image in equal proportions, hold down Shift while dragging the bottom right corner.

represented by a pencil icon), a scanned photo in a TIFF file (an X inscribed in a square icon), an image saved in EPS format (a PS icon), or a chart or graph document (from an object oriented-drawing, drafting, or charting program that saves a PICT file, represented by a pencil icon). PageMaker's pointer icons tell you what type of file you are placing.

To scale the graphic down in size to fit next to the title, hold down the Shift key and drag the bottom right corner of the image up and to the left (Figure 2-23). You can hold down the Command key along with the Shift key to scale the image in the proportions that will give best the results at your printer's resolution. If you use the Command key to size the images at optimal print sizes for typeset resolution (1270 dpi or 2540 dpi), select your printer (as described in chapter 5) in the Print command dialog box in the File menu, and print the file (or a single page) once, before you begin placing any images, and do not change printers until you have placed all of your images.

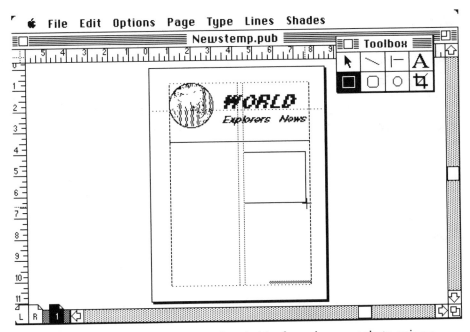

Figure 2-24. Drawing a box to act as place-holder for an image or photo, using a 1-point line.

Placing the Lead Article

The first article's heading should be in a size that is not too large to be confused with the newsletter title, but not so small as to be insignificant next to the text. It must also be close enough to the graphic image or photo that accompanies the article, so that when the readers' attention is drawn to the image or photo, the heading is the next item that is seen.

The best page designs will define an order, and balance the elements so well that the page may not appear to have been designed at all. (A good page design should catch the reader's attention, and direct the eye movement across and down the page, to facilitate faster comprehension of the content.)

Another decision to make is where to put a graphic or photo that accompanies the article. You should leave space on the first page for the image or photo, but you have the classic problem of not knowing how long

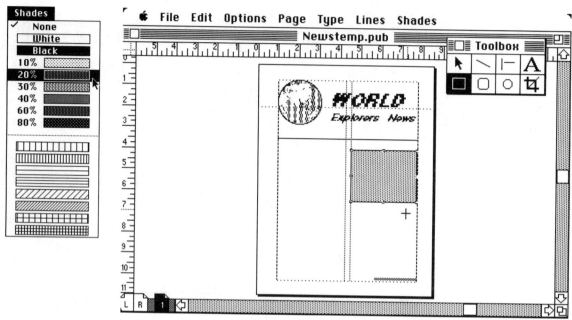

Figure 2-25. Setting a 20% shade for the place-holder.

the text will be when it is in typeset form. With PageMaker you can solve this problem by drawing a simple box to represent the image or photo, then placing the text of the article, and finally changing the size of the image area for the graphic or photo to accommodate the text, or adding other text or graphic elements to balance the page and avoid excessive white space. Figure 2-24 shows a box, drawn with the box tool, to act as a place-holder for an image or photo. Next, select a 1-point line from the Lines menu, and a 20% gray shade from the Shades menu (Figure 2-25).

You are now ready to place the text of the article. If your text file is already properly formatted as described in Chapter 1 (using Microsoft Word or another word processor supported by PageMaker), you can skip the type specifications. However, the word processor may not have used the proper leading (vertical spacing) value. For example, you may have picked 10-point type with 11-point leading in the word processor, but you really want 12 points of leading in the newsletter.

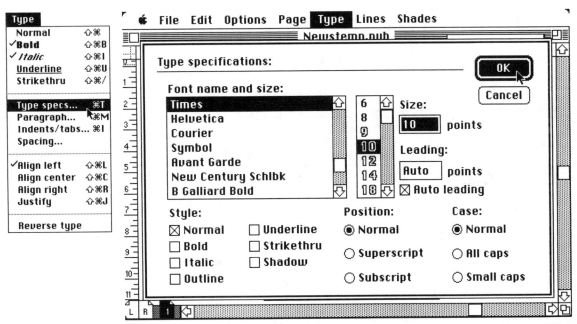

Figure 2-26. Type specifications for the text body, set before placing the text file so that they control the format of the text (overriding any format selected in the word processor).

We'll assume you did not format the text in advance, or you wish to override the format of the text set by the word processor. With the pointer tool selected, use the Type specs command in the Type menu, and select the Times Roman font at 10 points, with 12 points of leading, in the Type specs dialog box (Figure 2-26). In Figure 2-26 we did not need to type a value for leading, as PageMaker's Auto leading is 12 points at the selected 10-point type. You have the choice of using PageMaker's Auto leading (calculated as 120% of the specified point size, rounded to the nearest half point), or typing a number to specify leading (in points or half-points, such as 12 or 18.5). Click OK for the type specification settings, then check the Options menu to see if the Snap to guides option is on. (You should see a check mark next to the Snap to guides option.)

Choose the Place command from the File menu to place the text (Figure 2-27). Select a text file and click the circle next to the Text only option to

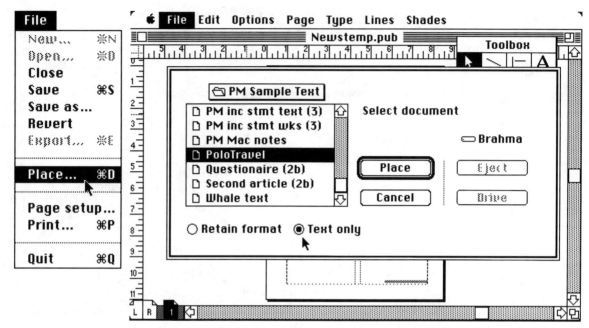

Figure 2-27. Using the Place command to place the text of the lead article, with the Text only option.

place the file without type formatting from the word processor (Page-Maker's Type specs settings are used). Finally, click Place (or press Return).

The pointer should turn into a text pointer icon, and you can place it appropriately in the left column as shown in Figure 2-28. Click the mouse. Text flows all the way down to the bottom of the page, and two handles on the text block (top and bottom center) appear (Figure 2-29).

The article's heading will be easier to work with, once separated into a block of its own, if it was part of the text file (otherwise you can simply type a headline at the position you want on the page). Holding down Option and Command and clicking the mouse while pointing to a specific spot on the page causes PageMaker to display an actual size view of the page. (Do it again and PageMaker jumps to fit-in-window view; the command toggles the displays.) Select the headline text by clicking the text tool, then dragging over the text to highlight it. Choose the Cut

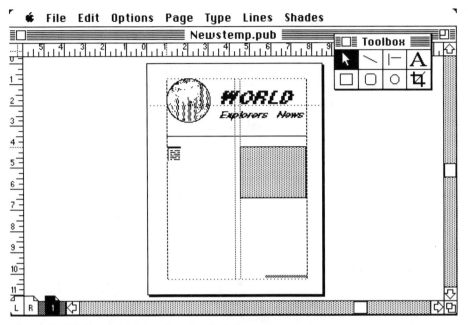

Figure 2-28. Text placement icon in the left column.

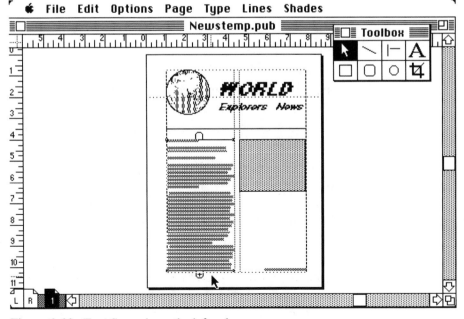

Figure 2-29. Text flows down the left column.

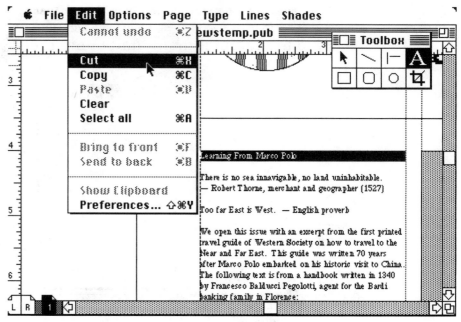

Figure 2-30. Cutting the headline text from the body text.

command from the Edit menu (Figure 2-30) and the headline disappears from the text block, leaving only the text in its proper place. You can use the text tool to continue editing the text if you wish; however, you should not do another Cut or Copy until you first Paste the headline.

Point to an area above the text block but below the title line, and choose Paste from the Edit menu (Figure 2-31). Use the text tool to select the headline text, then choose the Type specs command from the Type menu (Figure 2-32) to change the font of the headline to bold and italic 18 points, with 20 points of leading; then click OK. The headline should appear larger than before, but since it is only one column wide, you only see part of it on the first line.

To make the text block wider than a column, use the pointer tool and click the bottom right corner of the new text block formed by the Paste command, and drag it so it becomes a wider but shorter text block, so that the headline is one long line (Figure 2-33). With the headline fixed, you can move it into a better position by pointing in the middle of the text block

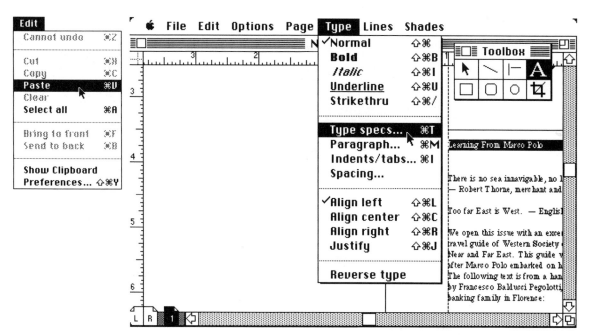

Figure 2-31. Pasting the headline in position, and choosing the Type specs menu.

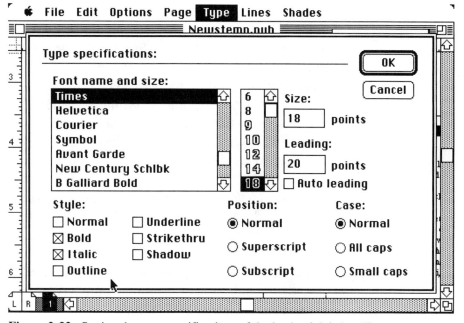

Figure 2-32. Setting the type specifications of the lead article's headline.

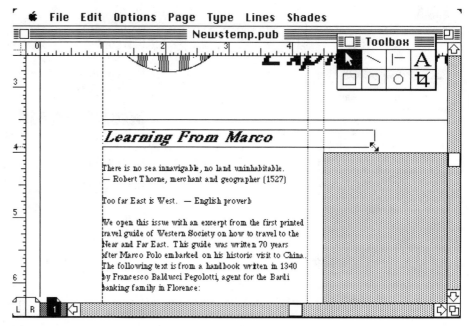

Figure 2-33. Stretching the headline text block to be wider.

and holding down the mouse button, then dragging the mouse when the double-arrow symbol appears. The entire block moves with the mouse, and you can position it properly. You can also click the body text block once to select it, then point in the middle of the handle atop the text block and hold down the mouse button while dragging the handle up or down, to align the text block to the image block. Or, hold down the Shift key and press the mouse button to constrain the block to horizontal or vertical movement.

The left column is too long — the bottom lines up with the page number footer. It helps to place a guide at the bottom of the page that runs across the text measure so that the right column's text can be aligned with the left column. Click the horizontal ruler at the top of the page and drag down a guide. Let go when the guide is at the 9 3/4-inch ruler mark (Figure 2-34).

The bottom handle of the left column has a + symbol, signifying that the text file has more text to place. To shorten the column, click the + symbol and drag the bottom handle up as if you were pushing up a window

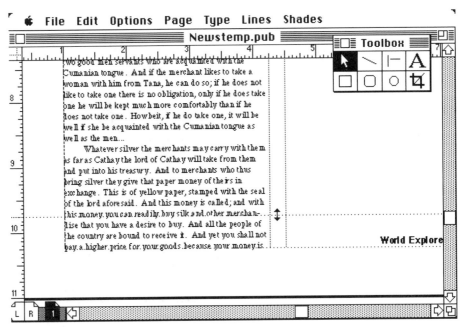

Figure 2-34. Setting a guide at the bottom of the page to help align text blocks.

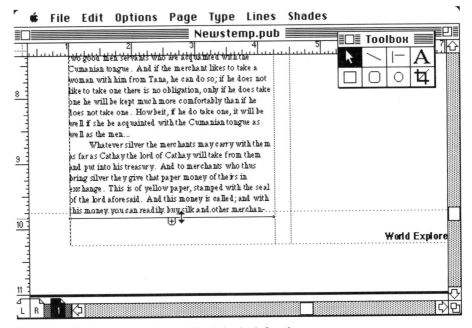

Figure 2-35. Shortening the text block in the left column.

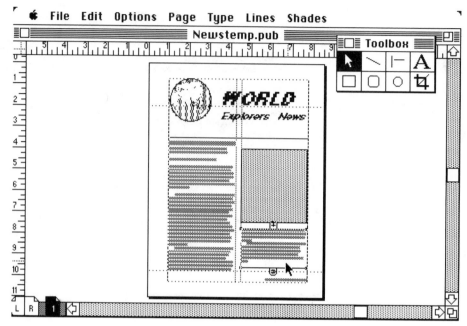

Figure 2-36. Placing the rest of the article in the right column.

shade; the text block is shortened as you move it. Align the text with the guide, then let go (Figure 2-35).

Change the display to a full-page view by typing Command W (or pick the Fit in Window option from the Page menu).

To continue the text to the next column under the image block, point to the bottom handle of the first text block and click it. The program changes your pointer to the text placement icon. You can still move around the page using the scroll bar, and you can select options from menus, change pages, and also insert new pages while the text placement icon is activated. But if you change to the arrow pointer, then switch back to the text tool, the text placement icon will no longer be loaded with a text file, but will instead show the text insertion pointer.

To place the next block of text under the image block, move the text placement icon to the mark at 7 3/4 inches, and click the mouse to place the rest of the article (Figure 2-36). The top handle of the right column contains a + symbol, indicating that the text continues from that location

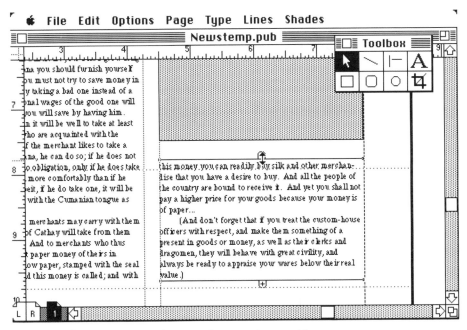

Figure 2-37. Lining up text in two columns using a guide.

back to another location (in this case, it continues to the bottom of the left column). The bottom handle contains a # symbol, signifying the end of the text file.

You can drag another guide down from the horizontal ruler to help align text, then push (drag) down on the top handle of the right column or pull up on the top handle to line up the text, as shown in Figure 2-37, and pull down on the bottom handle to display the end of the file (the # symbol).

Selecting and Changing Text

To change the type style of the quoted text in the article, switch to the text tool, click at the beginning of the text, and drag across the text to the endpoint before letting go, then select italic type from the Type menu (Figure 2-38) or use the keyboard shortcut Command Shift I.

To change the entire excerpted text in the article to italic, select the text by clicking a starting point and dragging the shortest distance (across both columns) to the endpoint. All text in both blocks between those points is

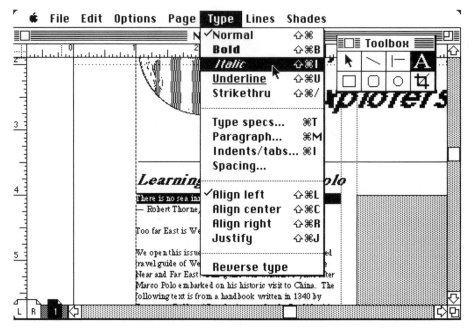

Figure 2-38. Changing selected text to italic.

highlighted (Figure 2-39), and you can press Command Shift I (or choose Italics in the Type menu) to change the selected text to italics.

You can also use the cursor keys to move an insertion point in the text to alter a selection after you have first selected an insertion point by clicking the mouse using the text tool. (Depending on your keyboard, your cursor movement keys may be numeric keypad keys, or they may be separate keys located to the right of the space bar.)

The left/right cursor movement keys move the insertion point by a single character or space, and the up/down keys move the point by a single line. Holding down Command when pressing a left or right arrow key moves the insertion point to the beginning of the next or previous word; when pressing an up or down key, Command moves the point to the beginning of the next or previous paragraph. You can also move up or down in the text block quickly, extending or shortening a selection, by holding down the Shift key and using the cursor movement keys.

There are several different ways to select text. Select a single word by

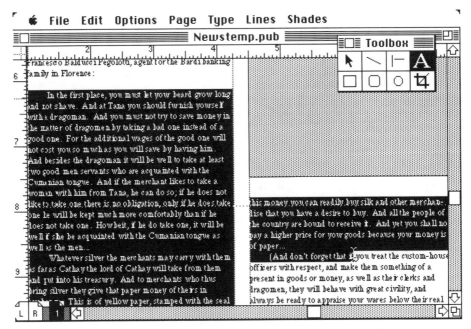

Figure 2-39. Selecting an area of text spanning two columns by dragging across them from starting point to endpoint.

double-clicking the word; you can then drag in any direction to select a group of words. To select a single paragraph, triple-click anywhere in the middle of it. You can extend a selection from an existing selection by holding down the Shift key and clicking a new ending point. (You can also use the cursor movement keys, as described above, rather than the mouse.) Another way to select a large area of text is to click a starting point at one end, then Shift-click the ending point at the other end. The easiest way to select all of the text is to click anywhere in the text once, then choose the Select all command from the Edit menu (or click an insertion point with the text tool and type Command A).

While the text is still highlighted (selected), another change to make is the tab spaces at the beginning of each paragraph. Select the Indents/tabs option from the Type menu and move the first tab marker on the ruler in the Indents/tabs dialog box (Figure 2-40) to approximately 1/8 inch. In the dialog box a fractional number changes as you move the tab marker —

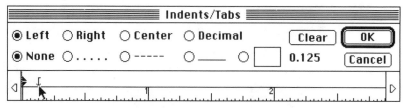

Figure 2-40. Indents/Tabs dialog box to change paragraph indents and tab settings.

when that number is 0.125, let go of the mouse. Click OK and the paragraph tabs change in the selected text. The increments you can set tabs at are determined by the page view size: if you can't select tabs at less than .25 increments, it is because you were at Fit in window page size when you issued the Indents/tabs command. Cancel the command by clicking the Cancel button, and switch to 200% page size (Command 2), then select Indents/tabs from the Type menu (or Command I) again, for maximum control of tab settings.

Note that these settings — type styles, tab settings, and even font size and leading — can be preset in the text file if you are using a word processor PageMaker recognizes (described in Chapter 1 and Appendix A), or set them (using the pointer tool, or the text tool *with no text selected*) for the PageMaker publication file before choosing the Place command and a text file, to place the text with new settings.

Adjusting Columns and Adding a Line
The lead article is one line too long, but there is one line of space near the beginning of the article. The easiest adjustment is to delete that blank line. (If you are practicing with a text file of a different length, add text until you reach the end of the page, then try this adjustment.)

You may want to change the display to Actual size (the Page menu). A quick way to do this is to hold down the Command and Option keys when clicking the mouse with the pointer tool — point to the area you want to see in actual size, then hold down Command and Option and click the mouse. Try this combination again and PageMaker changes the display to reduced size (Fit in window) so that the entire page is displayed. You can switch back and forth from actual size to reduced size with this key-click combination. Another way to switch to Actual size from any other view is to the use the combination of Command and 1.

Switch to Actual size to make most text adjustments, but for the most accurate page view, after you make changes at Actual size, you should always check the alignment by going to 200% size (Command 2), and then make any final adjustments in the 200% view. If you are using the built-in Macintosh screen, you probably don't want to be slowed down by working at the 200% size all the time, because it requires more scrolling. The fastest way to move the window is with the grabber hand (press Option and then drag), which can also be constrained by the Shift key to move vertically (Option Shift and drag up or down), or horizontally (Option Shift and drag left or right). When you move the window with the grabber hand or using the scroll bars, you must wait for the screen to redisplay. If you use a larger display screen attached to your Macintosh, you will find it is easier to work in the 200% size, because you can increase the size of your window to see more more of the page at once.

In fact, if you work with PageMaker full time, or even half time, you can quickly earn back the extra cost of a larger display, because you gain so much time by not switching page views and scrolling, then waiting for the screen to be redrawn each time you move your window. A large screen offers a larger window into the page, plus room to store your scrapbook, toolbox, and other tools, keeping them off the pasteboard and out of your way. Large screens today cost almost as much as your computer, so if that bothers you, work without one at first, and then add the display when you need it. (Several companies, such as Radius, SuperMac Technology, and E-Machines, sell large displays for the Macintosh. We suggest you test drive a few different models at your local computer store before buying, to determine which type you prefer.)

Choose the text tool to click at an insertion point at the beginning of the blank line (Figure 2-41). Press the backspace key to delete the blank line. The entire text block is reformatted, and the bottom lines of both columns should now line up.

What if you wanted to keep that blank line? Put it back by clicking the same insertion point again, and pressing Return. Now, of course, the text in the right column is one line shorter than the text in the left column. However, you can fix this problem in a number of other ways (besides

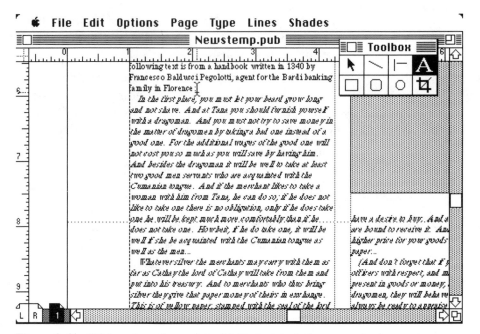

Figure 2-41. Click an insertion point with the text tool, then press backspace to delete a blank line, or press Return to add a blank line.

adding or subtracting a blank line): (1) you can edit the text to have more words and thereby extend one more line in the right column, or fewer words and thereby reduce by one the lines of text in the left column; (2) you can stretch the size of the image block to be longer so that the text in the right column is pushed down one line; or (3) you can change the word spacing in the article that PageMaker uses to determine line endings.

If you chose the first method, select the text tool and either add words somewhere in the text (enough to create a new line) or subtract words from the text (enough to reduce it by one line). If you subtract text from the right column, both columns will line up; otherwise, subtract the text, then push up or pull down on the bottom handles of the columns to line them up.

If you chose the second method, select the image block with the pointer tool, click the bottom handle of the block, and drag it down 1/6 inch. Then select the column text and push down on the top handle of the text by one line. The two columns should then be lined up.

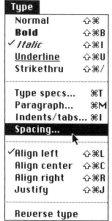

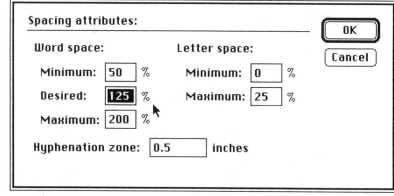

Figure 2-42. Choosing the Spacing option from the Type menu and increasing the desired word spacing to make ragged-right columns of text use more space.

The third method is perhaps the easiest. You can change the word spacing by first clicking an insertion point in the article using the text tool (or selecting an area of text), then choosing the Spacing option in the Type menu (Figure 2-42). The Spacing dialog box shows the minimum, most desired, and maximum percentages of the font's standard space amount used to make spaces between words and letters. These settings, and any changes made to them, control the spacing *for the entire text of the placed article*, not just the selected area of text or the column where you clicked the insertion point with the text tool. The entire article's spacing changes, but the newsletter title and other text that was typed or placed separately from this article is not affected.

Don't change the letter spacing (zero is the desired value, which is no extra spaces between letters), but change the Desired word spacing to 125% (by default it is set to 100%). With ragged-right columns of text, PageMaker uses only the Desired spacing value for all word spacing. The program uses the other values when it spaces words for justified columns (you'll experiment with justified text in the next chapter). The result of expanding the desired word spacing is that the right column now lines up perfectly with the left column (Figure 2-43).

You can now draw a line at the bottom of the page to provide an even look. Switch to the line drawing tool, and align the crosshairs cursor (+) to the left margin of the left column at the 9 3/4-inch ruler mark, and drag

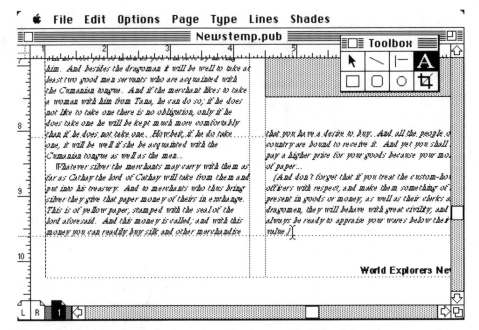

Figure 2-43. After the desired word spacing is expanded, the right column extends a line to be lined up with the left column.

across the column to the right margin of the right column. The program draws a straight perpendicular line (Figure 2-44).

Now would be a good time to save the publication, if you haven't done so already. If you have not, choose the Save as command from the File menu, and choose a new name for the publication (such as **ISSUE1.PUB**), thereby keeping the original version as a template.

Placing More Articles

PageMaker starts by default with one page ready for placing text and graphics. You could have changed that setting to several pages in the Page setup dialog box. This does not matter because you can add pages very easily by choosing the Insert pages command from the Page menu. The Insert pages dialog box (Figure 2-45) will automatically add two pages if

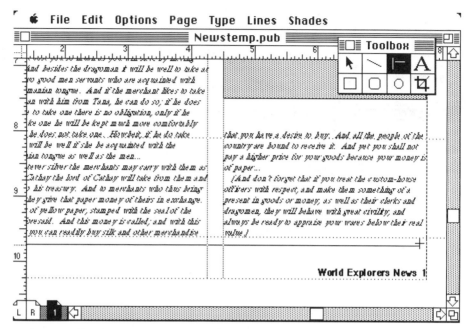

Figure 2-44. Draw a line across both columns at the bottom of the page using the perpendicular line drawing tool.

you click OK, or you can change that number to add more or fewer pages. PageMaker automatically uses the column settings and any images or text elements stored on the master pages, as long as both the Display master items and the Copy master guides options in the Page menu have check marks. (Normally the Display master items and Copy master guides options have check marks. Display master items, when not checked, hides the text and graphic items defined on the master pages so that they don't print. Copy master guides, when not checked, hides the column and ruler guides in the master pages. Keep these options checked unless you need to remove master items or guides from a page.)

To start the second article on page 2, click the page 2 icon (lower left corner of the screen). PageMaker will display facing pages (2 and 3), and you can choose page 2 by pointing to the left-hand page and clicking the mouse while holding down Option and Command.

By now you have learned a few tricks to perform before placing the text

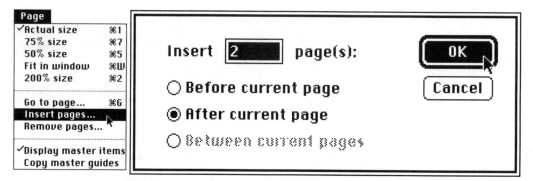

Figure 2-45. Using the Insert Pages dialog box to add two pages.

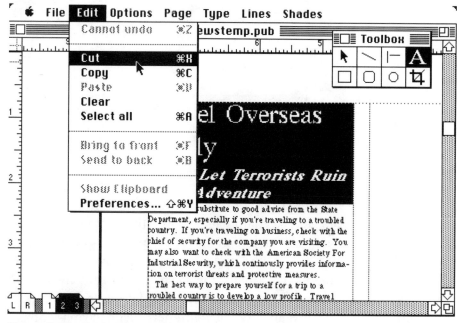

Figure 2-46. Cutting the headline text from the second article, to control placement and size.

of an article. If the article is not formatted, or you want to ignore any formatting and you will be placing only its text, first choose the desired Type specs (e.g., Times Roman, 10 points with 12 points of leading), then adjust the tab setting to 1/4 inch. (Both the Type specs and the tab settings

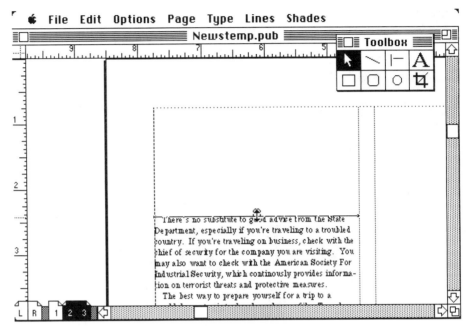

Figure 2-47. Pulling the text block down to make room for the heading.

should be already set from the last example; if not, be sure to use the pointer tool, or the text tool without any selected text, when you change the specs and settings.) Now place the second article the same way you placed the first: Choose Place from the File menu, click the Text only option, and point and click at the spot on the page where the second article should begin.

If the heading and subheading of the second article are not in the text file, you can type headings directly into the column. Select the headline with the text tool and change it to 30-point Times Roman bold, with 36 points of leading. Select the subheading and change it to 18-point Times Roman bold italic, with 20 points of leading. Then select both the heading and the subheading, and use Cut from the Edit menu (Figure 2-46). Move the text of the second article down by pulling down on the top handle (Figure 2-47), then use Paste from the Edit menu to paste the headline text. Click the middle of the headline and drag it into place, then drag the bottom right corner out toward the right margin to stretch the headline

Figure 2-48. Stretching the headline text block so that the heading and subheading each fit on one line.

block so that the headline fits on one line (Figure 2-48).

Drag a ruler guide down to the mark at 9 3/4 inches, then move up (use the scroll bar to move quickly) and drag another ruler guide down to the mark at 2 1/4 inches. Pull up the top handle of the text block to close up the space between the text block and the heading, lining up the text with the ruler guide, as shown in Figure 2-49. You can then line up the text with the bottom ruler guide, as shown in Figure 2-50.

You can continue the article in the next column by clicking the bottom handle of the text block (the pointer becomes a text placement icon) and clicking at the top of the next column. The text flows down to the bottom of the page. Extend the article to the next page by clicking the bottom handle of the text block to get the text placement icon, then clicking at the top of the column on page 3. If you had a very long text file, you could continue to place text in columns on pages by clicking the bottom handle to get the text placement icon, then switching pages by clicking the page

Figure 2-49. Adjusting the top of the text block using a ruler guide.

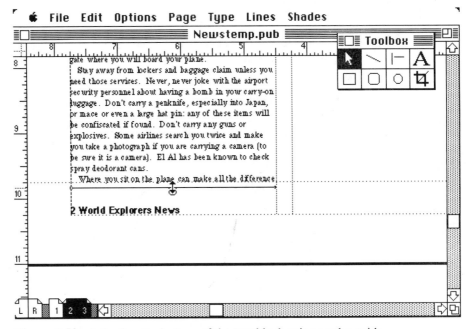

Figure 2-50. Adjusting the bottom of the text block using a ruler guide.

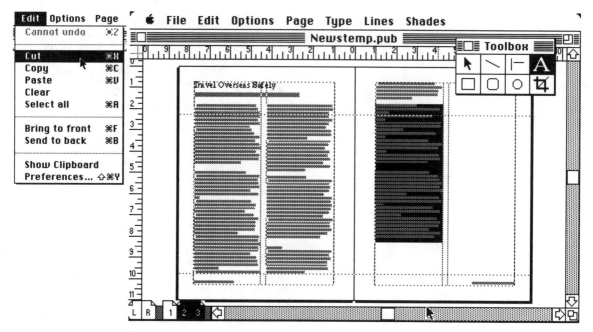

Figure 2-51. Using Cut to remove special text from the article to paste it separately.

marker icon. (You can switch pages or select options from some menus while using the text placement icon, but you can't switch tools without losing a loaded text file.) If you have not yet begun to place a file and you change your mind after choosing Place from the File menu (and the text placement icon has appeared), select another tool from the toolbox to cancel the text placement.

Changing the Layout

PageMaker is versatile — you can try one layout, then change it to another very quickly, without losing the first try. If you have enough space on disk, use the Save as command in the File menu to save the publication file as a second version, before changing the layout, so that you can later go back to the first version.

You may want to change the layout of the second and third pages. Assume that the second article does not fill up the entire two pages, and

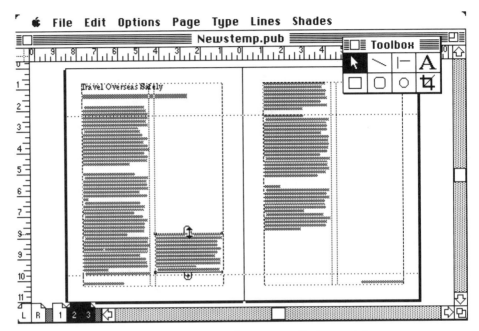

Figure 2-52. Moving the text block out of the way to fit the special text.

it includes a special section at the end that you want to move into a better position on the page. You can cut the text from the end of the article (Figure 2-51), then move the text block in the right column of page 2 (Figure 2-52) and in the left column of page 3 out of the way so that you can use the space for the special text. Paste the special text, then click in the middle of the special text and hold down the mouse button until you see the double-arrow symbol, then move the text block to the top of the right column (Figure 2-53).

The special section consists of two lists, each with seven numbered items, so they could be lined up side by side at the tops of the two columns, each boxed and shaded. Select the second half of the section and use Cut and Paste to separate it from the first half, then move both halves into position (Figure 2-54).

When you put a box around a text block in a column, you should make the text block thinner than the column, drawing the box so that it aligns with the column margins. To make the text block thinner, select it with the

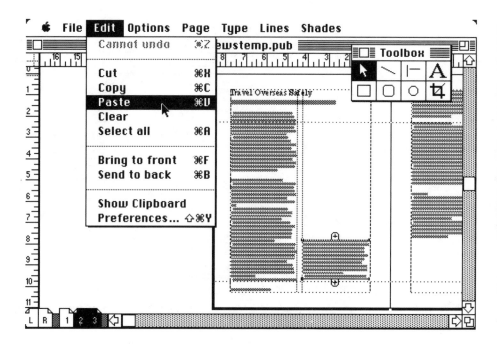

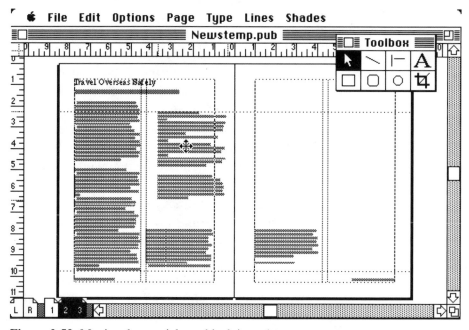

Figure 2-53. Moving the special text block into place.

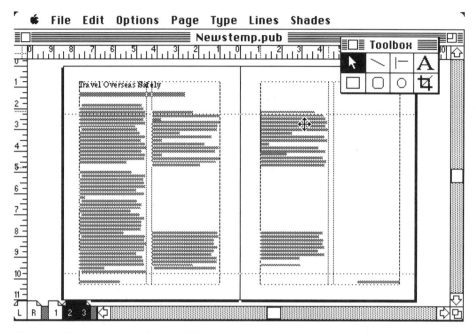

Figure 2-54. Separating the special text into two sections for placement next to each other.

pointer tool and drag the bottom right corner inward (Figure 2-55). You will have an easier time of moving the text block if you turn off the Snap to guides option in the Options menu (select it to get rid of the check mark to turn off the guides). When the block is not attached to guides, it can be moved freely to be very close to guides, without becoming attached.

Move the block so that it is centered in the column, then select the box tool and draw a box around the text by clicking a starting point above the top left corner of the text, and dragging across the text to a point below the bottom right corner, as shown in Figure 2-56. Line up the outer edges of the box with the column margins and, at the top and bottom, leave the same amount of space separating the box from the inside text. When you let go of the mouse button, the program completes the box; if you don't like it, select the Undo command from the Edit menu, or simply hit the backspace key since the box is already selected (it has handles), to delete the box. Or you can resize a selected box by dragging one of its handles with the arrow pointer tool.

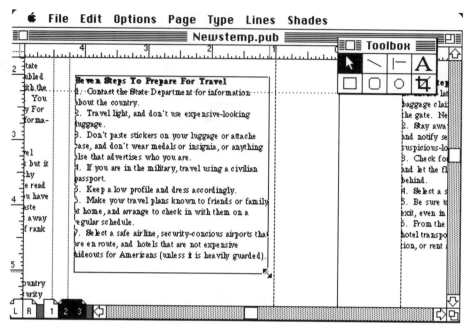

Figure 2-55. Changing the text block's width to accommodate a box around the text.

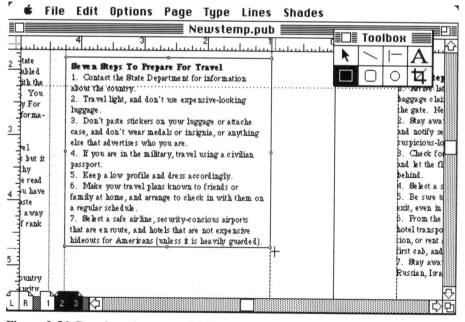

Figure 2-56. Drawing a box around the text.

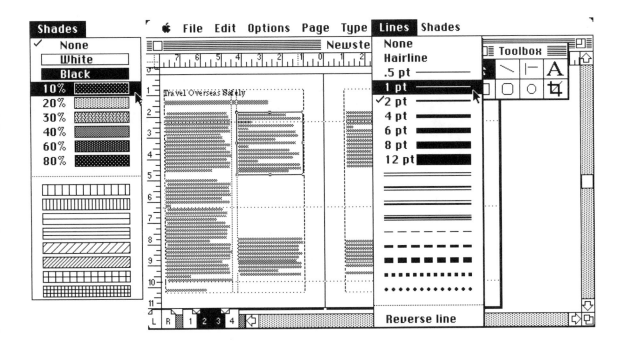

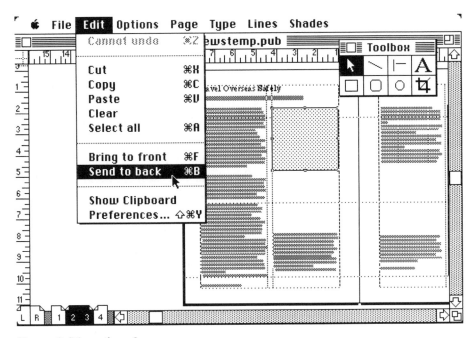

Figure 2-56 continued.

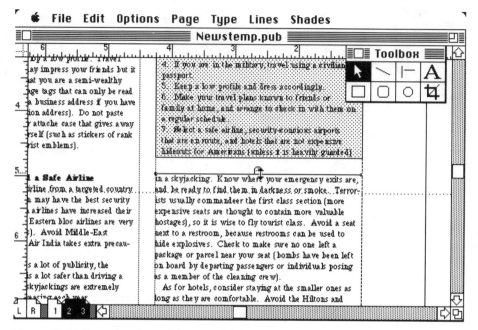

Figure 2-57. Dragging the article up to fill the space, using a ruler guide to line up the text in all of the columns.

While the box is still selected (i.e., displaying its handles), pick a line width from the Lines menu (such as a 1-point line), and a percentage of gray shading from the Shades menu (such as 10%). After selecting the shading, the box will look empty because the shading hides the text. To bring the text back into view, choose the Send to back command from the Edit menu, which sends the selected shaded box into the background (behind the text).

Now you are done with the first section; you can move over to page 3 and apply the same treatment to the second section. (Make the section of text thinner, center it in the column, draw a box around it, set the line width and shade, and send the shaded box into the background.) While drawing the box, move the display so that you can see the first box on page 2 and line up the second box on the same ruler guide. The pointer turns into a "grabber hand" if you hold down the Option key — you can move the

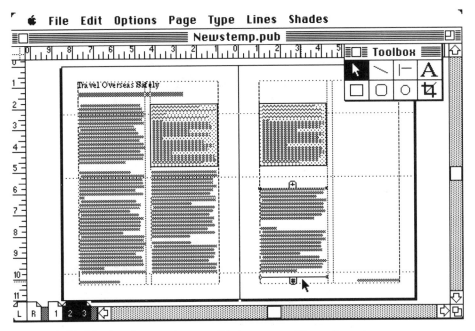

Figure 2-58. Moving the text down to fill the space with a pull quote.

display precisely and easily with the grabber hand. Use Shift and Option together and drag in the desired direction to constrain the window to vertical or horizontal movement.

Now you can drag the top handles of the article up to fill the space in both columns. Use a ruler guide to line up the text with the first column and the other columns (Figure 2-57). Drag the bottom handles down to the bottom ruler guide.

The article does not completely fill up the space, but we can push down the text in the left column of page 3 (Figure 2-58), and place a "pull quote" — an excerpt set in a larger font used as an attention-grabber. Highlight a sentence or fragment of text in the article using the text tool and choose the Copy command from the Edit menu to copy the text into the Clipboard. Paste the text back onto the page, and move it into position (point in the middle, hold down the mouse button until you see the double-arrow symbol, then drag the text block). Switch to the text tool, highlight the

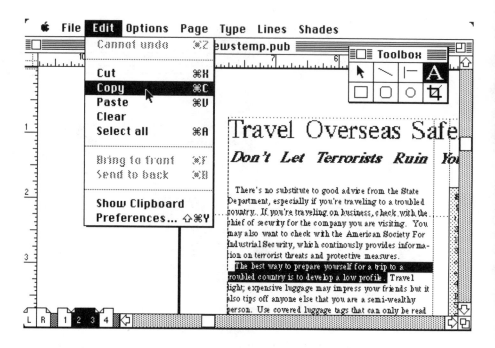

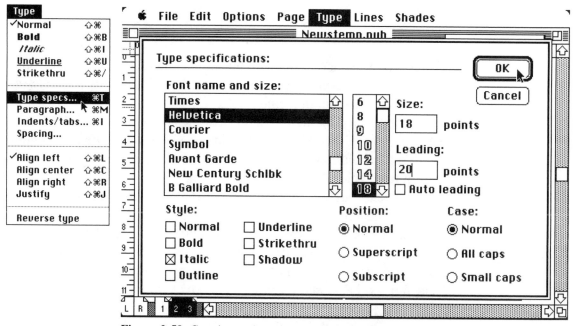

Figure 2-59. Copying and pasting a pull quote, then changing its type style and size.

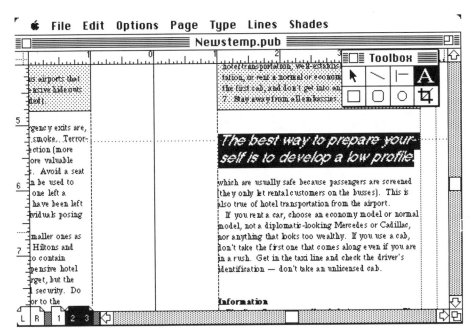

Figure 2-59 continued.

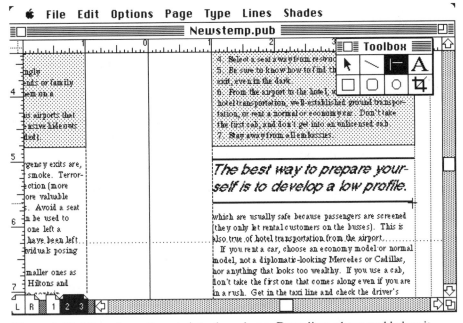

Figure 2-60. Move the pull quote into the column. Draw lines above and below it.

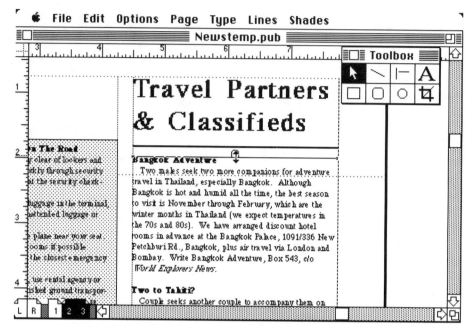

Figure 2-61. Placing formatted text and adjusting the beginning of it.

text, and change its font to Helvetica Italic, 18 points with 20 points of leading (Figure 2-59).

Drag a ruler guide down for alignment with the text on page 2 (at the 6 1/4-inch mark). With the pointer tool, select the text block under the pull quote and drag the top handle up to a point below the pull quote, then drag the bottom handle down to the bottom of the column. Push down on the top handle until the text is aligned properly with the text on the second page and with the bottom ruler guide. Then select the perpendicular-line drawing tool, and draw a 2-point line above and below the pull quote as shown in Figure 2-60.

Placing Preformatted Text

You now have a full first page, a full second page, and a half-full third page. You can place a third article (we use classified ad text) to fill the space on page 3, and another article (we use a questionnaire) for the fourth page.

Rather than place a file using the Text only option, this time you can place a file that has been prepared and preformatted on a word processor. As described in Chapter 1, word processors can be used to preformat text for PageMaker depending on how many formatting options are available in the word processor. For this article, assume you have used a word processor such as Microsoft Word, WriteNow, or MacWrite, all of which have options for italic and bold type styles as well as font selection. [MacWrite, however, does not have an option to specify leading. Use PageMaker's Paragraph command (Command M) to specify leading before or after placing a MacWrite file.] We selected a Times Roman 10-point font with 12 points of leading, with some text to be in bold and some in italic. PageMaker can read this information with the text and place it using these already-defined formatting options.

Before placing the article, type the headline for it (**Travel Partners & Classifieds**) in position, using Times Roman 30-point bold text with 36-point leading. Draw a 2-point line below the headline, using a ruler guide to align the 2 point line with the box top. Then choose Place from the File menu. The default setting for Place is to retain the formatting of the text file; until now you have been checking the other setting, Text only. This time, retain the formatting, and place the article starting near the top of the right column on page 3. When the article is placed, go back up to the top and align the text (Figure 2-61) using the same ruler guide you used to align the tops of the other three columns in this two page view (called a spread).

The text is already formatted to be 10-point Times Roman (with 12 points of leading), but the tabs at the beginnings of paragraphs are not the same point size (a 12-point tab would be best). To select the entire article text, click anywhere in the text with the text tool, and choose the Select all command (Command A) from the Edit menu. The entire article is highlighted, and you can change the type specifications or other settings. Change the tab setting with the Indents/tabs option (Command I) in the Type menu (Figure 2-62). Also, since the article is about one line too long, reduce the Desired word spacing with the Spacing command in the Type menu (Figure 2-63) to 75% (the Desired word spacing is the setting used

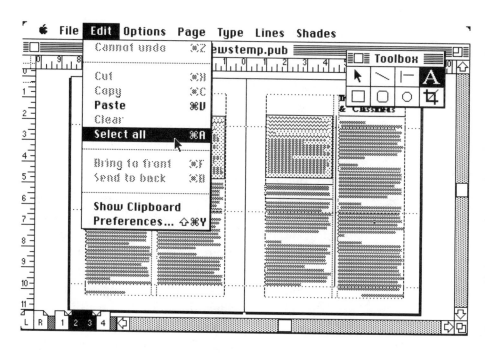

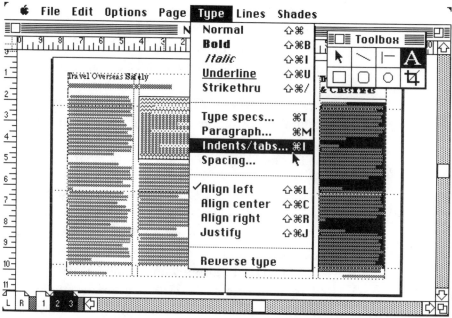

Figure 2-62. Selecting the entire text of the article, and changing the tab setting.

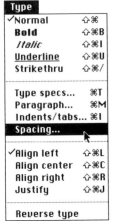

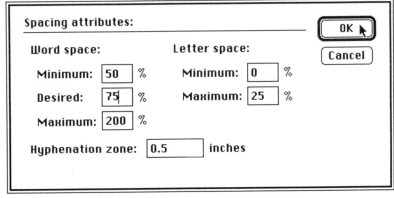

Figure 2-63. Reducing the desired word spacing (used for ragged right columns) to 75% of a regular space, to fit the text in the column.

for ragged-right columns). Now the text ends precisely at the bottom of the column.

You now have three pages of the newsletter filled with text. To add the last page, select the Insert pages command from the Page menu. The dialog box shows that the program is ready to add two pages (it assumes you are adding pairs of pages, because it is set for double-sided facing pages) after the current page. Change the number of pages to 1 and click OK, and PageMaker adds only one page and displays it.

In Chapter 1 and Appendix A we describe how to set up a text file to be completely preformatted so that you don't have to spend time formatting the text in PageMaker. The examples shown in Chapter 1 included a questionnaire prepared in advance with bold and italic text, assigned fonts (Times Roman, with Zapf Dingbats for the box symbols next to questions), leading values to space the questions properly (to leave room for people to write responses), and tabs to line up the multiple-choice answers. (Figure 1-14 shows how the text looks on the screen before placing it in PageMaker.)

Since the questionnaire is not formatted as a two-column article (it spreads across the page in one wide column), we first change the column setting for page 4 by choosing Column guides from the Options menu, and typing a 1 for the number of columns (in place of the 2). Now all you have

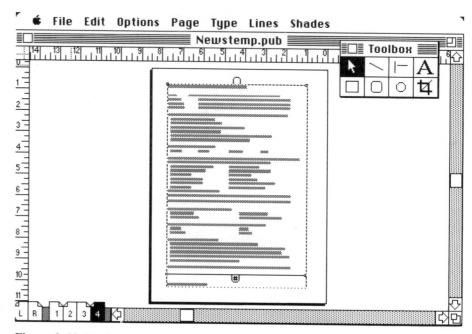

Figure 2-64. Placing the preformatted questionnaire on the last page.

to do is place the text file while retaining its format (keep the Retain format
selection active in the Place dialog box). Choose Place from the File
menu, select the file, click Place, and position the text placement icon at
the top left corner of the page.

Figure 2-64 shows the questionnaire placed on page 4; Figure 2-65
shows a close-up of the questionnaire — you can see that the tabs came
across to PageMaker, as well as the formatting. The Zapf Dingbats font
can be downloaded to a LaserWriter, and is included in ROM in the
LaserWriter Plus.

Figure 2-66 shows the printed version of the page using an Apple
LaserWriter Plus (a PostScript printer). If you haven't downloaded that
font, or it isn't a resident font in your printer, you can't use Zapf Dingbats
(unless a version of this font is supplied for your laser printer). You can,
however, use PageMaker's box tool to draw a small box (with no shading
or white shading, and a hairline or half-point line), then use the Copy and
Paste commands to copy the box for each multiple-choice answer.

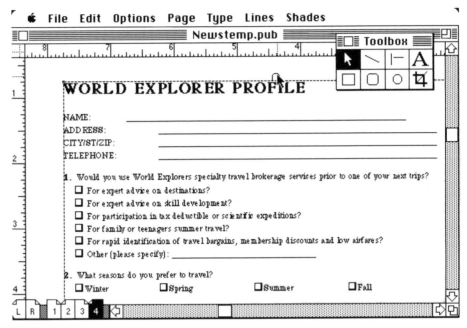

Figure 2-65. A close-up of the questionnaire: Each Zapf Dingbats box symbol is displayed on the screen and prints properly on a PostScript device.

The process is similar to selecting Zapf Dingbats or similar symbol font, typing the character that produces the symbol, and using Copy and Paste to copy the symbol for every multiple-choice answer, as we did in Chapter 1 using the word processor. The difference is that a pasted character (when in text mode) lines itself up on the text line, whereas a pasted graphic object has to be moved into position.

Adding Final Touches

You can add more graphic elements to the pages, such as vertical lines called "column rules" between the columns on each page. If you use hairline rules, the width is dependent on the resolution of your printer. The LaserWriter (300 dpi) harline is thicker than the Linotype L100 (1270 dpi) hairline, so ignore thickness of hairlines on the test pages from a LaserWriter, if you are using such a printer for proofing pages before

WORLD EXPLORER PROFILE

NAME: _____
ADDRESS: _____
CITY/ST/ZIP: _____
TELEPHONE: _____

1. Would you use World Explorers specialty travel brokerage services prior to one of your next trips?
   ❑ For expert advice on destinations?
   ❑ For expert advice on skill development?
   ❑ For participation in tax deductible or scientific expeditions?
   ❑ For family or teenagers summer travel?
   ❑ For rapid identification of travel bargains, membership discounts and low airfares?
   ❑ Other (please specify): _____

2. What seasons do you prefer to travel?
   ❑ Winter   ❑ Spring   ❑ Summer   ❑ Fall

3. Which of the following places would you like to visit in the next two years? (Put a 1 in the box of your first choice, a 2 in the box of your second choice; and fill any particular countries of interest)
   ❑ Continental US / Alaska / Canada   ❑ Orient: China & Japan
   ❑ Mexico & Central America   ❑ Indian Subcontinent / Himalayas
   ❑ South America   ❑ South East Asia
   ❑ Australia / New Zealand   ❑ Africa & Middle East
   ❑ Hawaii & Pacific Islands   ❑ Islands: Caribbean & Mediterranean
   ❑ South America   ❑ Europe (incl. Russia & UK)

Please indicate countries or states of interest:
Year 1: 1)_____ 2)_____ 3)_____
Year 2: 1)_____ 2)_____ 3)_____

4. If you are seeking travel services, what are they for?
   ❑ Family vacations   ❑ Trips open to all ages
   ❑ Active Baby Boomers   ❑ Summer adventures for teenagers

5. When travelling on a personal basis, what type of accommodations do you seek?
   ❑ Deluxe   ❑ Basic
   ❑ First Class   ❑ Bargain

6. Which type of trip are you interested in?
   ❑ Soft Adventures (exotic trips with deluxe / first class accommodations).
   ❑ Moderate Adventures (active tours for anyone in good physical health, may involve camping).
   ❑ Ultimate Adventures (very rugged and strenuous trips, high altitude treks and backpacking).
   ❑ Discovery Tours (informative travel; hone your photo skills, join and assist scientific expeditions).
   ❑ Leisure & Popular Tours (winter sun or powder skiing).

Date:_____   Signature:_____

4 World Explorers News

Figure 2-66. The printed page from a PostScript printer showing the questionnaire's Zapf Dingbats symbols.

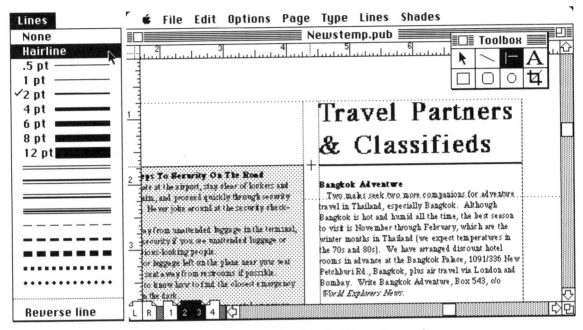

Figure 2-67. The starting point of the hairline column rules.

typesetting them. Many designers prefer to see white space rather than rules between columns. The goal is to balance all the elements on the page without crowding them, and white space is considered to be as much an element as are text, line art, rules, color, and halftones.

To draw a column rule, select the perpendicular-line drawing tool and a hairline from the Lines menu, then click the starting point for drawing at the top of the column above the 1-point dividing line (Figure 2-67). The pointer turns into a crosshair (+) so that you can line up the hairline to the ruler guides. Drag downward (Figure 2-68) to draw the hairline to a point where the body text ends, then release the mouse button.

With the perpendicular-line drawing tool still selected, continue drawing the line below the dividing line, until you reach the bottom of the column of text. Turn to page 2 and add a hairline column rule to separate the two articles from the top to the bottom of the columns (Figure 2-69).

You can tinker with the newsletter title to make it more attractive. You can try a different font or manually kern some of the letters (bring them

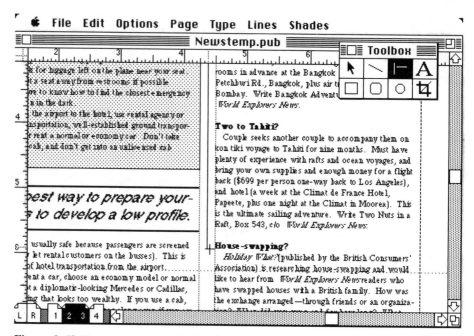

Figure 2-68. Drawing a perpendicular hairline column rule.

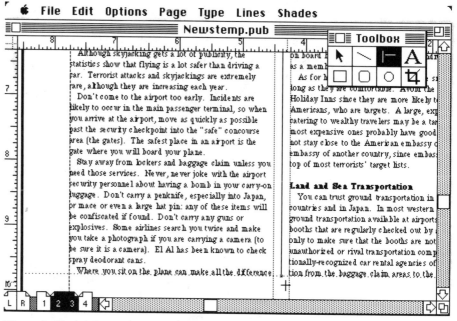

Figure 2-69. Adding a hairline column rule to page 2.

Figure 2-70. Manual kerning of letters in the newsletter title.

closer together), especially at large sizes. To kern a letter so that it is closer to the previous one, click with the text tool just before the letter, hold down the Command key, then press the Backspace key for each increment of space to delete between the letters (Figure 2-70). The first stroke deletes automatic kerning, and the second stroke begins manual kerning. To add space between letters, use the same procedure, except hold down both the Shift and Command keys as you press the Backspace key for each increment of space to add between letters. The amount of space added or deleted is calculated as 1/24 the point size of the character to the left of the insertion point you click with the text pointer.

For the final touch, return to the title page (page 1) and select the Display master items option from the Page menu. This option, which is usually turned on (a check mark is displayed next to it), means that PageMaker copies text and graphic items (such as footers) from the master pages to the selected page for displaying and printing. The only master item in this example is a page number footer, which is usually left

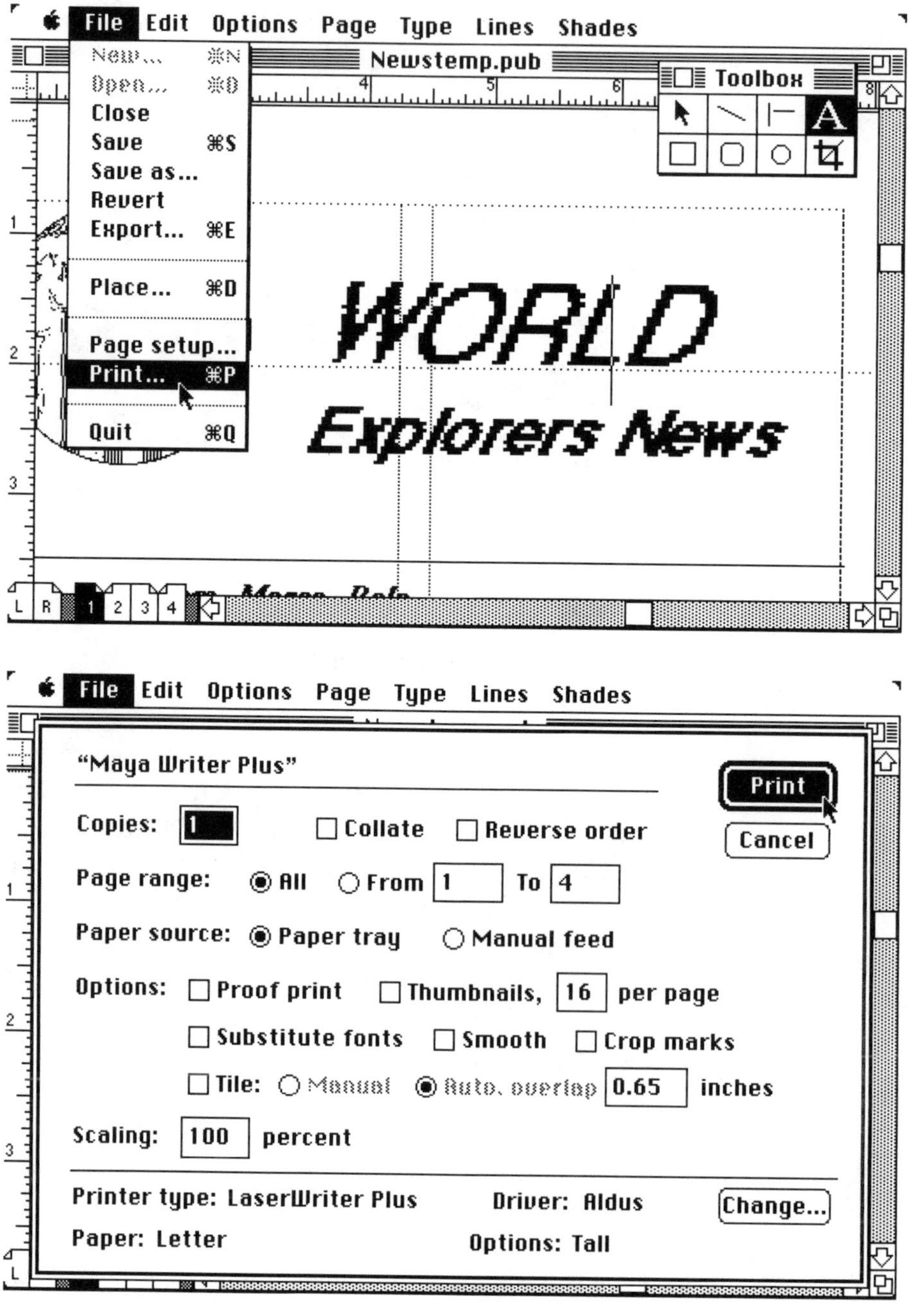

Figure 2-71. The Printing dialog box.

off the title page. Turn off the display (and printing) of master items for page 1 by selecting the option again (the check mark disappears).

Save your file when you have finished making changes. PageMaker does a "mini-save" whenever you turn the page, so if the system bombs or the power fails, you will not lose more than a page or two. You can revert back to the way the publication file was at the last full save operation, or you can revert back to the last mini-save operation by holding down the Shift key when selecting Revert.

Printing the Publication

We are now ready to print the pages we've assembled. Select the Print command from the File menu, which displays the dialog box shown in Figure 2-71.

Depending on the printer you are using, you can select several print options, or click OK to accept the default settings or the last settings you chose for printing (one complete copy at 100% scaling factor printed in the usual order of pages for your printer). You can select any number of copies and/or specify a specific range of pages to be printed. Other options include thumbnails (mini-pages useful in design and production planning), collated copies, reverse order, crop marks (also called trim marks), and printing larger or smaller than original page size (type a Scaling factor, as a percentage of original size), with the option of using tiling settings for oversize pages. (Tiling is printing a large image on several pages with edges that can be overlapped and pasted together.) If you select Change (Printer type), you can even use Mirror and Invert to print film negatives, emulsion side up or down.

You specified the margins for your page in the Page setup dialog box when you first created the publication file. You should have referred to your printer manual to be sure your design does not extend beyond the maximum print area of your printer. You can choose Page setup from the File menu to change the margin settings, but that will affect your layout and make changes you may not want. To print the complete pages without changing the layout, scale the publication to less than 100% in the Print dialog box, selected from the File menu at print time.

Summary

You have successfully completed four pages of a newsletter and printed them with excellent results. You've learned the following in this chapter:

Starting PageMaker
First, choose a final printer. Then either open a predesigned model or template file (such as *Aldus Portfolio: Designs for Newsletters*), or choose New from the File menu and use or modify the default page setup (for double-sided, facing 8 1/2- by 11-inch pages, with a 1-inch inside margin — to allow an extra 1/4 inch of space for binding — and 3/4-inch outside, top, and bottom margins).

Designing Master Pages
Choose Column guides from the Options menu to specify the number of columns (set up a layout grid, which can be changed later). Use the toolbox to create left- and right-hand footers, place automatic page numbering markers, and position all other elements that you want to repeat on all left- or right-hand pages on the left and right master pages.

Saving Your Publication File
Choose Save from the File menu, and give your new publication file a name. Or, if using a template, choose Save as from the File menu, to give your new publication file a new name, while preserving the template file intact. Continue to Save your file as often as necessary to prevent lost work.

Designing Title Page
The Option menu offers Rulers, with a selectable unit of measurement (default rulers measure inches, or select Preferences from the Edit menu to display millimeters, ciceros, picas, or points), and Snap to guides (default is on), used to create an attraction between the elements you are placing and any column guides you have set, so that elements will automatically attach to the column guides they are closest to, for automatic precision alignment of elements to columns.

Typing Text

Select Type specs from the Type menu and choose a font, style, size, and leading, then click the text tool. Move the I-beam pointer into position, click the mouse button to establish an insertion point (if Snap to guides are on, the insertion point will snap to the nearest guide), and start typing. Text automatically wraps (and hyphenates, if hyphenation is set to automatic) to the next line if it extends past the right margin setting.

Changing Width of a Text Block

Select the pointer tool (the I-beam pointer changes back into an arrow pointer) from the toolbox and drag the bottom right corner of the text block to the desired width.

To move the title into position on the page, position the pointer tool over the title and press down, but don't release the mouse button; the double-arrow symbol will appear. The double-arrow symbol tells you that you can move the selected text or graphics element to a new position on the page; then release the mouse button to fix the element at the new position (if Snap to guides are on, they will affect the placement).

Drawing Circles and Horizontal Rules

To draw a circle, select the oval drawing tool and move the crossbar icon into position on the page, then hold down the Shift key, while dragging to the right and down, to size the circle. (If you don't hold down the Shift key, you will draw an oval.)

To draw a horizontal rule, select the perpendicular-line tool, then move the crossbar pointer to the starting position, click the mouse to start drawing your line, then drag the line until you have reached the end position.

Placing Graphics

With the pointer tool, select Place from the File menu, then select from a list of suitable graphics files (paintings, drawings, scanned images, or charts or graphs in formats PageMaker recognizes) and click the place button, or double-click the file name. Move the icon into position on the page and click to place the file. After placement, you can scale graphics by dragging a corner handle of the selected image (you can also select an image at any time and scale or crop it). Scale in proportion without distortion by holding down the Shift key while dragging a corner handle of the image. For paint-type graphics, use built-in sizes optimized for your printer's resolution by holding down the Command key while dragging. Use both Command and Shift to resize a paint-type graphic in proportion and get the best resolution on your printer (use Print in the File menu to select your printer).

You can also place a graphic by using the Copy (or Cut) command from the Edit menu to copy the graphic from the Scrapbook, Clipboard, or other desk accessory, together with Paste to place the image on the PageMaker page.

Placing Articles

You have a choice of placing formatted text (if the text is preformatted) or placing with the Text only option (ignoring any formatting from your word processor). First change any of PageMaker's default type specs you need to before you place the file. Select a file to place, and move the Text placement icon to the desired position on the page, clicking once to place the first column (if Snap to guides are on, the column flows within the preset columns). Cut the headline from the top of the text file, paste it on the page as a separate block, and use the Text tool to select the headline text. Change its type specs (from the Type menu) to be bigger and bolder. Adjust the headline to be wider and reposition it on the page, then pull the first column text block to a better starting position by pulling up on its top handle. Push up or drag down on the bottom handle of the text block to position the end of the column, then click on the bottom handle to continue placing text in the next column.

After placing you can separate text into separate blocks, move blocks on the page, select text and change type specs, change tab settings, change letter and word spacing for the entire article, edit text on the page, and change page size view. You can insert pages, change settings that affect the page (such as Display master items and Copy master guides), turn the page, and place more text (with new Type spec settings if you need to). Change the type specs and position of headings and subheadings by selecting them with the text tool.

Changing the Layout

Change the layout to include a sidebar of boxed text (adjust column widths to be narrower to fit within a box; set the box line style, width, and shading), then move the sidebar forward to a previous page in the publication file. Create and place a pull quote by copying a section of text, pasting it down in a separate block, changing the type specs, and resizing the column width of the separate block.

Placing Preformatted Text

You can place preformatted text (retaining formatting) and still apply new settings for tabs and word spacing or change the Column guide settings (to place a file that was formatted to be one column wide onto a two-column page, with the same line endings). Add special symbols and characters by using defined Command key sequences (see Appendix C).

Final Touches

Add column rules and kern headline type (if necessary) to bring letters closer together. Draw vertical rules if desired as column separators.

Printing the Publication

Select the Print command from the File menu, then specify print options such as thumbnails, all pages or a specified range, the number of copies of each page, collated or not, in reverse order or not, with or without crop marks (trim marks), scaled in size to print smaller or larger than the original 100%, and tiling (controls options for printing oversize publications across several pieces of paper).

3 | Business Reports and Manuals

This chapter describes how to design and produce mid-sized to large publications, such as an annual business report or a full-size instruction manual. One characteristic these publications have in common is that they should be designed with a consistent format, both to present a unified image of the company and to make them more readable. Since the readers of such documents usually do not read them by choice, use a simple design, with consistent treatment of titles, headings, subheadings, charts and figures, and so on, to present the information more clearly. Your company logo and a unified design scheme can be effectively used for all your documents — business cards, letterhead and envelopes, product packaging, documentation, annual reports, and advertising — to present an image that will be remembered.

You can enforce a uniform style for a publication by creating master pages and saving the publication as a blank template publication file. Graphics from one publication can be easily copied into another, using the Copy and Paste commands in the Edit menu. You can also start with a template for one type of publication, modify it for another type, and use the Save as command to save the modified publication as a new template without changing the first template.

PageMaker is a good choice for producing an annual report or manual because it can accept charts, graphs, and illustrations from different programs or even different types of computers. The report or manual can be printed on a laser printer for final proofing, updated very quickly, then transferred to a typesetter for a very professional look. (The typesetter prints with a much higher resolution — 1270 or 2540 dpi, compared to the typical laser printer at 300 dpi.)

PageMaker can handle any type of document up to 128 pages. Since most instruction manuals and reference manuals are broken up into sections, you can use PageMaker to produce each section. You would create a publication file for each section or chapter (each can be up to 128 pages). PageMaker can provide automatic page numbering (up to 9999) starting with any page number and can even produce page numbers such as "page 4-2" (section 4, page 2).

Annual Business Report

Reports usually include charts, spreadsheets, and specialized graphics. (Chapter 1 and Appendix B describe all of the programs that can generate such elements for PageMaker pages — nearly every popular program for the Macintosh is supported by PageMaker.) A report should also have the company logo (perhaps placed on every page in the footer), a title page, and perhaps graphics or photos.

You can follow along with the example by typing enough text to fill a few pages, or borrowing text from a file you already have, as long as the text has subheadings (or add subheadings to your text file). You can also create a company logo like the one in the following example by altering one of the supplied graphic files in the PageMaker tutorial using MacPaint (if the image is a paint-type image), MacDraw (if the image is saved in a PICT file format), Adobe Illustrator (for PostScript and EPS format images), or some other painting or drawing program. Charts and graphs can be produced by various programs including Cricket Graph; we used Microsoft Excel on the Macintosh to enhance a set of Lotus 1-2-3 charts and graphs before placing them onto PageMaker pages.

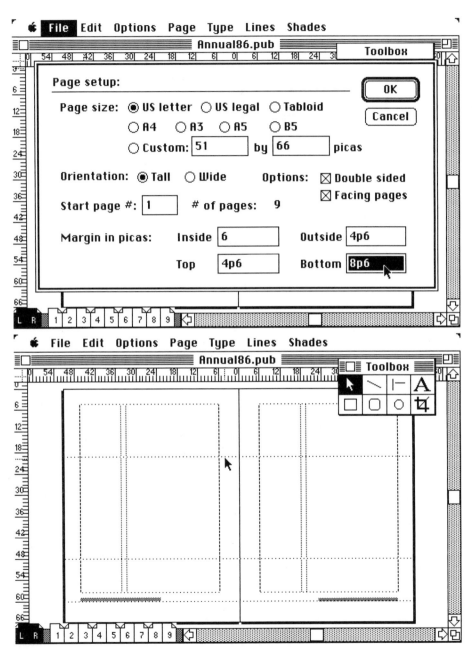

Figure 3-1. Master left and right pages for an annual business report.

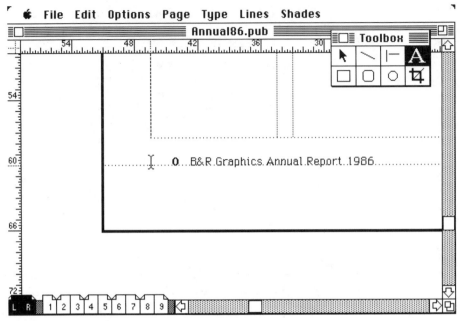

Figure 3-2. A different footer for left and right pages, with space to drop in a logo.

Setting up the Master Pages

Start by designing a new publication file's master pages. You can choose the standard page setup, and define a left-right page orientation, so that PageMaker creates two master pages: one for the right and one for the left. However, you should change the default image area to the actual dimensions of the image area you want for the report. In the following example, the bottom margin is redefined to be 8 picas rather than 4, leaving enough space at the bottom of each page for a footer and white space (always design pages with some thought to leaving white space for a more pleasing, less crowded look).

Figure 3-1 shows the master pages defined for the left and right pages, with ruler guides added. Figure 3-2 is a closeup of the footers defined for these pages, which include automatic page numbers (as in the newsletter example in Chapter 2) and space for a logo, created by typing two em spaces (Command Shift M for each space) next to the page marker. Em

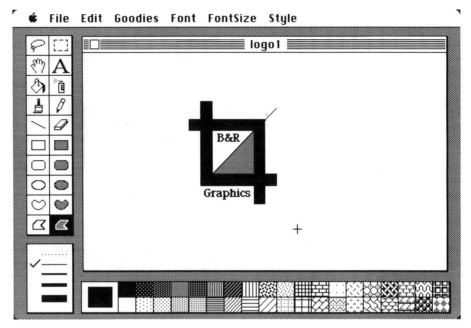

Figure 3-3. Editing a logo image using MacPaint.

spaces are fixed spaces that are the width of a capital "M" in the chosen font, and unlike regular spaces between words, they are not changed by PageMaker. Also type one em space after the page marker to separate it from the text of the footer.

In the master pages, define a single body text column 28 picas and 6 points wide, and a column for headings and subheadings that is 12 picas wide, leaving 1 pica and 6 points for a gutter between the columns. The master pages automatically set all of the publication file's pages to start with these column settings, but these can be altered when you want different column settings on a particular page.

Corporate Logo

You can place a company logo on the master pages so that it appears in the report on every page at the same location. To create the logo, you could start with a sketch or a previously designed logo on paper, and digitize it

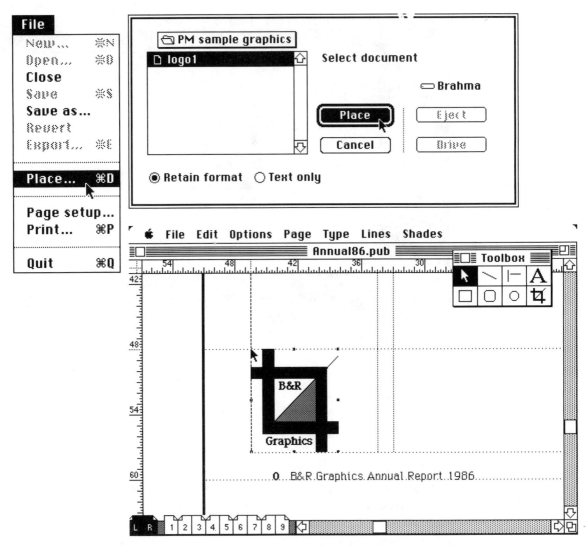

Figure 3-4. Placing a logo on the left master page.

with a desktop scanner. The scanner creates a file containing a bit map of the logo, and you can edit and retouch the pixels on the screen using a paint program (MacPaint, SuperPaint, FullPaint, and others described in Chapter 1 and Appendix B).

For the example, we copied and edited the cropping tool image supplied on the PageMaker Tutorial disk (supplied as a paint-type graphic) using MacPaint. Figure 3-3 shows the MacPaint display and the edited logo (we added a triangle with a gray shade). The logo is now ready to manipulate with PageMaker.

Note, however, that the logo is still a resolution-dependent bit-mapped image, which means the number of dots per inch is the same as shown on the display (72 dpi). A 300-dpi laser printer will print the image very well, but the sharp edges (sometimes called the "jaggies") will remain. Sometimes, leaving the sharp edges is an artistic decision, but if you want a smoother appearance, you can use a *drawing* program rather than a painting program.

For example, when you design a logo using MacDraw or Adobe Illustrator, the logo is comprised of lines, curves, and shapes (referred to as "objects") that are resolution *independent*. The dots per inch used to print such objects depends on the printer — high-resolution typesetters and laser printers will print a better, smoother image (using more dots per inch).

No matter which method you choose to create a logo, you can manipulate the logo in PageMaker as long as you use a graphics file format compatible with PageMaker (Chapter 1 describes graphics file formats and graphics programs).

When you place a bit-mapped image (from a paint program, or a scanned image saved as a TIFF file) larger than 64K onto a page, PageMaker stores a lower-resolution display version in the publication file and establishes a link to the original version for printing. For faster printing, PageMaker prefers that the original image file be stored in the same folder as your publication file, and in the same place it was when you placed it; or else, if you move the image file after it has been placed on a publication page, PageMaker won't find it when it prints the publication file, and it displays a dialog box asking for the image file. You can type a file name to tell PageMaker where the image is stored and continue printing, or else let PageMaker print the lower-resolution display version of the image.

To use the logo with PageMaker, switch to actual size display, then place the logo's graphic file using the Place command from the File menu.

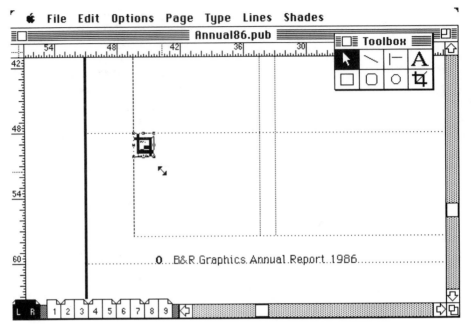

Figure 3-5. Scaling the logo down in an equal ratio.

Select the left master page and click the mouse to place the image (Figure 3-4). If the graphic is a line drawing (without patterns and a lot of details), you can resize it by dragging a handle until the graphic is the right size for your layout. If, however, the graphic has a pattern or has fine detail, you should hold down the Command key to automatically select the optimal sizes for your target printer. In addition, hold down the Shift key while resizing, in order to keep the same proportions (and then let go of the mouse button before releasing the Command and Shift keys); otherwise you can distort the image by stretching or compressing from any side of the image. In Figure 3-5 the logo is resized by holding down the Shift and Command keys while dragging the lower right corner inward, scaling the logo down in size and by equal proportions.

When you've scaled the graphic to a size that fits in the space to the left on the footer, let go of the mouse button (and then let go of the Command and Shift keys). While the graphic is still selected, choose Copy from the Edit menu to copy the logo into the Clipboard, then switch to the master

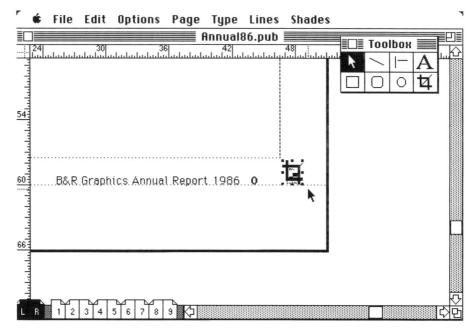

Figure 3-6. Logo placed on the master right page.

right page and choose Paste from the Edit menu. Move the newly pasted graphic into position next to the footer on the master right page (Figure 3-6). The logos and footers will be repeated on every left and right page, unless you choose to turn off the automatic Display of master items (Page menu) on any particular page.

To include the logo in a different location on the first page of the report, move to the first page and choose Paste again. Resize the logo by clicking the bottom right handle while holding down the Shift key. Turn Display of master items off for page 1 to suppress the footer, so that the page will not print with two logos.

The First Page
An annual report should have the look of sophistication and importance. You should lay out the text with enough white space surrounding it to make the text look important. The design we chose — one wide ragged-right margin, with headings, subheadings, and pull quotes in a thinner

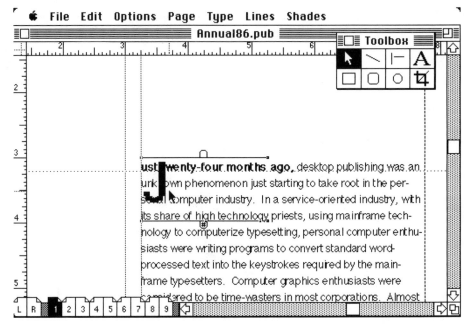

Figure 3-7. Moving the large first character into position.

marginal column — helps preserve white space. The one-column body text design also makes it easier to flow the text from one page to the next quickly, without the need to adjust columns.

The text of the report can be preformatted, with font, size, and leading already set, and brought into PageMaker using Place and the "Retain format" option. Alternatively, you can select the font, size, and leading in the Type specs dialog box, then bring the text into PageMaker using Place and the Text only option. We used a 12-point sans serif font (such as Helvetica) and 16 points of leading and set the first tab at 16 points because it is a good design practice to use the same amount of space in the indent of the first line of a paragraph as you are using for leading.

Place the text on the first page in the wide column at the 3-inch mark (select the Rulers option in the Options menu; to change from inches to picas or other measures, choose Preferences in the Edit menu). The first phrase in the text file should be in a bold style. Continue placing the text over pages (in only the wide column) until all of the text is placed. Then move back to the first page (click each previous page icon, one at a time,

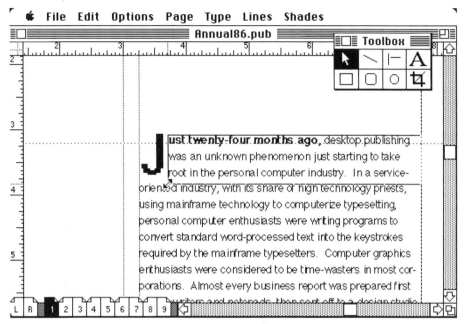

Figure 3-8. Adjusting the first three lines to accommodate a large capital letter.

or click the page icon scroll arrow, or use Command Shift Tab to move back one page at a time (Command Tab moves forward one page at a time). Click the page 1 icon to move quickly to the first page, or if you have turned off the scroll bar display (using the Scroll bar command in the Options menu), use the Go to page command (Command G) in the page menu, and specify page 1).

To make the first letter a large capital letter that extends below the baseline of the first line (sometimes called a large "dropped initial" or "dropped cap"), highlight the letter by choosing the text tool and dragging across it, cut the letter from the text, then paste it back onto the pasteboard area, or on the page above the body text. Click an insertion point immediately after the big letter and press Return — this ensures that the line length of the large character is accurate. Choose the Type specs menu, and change the font size to 60 points with 70 points of leading.

Move the big letter back into the top part of the text (if its handles are too wide, drag the top or bottom right handle to the left, to make the block only as wide as the character), flush to the left margin of the wide column

Figure 3-9. Stretching the title to fit across the page.

(Figure 3-7). Choose the Send to back command from the Edit menu, so that you can select the body text without selecting the big letter. Push the top handle of the body text block down below the big letter, then click the mouse on the top handle to get the text placement icon. Click again at the left margin of the column where the text block used to begin, and a few lines from the beginning of the text block should appear. Push the bottom handle of this text block back up so that only three lines of text remain. You have just separated the first three lines of the text from the rest of the text block. Click the bottom left corner of this small block, and drag it inward and adjust the width to accommodate the capital (Figure 3-8).

Due to limited resolution of the screen, PageMaker can't accurately display the width of a letter in the Actual size page view. Use the 200% view (Command 2, or Shift Option Command and click the mouse button) for an accurate display when adjusting the column width, or print the page, and then adjust the column width next to the letter if necessary. The rulers

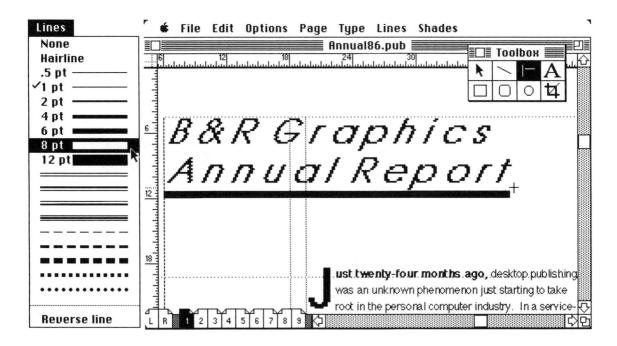

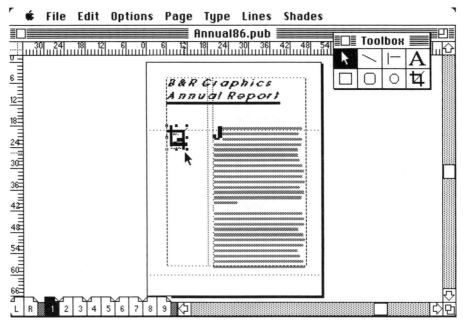

Figure 3-10. Drawing an 8-point line under the title, and placing the logo.

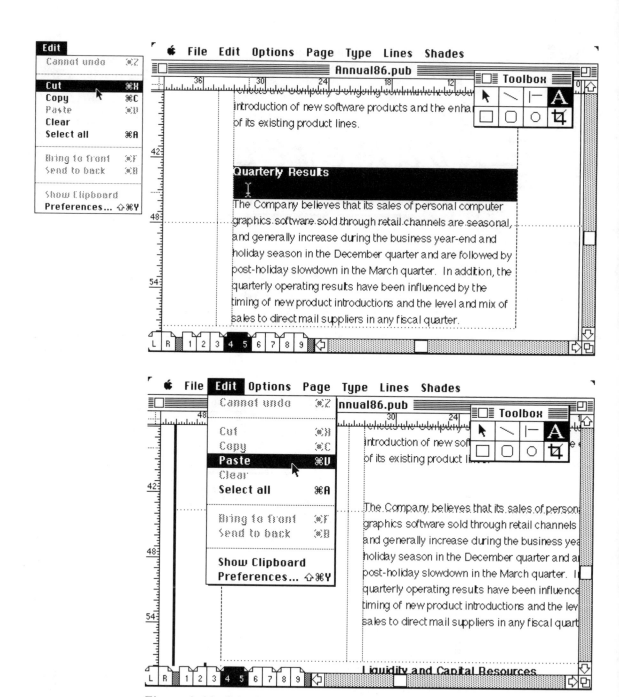

Figure 3-11. Selecting a section heading using the text tool.

are most accurately calibrated for measurements at actual size, but to position elements precisely, switch to a 200% view.

To add a title to the report's first page, choose the text tool and click an insertion point at the left margin of the page and near the top of the page; then type the title with one space between each letter and two spaces between each word. Highlight the title and change the font to a sans serif font such as Avant Garde (a PostScript font) or Helvetica, bold italic, 36 points with automatic (auto) leading. Stretch the title block by dragging the bottom right corner out to the right margin and down to display both lines of the title (Figure 3-9).

Change the rulers back to picas (Preferences in the Edit menu), and then switch to the perpendicular line tool, choose an 8-point line from the Lines menu, and drag a line at the 12-pica mark across the page (Figure 3-10).

Complete the first page by moving the logo into place and resizing it by shift-clicking and dragging the bottom right corner handle on the image. You may also want to remove the footer from the first page, since the first page already has a logo and does not need a page number. By selecting the Display master items option in the Page menu, you turn the option on (check mark displayed) or off (no check mark).

It is a good idea to position all of the text first so that you can readily see how many pages of text you have. It is then easy to change the layout repeatedly and experiment. If you plan to use graphic elements, you might prefer to decide their position and place them before placing all of the text.

Subsequent Pages

The annual report may have sections dealing with market analysis, product information and life cycle, financial summaries, media campaigns, and anything else relevant to describing the business. Each section should follow a consistent heading and subheading format. To move a heading from the body text column to the narrow column, choose the text tool, then click and drag across the entire heading (Figure 3-11), and use Cut from the Edit menu. Click an insertion point at the left edge the narrow column, and use Paste from the Edit menu. Drag across the heading again (while still using the text tool), choose the Type specs menu, and change the font size to 14 points with 18 points of leading. Finally, draw a 2-point line under the heading (Figure 3-12). You can repeat these steps for each

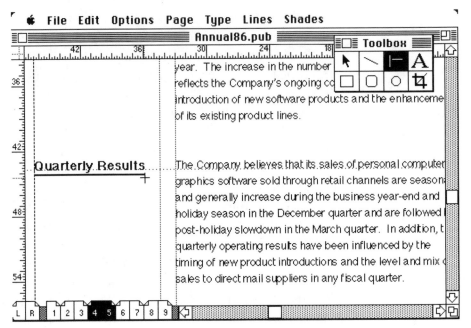

Figure 3-12. Drawing a 2-point line under the heading.

heading in the report. Using the text tool, insert a Return (carriage return) to break a long headline where you want it broken, since headlines should not be hyphenated (Figure 3-13). Subheadings should remain in the text block, but should be changed to 14 point bold.

If a page of text ends with a single word or very short line (an *orphan*), or pushes a single word or short line less than half the width of the column to the next page (*widow*), you can reduce or expand the percentage of a space used to determine word spacing, and then hand-kern letters if necessary. (See Figure 2-70 for kerning, and Figure 2-42 for type spacing.) Use the Spacing command from the Type menu, and change the percentage (default is 100%) for the Desired word spacing in the Spacing dialog box. For ragged-right text, PageMaker uses only the Desired percentage; the other word spacing percentages (minimum and maximum) are used only for justified text. You can also set a Hyphenation zone for ragged-right text, to control line length: The smaller the size of the

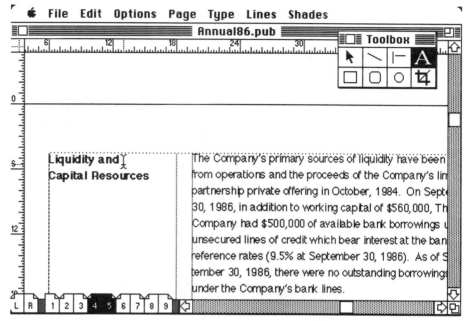

Figure 3-13. Breaking a headline by typing a Return (carriage return) while in text mode.

zone, the more PageMaker will hyphenate words at the ends of lines, and the less ragged the text will look (line endings will be more ragged if you use a larger hyphenation zone).

The spacing settings are in effect for the entire article over all of the pages it threads. You can try a different percentage, then check other pages to be sure it doesn't cause other widows or orphans. You can undo the operation immediately after doing it. You can also change the percentages back to their original values at any time.

To make room in a text block for spreadsheets, charts, graphs, or other elements, select the pointer tool, then click anywhere inside the text block. Drag the bottom handle up to the top of the area to be reserved, and let go. You can continue text below a reserved area by clicking the bottom handle and clicking a starting point for the rest of the text.

Move a text block the same way you move a graphic — point in the middle, hold down the mouse button until you see the four arrows, and

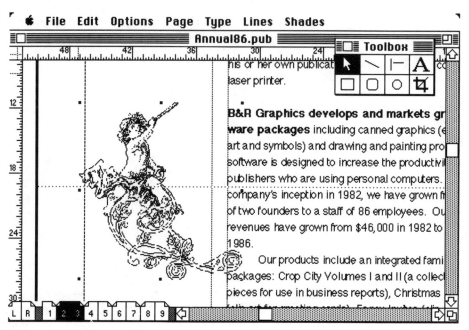

Figure 3-14. Placing graphics in the narrow column.

Figure 3-15. Adding a caption and vertical rule for emphasis.

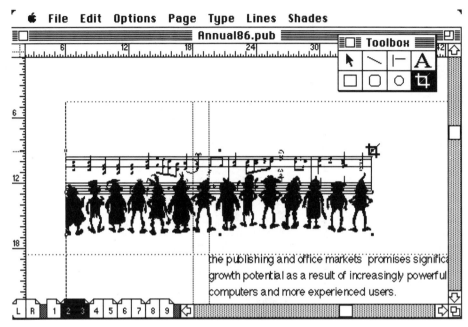

Figure 3-16. Selecting a resized graphic with the cropping tool.

drag it into position. With Snap to guides on, you can attach a text block or graphic to a column guide or ruler guide. Use a ruler guide to help align text columns side by side.

Adding Graphics

The narrow column is useful for displaying images and graphics. Figure 3-14 shows a graphic image placed in the narrow column, resized (with Command Shift drag) to fit, and positioned to intrude slightly into the text. Place another graphic below it in the same manner. Switch to the text tool and type the caption in the narrow column, then resize the caption block to fit a 4-point vertical line for emphasis (Figure 3-15).

Add another graphic to the next page (a facing right page) and resize it using the same Command Shift drag method. Figure 3-16 shows how you can align the cropping tool over the handle, and Figure 3-17 shows the result of dragging the cropping tool icon and cropping the image. After adding a caption formatted just like the last one, switch to the full-page

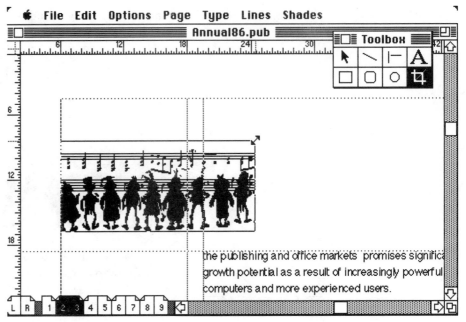

Figure 3-17. The result of dragging the cropping tool to crop the image.

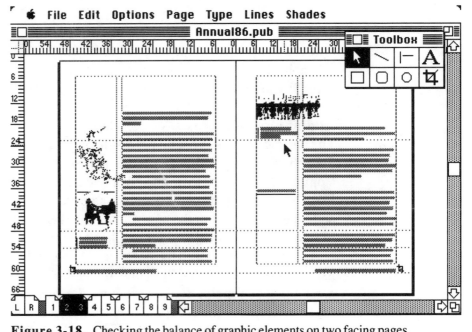

Figure 3-18. Checking the balance of graphic elements on two facing pages.

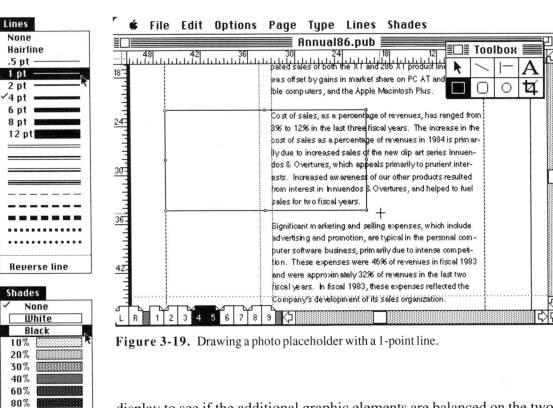

Figure 3-19. Drawing a photo placeholder with a 1-point line.

display to see if the additional graphic elements are balanced on the two facing pages (Figure 3-18).

You can also separate text with a graphic or photo in such a way that the element adds visual balance and makes the page more interesting. Desktop scanners can save a file in the TIFF format for placing in PageMaker, but scanned images might not provide enough gray scale or color information to reproduce a black-and-white or color photo with the same quality as conventional photographic reproduction (some inexpensive scanners can provide enough gray scale to reproduce newspaper quality halftones). To include a conventionally produced black-and-white halftone or color-separated image, have your print shop combine the image with the desktop-produced page. Draw a placement box on the PageMaker page to represent the image by selecting a 1-point line for the box edge from the Lines menu; then select the box tool, click a starting point at one corner of the box, and drag the mouse to draw the box (Figure 3-19). While the box is still selected, add a black or gray shade by

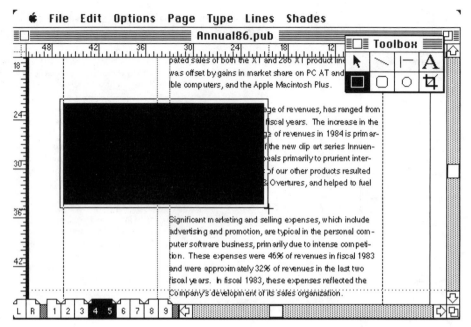

Figure 3-20. Drawing a keyline around the photo box.

choosing that option from the Shades menu. This box is just for placement and will be replaced by an actual halftone or color-separated image by the printing service, so it is wise to use 100% black, which leaves a solid area on the film (called a window) on which a photographic image can be overlayed.

You can draw a second box (called a keyline) around the shaded area if you want to have the photo framed on the page (Figure 3-20). Or, your printing service may prefer an empty white box with a black keyline (which frames your photo or not, as you wish) to be used as a guide to place a photo. Ask your print service which method they prefer before you place graphics on pages, or make changes just before printing final pages. It is very easy to make such changes with PageMaker at the last minute, but there is no substitute for establishing a good dialogue with your printer.

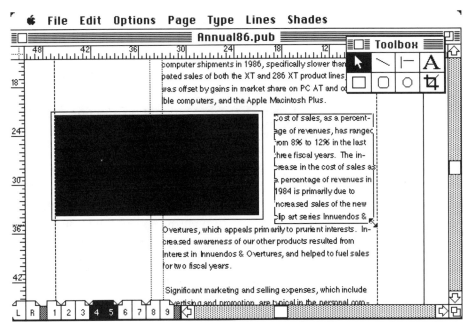

Figure 3-21. Wrapping text around the photo box.

By stretching or reducing a column's width and moving the column, you can wrap text around images. To flow text around the box, select the text block and drag the bottom handle to a point just above the box. Click the bottom handle and place the separated block in the narrow part of the column next to the box. Then click the bottom handle of this narrow block and place the rest of the text in the normal column width below the box. Finally, select the narrow block of text, drag a corner inward to reduce its width, and then click in the middle of the block to position it closer to the right margin, leaving enough space between the box and the text (Figure 3-21).

You can prepare the camera-ready pages for your high-volume printer with the black box for placement, then have your printer splice the halftone or four-color separation film negatives with the negatives prepared for the printing plates.

Adding Spreadsheets

Reports usually contain financial data displayed in tables, which are called spreadsheets in personal computer terminology. A spreadsheet is likely to consist of numerical information organized in rows and columns. Each number or text element is referred to as a *cell*.

Cells in a spreadsheet should line up properly. Regular tabs can align text or numeric items, either on the left edge of the cell or the right. An alternative is the decimal tab which aligns numbers according to their decimal points (similar to right-justifying the numbers in the cells).

Spreadsheet programs are designed primarily for entering and calculating numbers, not for preparing the information for presentation on the pages of a report. Some programs will let you designate fonts for the text and use different widths for columns. However, PageMaker can't place a spreadsheet directly from a spreadsheet program, unless it is in a format PageMaker recognizes. Most spreadsheet programs can save the spread-

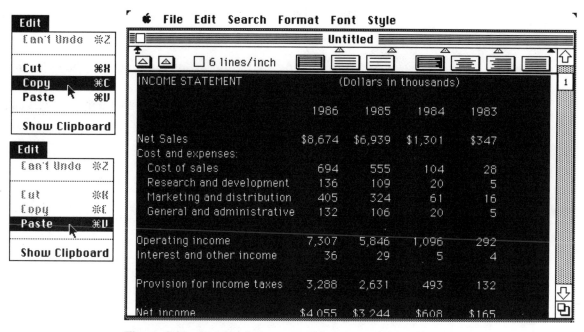

Figure 3-22. Copying from a spreadsheet program into MacWrite, which can format the spreadsheet for use with PageMaker.

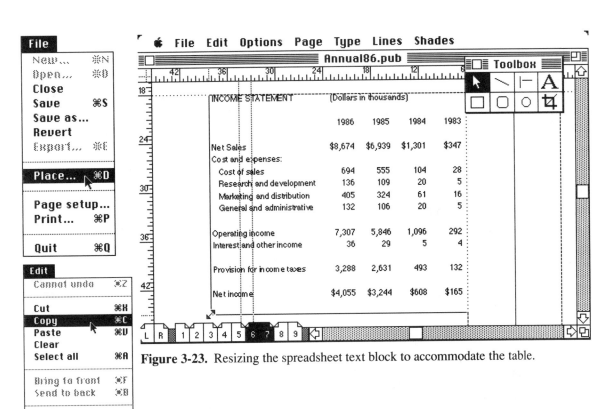

Figure 3-23. Resizing the spreadsheet text block to accommodate the table.

sheet in a text format (text only), or a PICT format, which you can place with PageMaker.

With some spreadsheets, it may be necessary to adjust the delimiters (commas, tabs, carriage returns, etc.) with the search and replace function of a word processor before placing the text into PageMaker. It is also a good idea to first edit the spreadsheet file with a word processor to set decimal tabs and fonts if your spreadsheet program does not allow such formatting. You can use a word processor file format recognizable by PageMaker, or simply use a text only file with no formatting options. Be sure to give your file a name that PageMaker can recognize (usually the same as the default file name extension your word processing program assigns when you save the file, but see Appendixes A and B for suggested file name extensions).

The Macintosh has a Clipboard that lets you cut or copy data from one application and paste it into another, so you can quickly transfer a spreadsheet from a program such as Microsoft Excel to MacWrite using

Copy and Paste (Figure 3-22). MacWrite can designate fonts, sizes, styles, and tab settings, all of which are recognized by PageMaker.

A Lotus 1-2-3 or Microsoft Excel spreadsheet can be saved as a text only file (also known as an ASCII file), then opened with Microsoft Word and formatted the same way. Other spreadsheet programs can save the information as a text file in a similar manner, and you can read them into

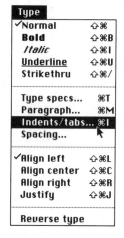

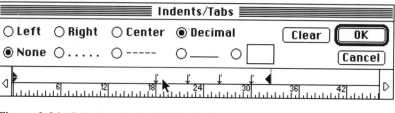

Figure 3-24. Selecting decimal tabs for the spreadsheet.

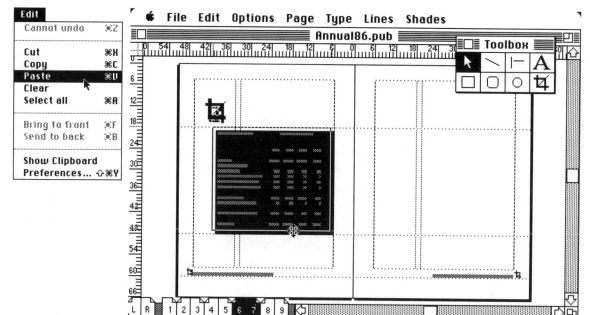

Figure 3-25. Drawing a drop shadow of a frame by copying it, moving the copy to the shadow position, changing its shade to black.

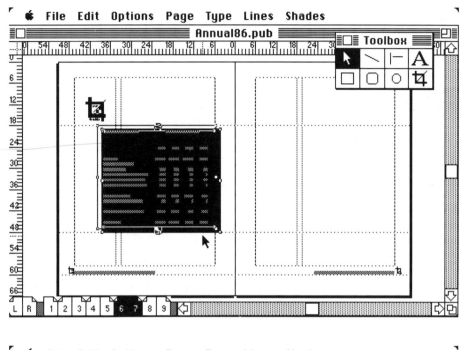

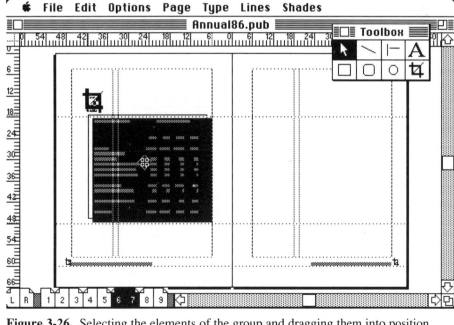

Figure 3-26. Selecting the elements of the group and dragging them into position.

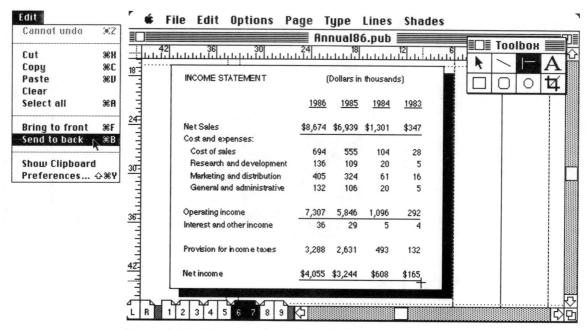

Figure 3-27. Selecting only the black shadow, and sending it back behind the frame and text elements.

your word processing program to save them again as text only, then place the files with PageMaker.

Place the spreadsheet text file as you would any other text file, but resize the block (Figure 3-23) so that the spreadsheet cells line up according to its tab settings. You can adjust the tab settings by selecting the spreadsheet with the text tool and choosing Indents/tabs from the Type menu in PageMaker. Be sure to select decimal tabs (Figure 3-24) for each number column if you want the numbers to line up on their decimal points.

You can jazz up the spreadsheet by drawing a frame and drop shadow around it. To draw a drop shadow of the frame, copy the frame to the Clipboard, paste the copy back to the page, move the copy to the shadow position (Figure 3-25), and change its shade to black. To move all of the elements at once, hold down Shift to select the frame and the text without deselecting the already-selected black shadow (Figure 3-26); then release Shift and click in the center of the group until you see the double-arrow

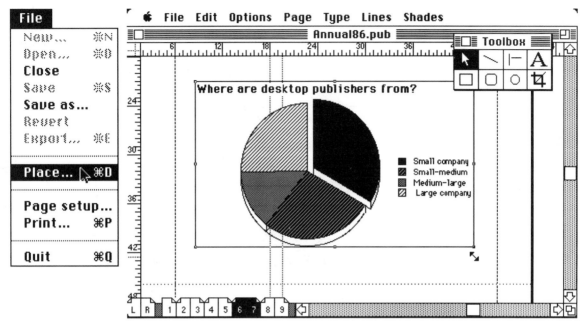

Figure 3-28. Placing and resizing a PICT chart from a graphics program such as CricketDraw.

symbol, then drag to move the entire group. Finally, to move the black shadow behind the frame and text, deselect by clicking the pointer tool again, then select only the black shadow and use the Send to back command.

Figure 3-27 shows the result, including lines drawn to emphasize rows. These were made with the line drawing tool; if you want individual strings of text or numbers underlined, use the text tool, highlight the text to be underlined, and choose Underline from the Type menu.

Adding Charts and Graphs

PageMaker reads the graphic output of some spreadsheet and graphics programs, such as the charts and graphs produced by Cricket Graph, in several ways. If the graph or chart can be copied to the Clipboard, it can be pasted into MacDraw or some other drawing program for editing, before placing in PageMaker. You can then save the file in PICT format.

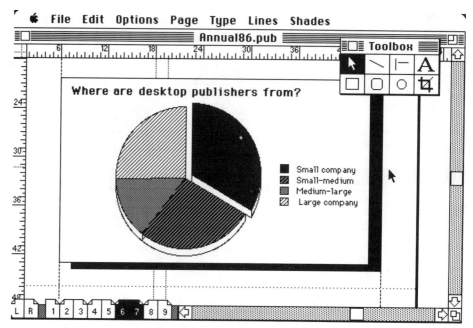

Figure 3-29. Scaling the fonts with the graphics.

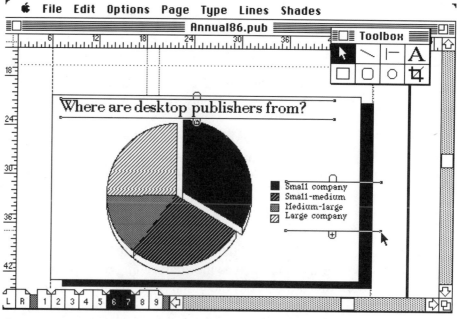

Figure 3-30. Alternatively placing only the graphics and adding text using PageMaker.

Some programs (such as CricketGraph) can save the file as PICT. You can also use an accessory program called Glue (Solutions, Inc.) to save a PICT file, even if your application program does not ordinarily save a PICT file.

We suggest that if you use a graphing program, save the file in PICT (or EPS) format to produce high-quality and high-resolution images with PageMaker. The pie and bar charts in this example were saved first as Cricket Graph files, then saved as PICT files before placing them with PageMaker.

Use the Place command as you did before with the MacPaint file. If the file is from an object-drawing program (PICT format, as described in Chapter 1), you can resize the graphic as desired without holding down the Command key. For example, for any PICT files (signified by the pencil placement icon), just drag a corner of the image (hold down Shift to maintain the proportions) to the size you need to fill (see Figure 3-28). If the file is not from an object-drawing program (placed with a pencil icon) but is a bit-mapped image (signified by the paintbrush placement icon) from a program such as MacPaint, you should hold down both Command and Shift while dragging to resize the image to an optimal size for your printer.

When a PICT image is resized on the PageMaker page, the fonts are also reduced in size. Object-drawing programs use PostScript fonts for text, and these fonts are carried over into PageMaker, but they are scaled along with the image, and you can't change their point sizes or styles. (Graphics (bit-map) fonts used in MacPaint are also reduced or enlarged with the image as you resize the image, but they do not correspond directly to PostScript fonts.) Figure 3-29 shows how PostScript fonts are scaled with the chart, and it shows a black shadow behind the chart added with PageMaker (the same method used in Figures 3-25 through 3-27 with the spreadsheet).

You can alternatively place just the graphics in PageMaker without the text and then add text with PageMaker, which gives you more control over text size and styles of the font within a text block (Figure 3-30). However, if you want text to run vertically alongside a vertical axis, or in any other orientation besides the usual horizontal orientation, use MacDraw or another graphics program (such as Illustrator) to define it, since Page-Maker does not offer the ability to rotate text. Scale the image to final size,

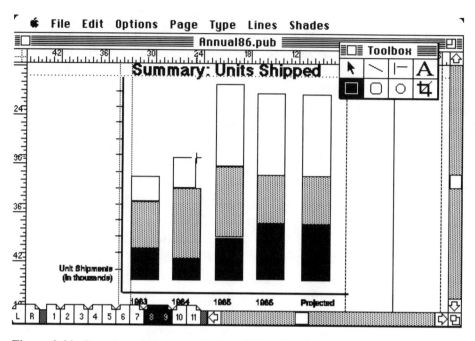

Figure 3-31. Drawing a bar chart with PageMaker drawing tools.

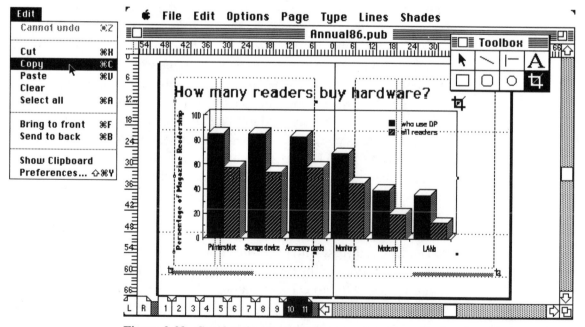

Figure 3-32. Copying the chart across two pages, then selecting the cropping tool.

and then set the text font and point size, before placing it on the PageMaker page.

You can draw an entire chart or graph using PageMaker's line drawing, box drawing, and circle drawing tools and gray shades. PageMaker's Snap to guides feature makes it easy to line up several distinct boxes to form a bar chart (Figure 3-31), and you can draw perfect circles by holding down the Shift key while dragging with the oval/circle tool, or perfect squares by holding down Shift while dragging with the box tool.

However, spreadsheet and business graphics programs can do the calculations and produce a bar or pie chart or an x–y graph that is accurate in proportion to the calculations. It is therefore better to use the output of these programs, at least as a template for the purpose of tracing new shapes that are accurate. You can bring the template into a program such as MacDraw or Illustrator, or directly into PageMaker, and draw your own shapes based on the template, then delete the template. Most spreadsheet and business graphics programs for the Macintosh (such as Microsoft Excel) can save a PICT format file, which PageMaker can place directly.

Whether you draw your charts and graphs in a graphics program or in PageMaker, you can still change the chart or graph at the last minute before publication. If the chart is from a graphics file larger than 64K in size, PageMaker will use the original file when it prints the report, so update the original file first. Then, if you have time, place it in PageMaker, replacing the older image; if you don't have time, simply update the original and print the report.

Remember, when you place a bit-map graphic larger than 64K in size, PageMaker places a lower-resolution version in the publication file for display, and uses the original for printing. However, line art drawn by object-drawing programs (PICT or EPS format) is placed at the highest resolution. In the case of PICT files, you can either change the PageMaker page directly or change the original file and place it back on the page, replacing the older version. EPS files may not display the actual image. Unless the EPS file contains an embedded TIFF or PICT format image, a gray box with information about the image will be placed on the page, at the size and shape of the final image. You can crop or resize the image to fit your page layout; however, you may prefer to use the application that created the file to edit it to a final size before placing it in PageMaker.

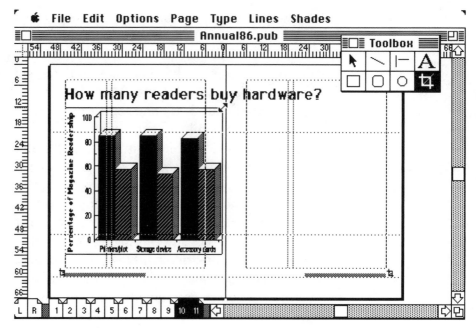

Figure 3-33. Cropping the chart to show half on one page.

Cropping and Scaling

To extend a bar chart across two pages, first place the chart on the left page, then hold down Shift and Command (if it is a paint-type graphic — signified by a paint brush placement icon), or hold down Shift (if it is a PICT, or draw-type graphic — signified by a pencil placement icon) while dragging the bottom right corner out to the bottom page guide of the right page. The chart straddles the unprintable middle at the moment, but it is the right proportions and size, so use the Copy command to make a copy of it in the Clipboard. Then choose the cropping tool and select the top right corner (Figure 3-32), dragging inward to crop half the image in width, while leaving the height the same (Figure 3-33).

Paste the copy and align it directly on the cropped chart (Figure 3-34) so that the text areas disappear, indicating a perfect match. Drag with the cropping tool from the top left corner to the right of the selected graphic, cropping the area that is already placed on the left page (Figure 3-35).

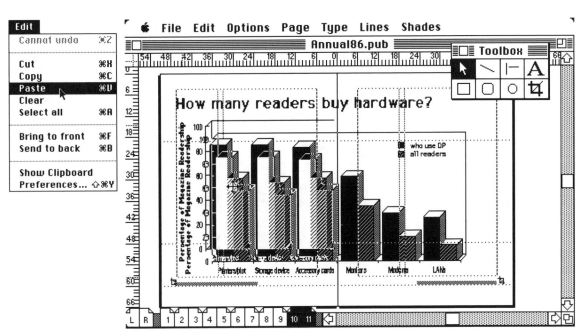

Figure 3-34. Aligning a copy of the chart with the cropped chart.

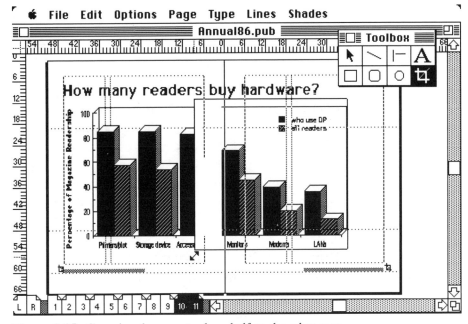

Figure 3-35. Cropping the copy to show half on the other page.

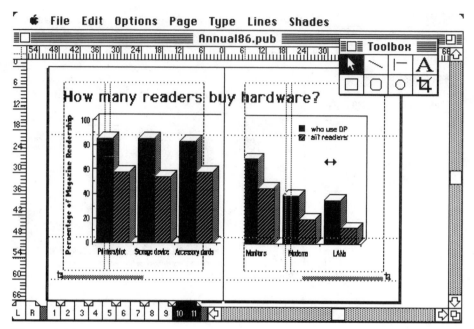

Figure 3-36. Dragging the cropped copy to the other page, holding down Shift to drag evenly.

Hold down the Shift key and drag the cropped copy horizontally across to the right page. The Shift key lets you drag evenly, without moving up or down (Figure 3-36), or, if you accidentally drag up or down first with the Shift key depressed, you will be constrained to up and down (vertical) movement. If this happens, let go of the mouse button and keyboard and immediately undo the move (Edit menu), before doing anything else. To constrain the Shift-drag to horizontal rather than vertical movement, be sure to drag in the left–right direction first, and do not use an up–down movement.

Printing the Report: Using Different Devices

If you are using the same system and printer with PageMaker that you used with your graphics program, you should obtain optimal results. If, however, you created graphics with text for a different system or printer, you may have problems with the text and the graphics.

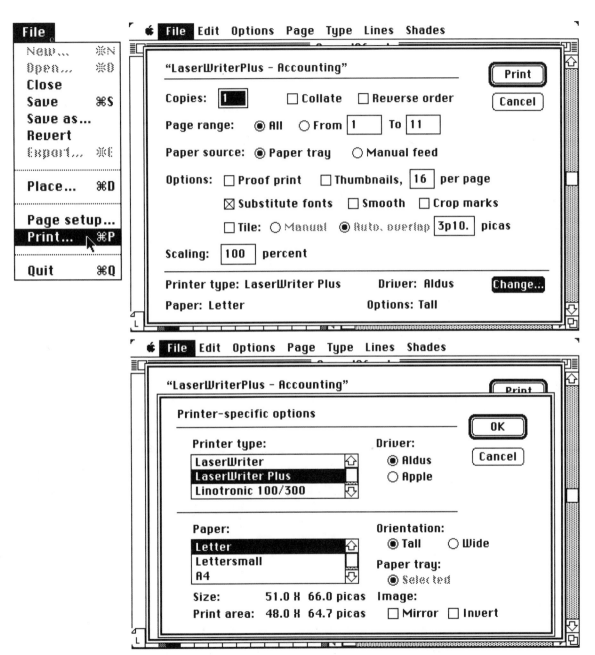

Figure 3-37. Before placing any text or images, first choose the Print command from the File menu, then the Change button to change to the final printer you plan to use, and print to it once to tell PageMaker the resolution setting in its APD file.

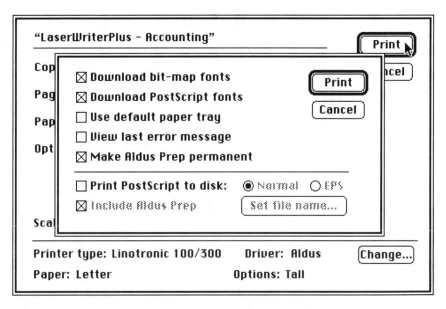

Figure 3-38. Changing the printer for a PageMaker publication file in the list of printers for which you have APDs installed. Holding down the Option key while pressing the Print button allows you to choose other PostScript options, such as printing to a disk file.

For example, assume that you composed a pie chart with text using bit-map MacPaint fonts. Assume also that you have installed a PostScript laser printer (300 dpi) and typesetter (1270 dpi) and that you want to print the final version of the report on the PostScript typesetter, using the higher resolution PostScript fonts.

Before placing the MacPaint file, edit it with a painting program to remove the text, and then use PageMaker's text tool to add the text, after placing the graphics file. Use the Print command in the File menu to change the printer to the final PostScript printer (such as an Apple LaserWriter printer or Linotype Linotronic typesetter): choose the Change printer command from the Print dialog box, which displays a dialog box with each type of installed printer driver on your system (Figure 3-37) and print options pertaining to the selected printer. After printing the file once, you will be able to size images at an optimal size for the printer's resolution.

You can change the paper orientation to wide (also called landscape), which is for sideways printing, or tall (also known as portrait), which is separate from the page orientation you set in the Page setup dialog box in the File menu), as well as the source of paper (the manual feed or the paper tray), and the number of copies of each page to print. You can print all pages, or specify a range of pages to print, as well as the number of copies and whether or not to collate copies.

After clicking OK to accept the specific printer setting and options, you can change the fonts in the graphics file to be substituted with PostScript fonts (click the Substitute fonts box in the Print dialog box to substitute PostScript fonts to be used in the final printing) and use the graphics file with PageMaker.

To change other PostScript settings — for example, to use downloaded fonts — instead of simply clicking the Print button, hold down the Option key and click Print while the Option key is depressed (Figure 3-38). You will see another dialog box, with settings for additional PostScript options such as downloading bit-map or PostScript fonts, or printing PostScript or EPS format files to disk (usually you will use this option before transmitting your file over a modem to a service to be typeset). You can then click the Print button, or the Cancel button to ignore any changes you made. The PostScript print options dialog box appears, and you can set various print options, or Change printers, just as before.

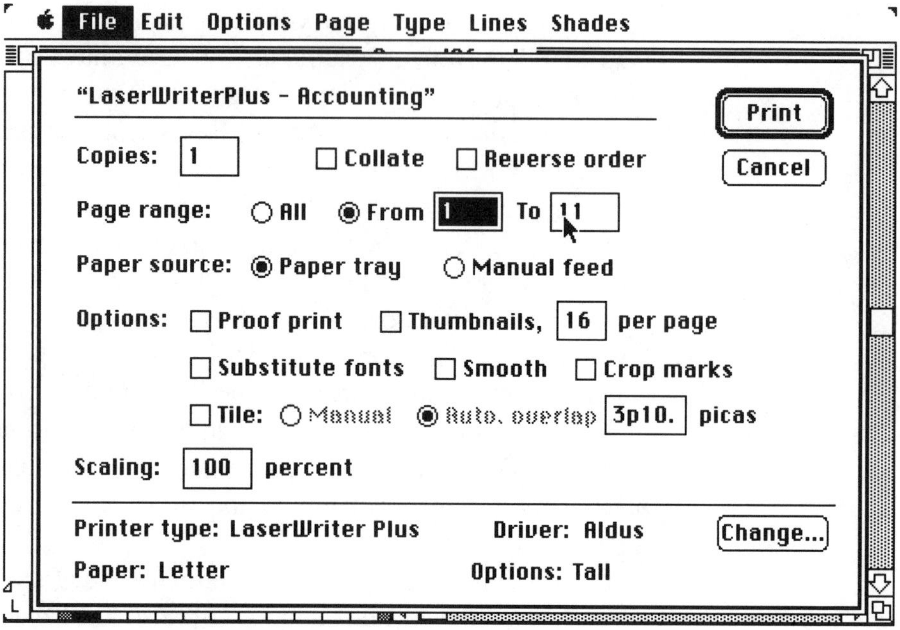

 File   Edit   Options   Page   Type   Lines   Shades

"LaserWriterPlus - Accounting"   ⌈ **Print** ⌉

Copies: ⌈1⌉   ☐ Collate   ☐ Reverse order   ⌈ Cancel ⌉

Page range: ○ All   ◉ From ⌈**1**⌉ To ⌈11⌉

Paper source: ◉ Paper tray   ○ Manual feed

Options: ☐ Proof print   ☐ Thumbnails, ⌈16⌉ per page

           ☐ Substitute fonts   ☐ Smooth ☐ Crop marks

           ☐ Tile: ○ Manual ◉ Auto. overlap ⌈3p10.⌉ picas

Scaling: ⌈100⌉ percent

Printer type: LaserWriter Plus   **Driver: Aldus**   ⌈Change...⌉
Paper: Letter   **Options: Tall**

Figure 3-39. When printing the report, you can select a number of copies, or select a range of pages to print rather than the entire publication.

Once you are in the PageMaker document, your printer may have to be changed if you had first composed the pages with another system and printer, and you do not want PageMaker to substitute its default font for any fonts not available in the system or the printer you now have selected. Choose the Print command from the File menu and select the final printer from the list of installed printers. If you also make changes in the Page Setup dialog box (in the File menu) to change the page size, PageMaker will recompose the entire publication, which may change the layout, so look over your publication carefully afterward. It is for this reason that you should always have the final page size and printer in mind at the outset. Set your publication for a final page size, and choose a system and printer with the fonts you want to use, before you begin to place text and graphics.

You do not need to have the printer connected to select it, but if you know what fonts you will use, you can install (using the Font/DA Mover) display versions of the printer fonts, so that your displayed page is the closest possible match to the final printed result. (If you are using a laser printer for proof pages, and a service bureau for final typesetting, Chapter 5 explains how to edit an APD file to change the laser printer's resolution to match the typesetter's resolution, so that bit-map images can be printed without distortion.)

To print the report, simply choose the Print command from the File menu, which presents the printing dialog box (Figure 3-39). The printing menu also allows you to specify the number of copies of each page, a range of pages rather than the entire publication, the order of the page printing, and the percentage of scaling the pages (if any). Scaling is useful when you design pages that are larger or smaller than the final size, and you want to print the page in its final size. You can also print a page at, say, 200%, then reduce it with a camera to regular size, gaining resolution and reducing jagged edges. Tiling is also available for printing an oversize image on a standard laser printer with an overlap, so that you can line up the pages to form the large page. You can even specify the amount of the overlap for tiling.

You can at any time change to another printer, but PageMaker does not recompose the publication for that printer. Problems can occur with bit-map images that were sized using the Command key, and with fonts. If you print to a Linotronic 100 or L300, and then place images with the printer set to Linotronic 100/300, you will get more choices when using the Command or Command and Shift keys to resize images than after switching to a LaserWriter Plus. Once you set the printer to LaserWriter, and print a page on the LaserWriter, you will be able to choose only standard LaserWriter sizes. To change them, resize without the Command key (which does not calculate optimal sizes), or switch the printer back to Linotronic 100/300.

You may want to use Adobe Systems' Font Downloader to download fonts to the printer's memory to speed up printing operations (Figure 3-40). If you are using Adobe's older copy-protected downloadable fonts (Adobe fonts are no longer copy-protected), and you switch to a new printer that has had those same downloadable fonts installed from another initializer disk, do not use the Option key when you click Print; if you do, and then check the PostScript option to download PostScript fonts to the

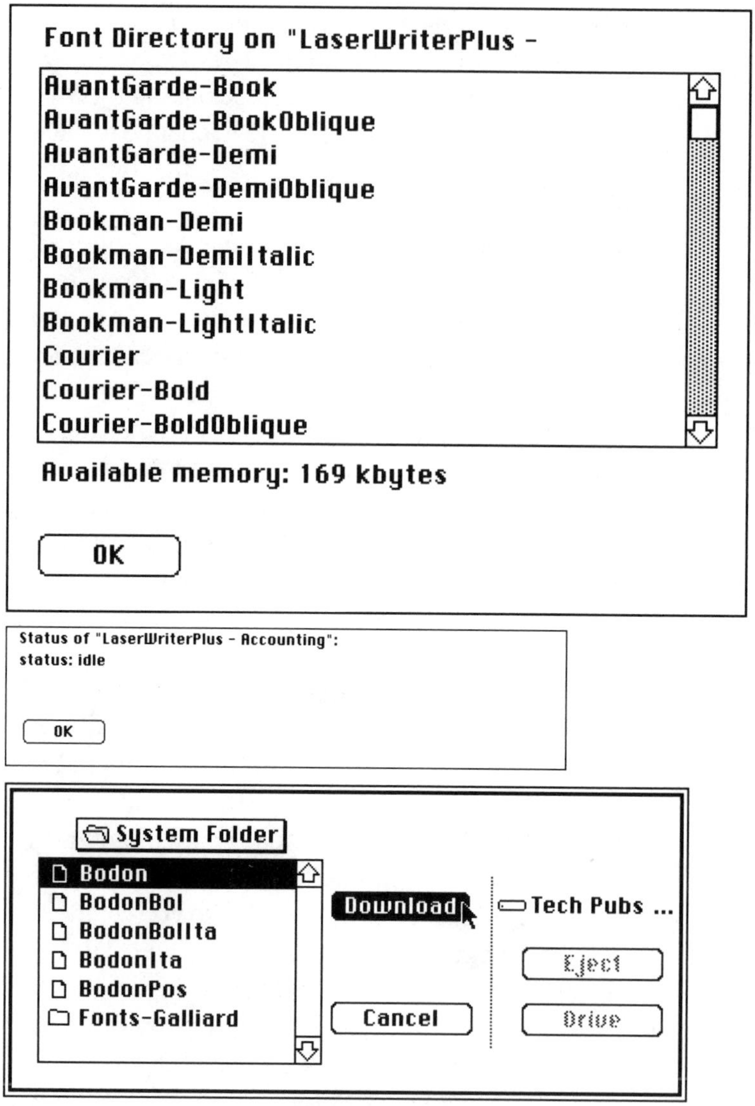

Font Directory on "LaserWriterPlus -

AvantGarde-Book
AvantGarde-BookOblique
AvantGarde-Demi
AvantGarde-DemiOblique
Bookman-Demi
Bookman-DemiItalic
Bookman-Light
Bookman-LightItalic
Courier
Courier-Bold
Courier-BoldOblique

Available memory: 169 kbytes

OK

Status of "LaserWriterPlus - Accounting":
status: idle

OK

🗁 **System Folder**

🗋 **Bodon**
🗋 **BodonBol**
🗋 **BodonBolIta**
🗋 **BodonIta**
🗋 **BodonPos**
🗀 **Fonts-Galliard**

Download   ▭ **Tech Pubs ...**

Eject

Cancel   Drive

Figure 3-40. The Font Downloader from Adobe Systems.

new printer, your document may not print because the downloaded font serial numbers don't match. You can print the publication and close it without saving changes to avoid problems: The publication will retain the form it had before you changed printers.

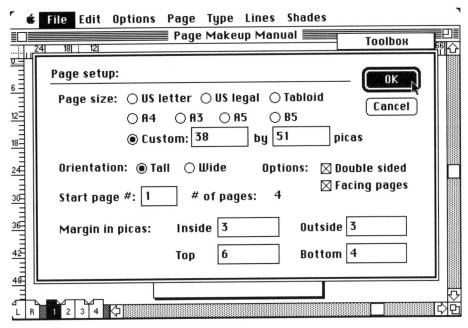

Figure 3-41. Page setup for a technical manual about the same size as the Page-Maker manual.

Changing the resolution (dots per inch) can affect the appearance of draw-type graphics. The lower the resolution, the coarser the draw-type graphics, and hairlines will not print at all on an ImageWriter. In addition, if you compose your publication for an ImageWriter at legal (11- by 14-inch) paper size, and then you switch to a LaserWriter for final printing, you may find the right edges of your pages have been cut off, because the ImageWriter has a wider legal page size than the LaserWriter and LaserWriter Plus legal page size.

Technical Manual

The technical manual is an example of a lengthy publication that can be handled by PageMaker. The Aldus PageMaker manual itself was produced with PageMaker, as was this book (you'll see how to design those pages later). The following example, however, is simpler in design and execution. The idea is to produce a publication in which all the pages have a similar format, but contain certain differences such as illustrations, photos, or footnotes. It is very important to keep the design simple for two reasons. First, you need to attract and hold the reader's attention without too many distractions or arresting items. Second, you have to streamline the production process to be able to produce many pages quickly.

To compose sections of the technical manual easily, you can use the text and graphics files supplied in the PageMaker tutorial folder (PM Tutorial).

Designing the Pages

Start a new publication and change the default settings for the Page setup (File menu) to the dimensions of the pages you will produce: a custom page that is 38 picas wide by 51 picas high, with tall (portrait) orientation and double-sided pages. The image area is defined by margins that are 3 picas in from the binding, 3 picas in from the edge of the page, 6 picas down from the top of the page, and 4 picas up from the bottom of the page (Figure 3-41).

Part of the overall design is the layout of the title page. Design page 1 by specifying a two-column format with 1 pica and 6 points (1p6) space between the columns. The column guides show the middle of the page. Figure 3-42 shows the scaling of a placed title logo prepared in a drawing program (the PS icon signifies the graphic is in the EPS file format). This logo is called "Tips Logo," and can be found in the PM Tutorial folder supplied with PageMaker. The "Tips Logo" file has a display version embedded in the PostScript file to display the logo on the screen; it can be resized, and will print as it is displayed, but at the selected printer's high resolution, rather than at the 72 dpi display resolution. Some application programs, such as Cricket Draw, create an EPS file that does not contain a display version of the image embedded in the PostScript file. When you place an image from such applications, you may see only a properly sized gray box, including some information about the image (such as file name, the name of the program that created the image, and the date the image was created). You can still resize such images in PageMaker; however, since you can't see the image on screen, you should print the page to check it.

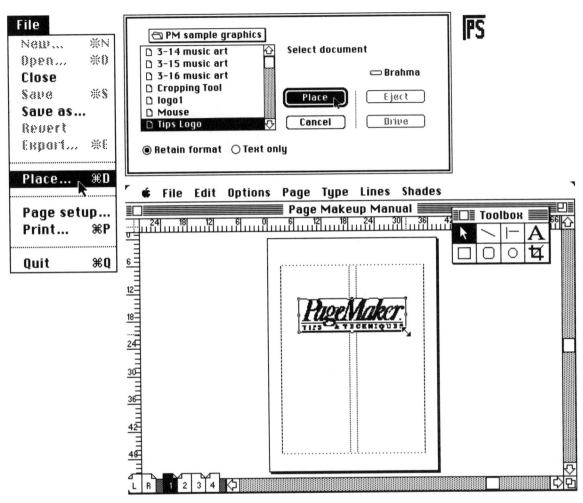

Figure 3-42. Producing the title page of the manual by scaling a logo that serves as a title. A title can be typed directly into PageMaker or prepared in a graphics program as a logo and brought into PageMaker as a graphics file. This logo was created with Adobe Illustrator, and saved in EPS format.

To scale a logo created with a paint-type program properly, hold down the Command and Shift keys while dragging a corner of the image. For PICT or EPS files, you do not have to hold down the Command key while

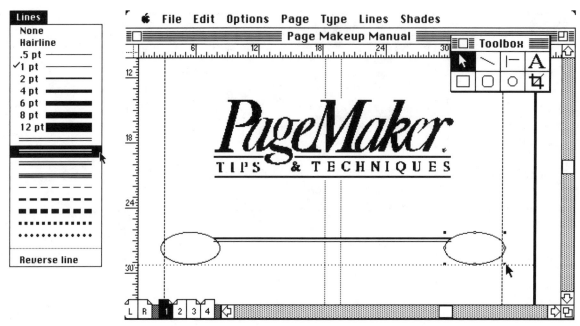

Figure 3-43. Overlapping a line ending with an oval that will define the edge of the line ending.

resizing — such images are resolution independent and will print at the printer's best resolution without distortion. If your image is distorted by dragging a side handle, you can restore it to the size you first placed it at by holding down the Shift key and clicking any handle; then resize it to the desired size.

A variety of line styles are available. Here, we customized the line endings by drawing an oval to overlap the line ending (Figure 3-43). Pull a guide down from the ruler to the base of the oval, select and copy the oval, and then paste and move the copy to the other end of the line, resting on the same horizontal and vertical guides. This result would be easier to achieve with a painting or drawing program (or program such as Adobe's Illustrator, which has a Reflect option) suitable for complex image construction, rather than with PageMaker.

Next, set the type of line in the Lines menu to None for the selected oval (so that the oval itself disappears), and set the type of shade to White in

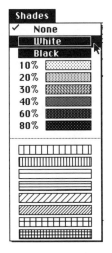

Figure 3-44. Changing the oval's line to None and its shade to White turns the oval into a mask that defines the edge of the line ending.

the Shades menu (Figure 3-44). Other types of lines can be drawn to give the title page an interesting, inviting look. One line style popular in advertisements and instruction manuals (such as the PageMaker manual) is the line of small dots, which can add a "well-designed" look to an otherwise boring page. Figure 3-45 shows the use of such lines on the title page of the manual; the lines are drawn out beyond the edges of the paper on purpose, for the "bleeding line" effect. Create custom line effects by drawing a long, thin rectangle with different fill patterns to vary the line, or use PageMaker's leader dots or dashes (Indents/Tabs in the Type menu).

To define the layout of the regular pages, switch to the left–right master pages and unlock the guides if they are locked. (A check mark next to the Lock guides option means the guides are locked.) You can now move the guides: drag the right-hand column guide on the left master page (Figure 3-46) over to the left side of the page and line it up with the 25-pica marker.

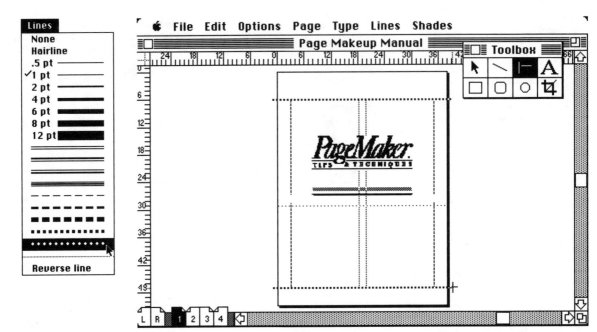

Figure 3-45. The title page of the two-column technical manual.

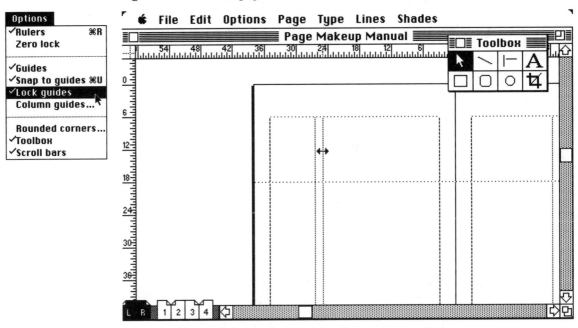

Figure 3-46. Moving the unlocked column guide on the left master page to a custom position for all of the left-hand pages in the publication.

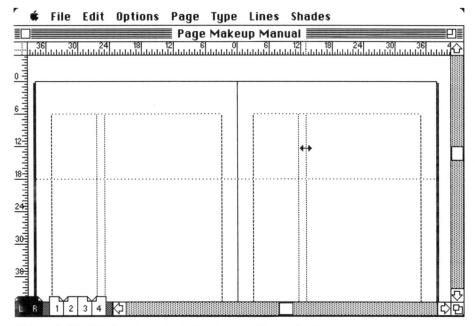

Figure 3-47. Moving the unlocked column guide on the right master page to a custom position for all of the right-hand pages in the publication.

Scroll the screen over to the right master page and line up its right-hand column guide on the 13-pica mark. (If the toolbox is in the way, you can move it by dragging its title bar, or you can temporarily hide it by clicking its close box or by selecting the Toolbox command from the Options menu. Select Toolbox from the Options menu again to redisplay the toolbox.) Both pages should now have the same column layout (Figure 3-47). Add page number footers to the master pages as shown in previous examples.

Save the publication file as the title page (call it **Title Page**), and save it again as a manual template (called **Manual Template**) for use with other sections or chapters of the manual. Use the Manual Template file to start the first section of the manual. Save the publication once more as **Page Makeup Manual** (for the first section).

Create the chapter title page text by typing the chapter title with the text tool, highlighting the text, and changing the Type specs (in the Type menu, or use Command T) to Times Roman 36-point bold italic with 40

Figure 3-48. The first chapter's title page is a right-hand page; each chapter is stored in a separate publication file.

points of leading. To fix the column breaks, stretch the column width of the chapter title and position the title as shown in Figure 3-48 (note the use of a vertical dotted line next to the chapter title). To produce the typographic apostrophe in the chapter title, use Option Shift]. Alternatively, type the single quote, then select it using the text tool, then hold down the Option and Shift keys as you type the] character, and the single quote character will be replaced by the apostrophe. (PageMaker can produce other special symbols and characters, described in Appendix C.)

Preparing Text and Graphics
The text for the manual should be preformatted to have italic and bold styles and tabs already set, so that you can bring tables and formatted text into PageMaker with styles intact (using the Retain format option in the Place dialog box). Microsoft Word has the closest relationship to Page-Maker, and PageMaker can export selected PageMaker text as a Word text

file. (PageMaker also exports WriteNow text files and Text only files. Other "export filters" are being developed by Aldus and other vendors.) PageMaker also allows you to copy and paste selected text to another program using the Clipboard. If you have several blocks of text to move, you can use the Clipboard and Scrapbook. This text updating process is most important in the production of manuals that are frequently updated.

Tables of data should be prepared so that the same number of tabs are used between columns of a table. Set the tabs so that the table columns line up in the word processor with one tab between each column item. In PageMaker you can change the tab settings to fit the column format, or use the tabs already set in the word processing program.

You should also use a tab if you want to indent the first line of each paragraph (or, in Microsoft Word, you could instead use the first line indent for a paragraph format). PageMaker recognizes the left margin setting as a starting point, and uses the right margin setting, but you can change these settings in the Paragraph dialog box (in PageMaker's Type menu). PageMaker also recognizes the first-line indent of a paragraph in Microsoft Word and other word processors (see Appendix A), whether that indent is positioned to the left of the left margin (a hanging indent) or to the right (a regular indent).

Technical manuals usually require a lot of illustrations, chiefly line art rather than paintings with gray scale. (Drawings of equipment and schematics are "line art" because they consist of lines, curves, and geometric shapes, without rough edges and blurred details.) Therefore, you will want to use a drawing program rather than a painting program, so that the fine lines and curves will be reproduced with the highest possible resolution (and therefore the highest quality).

If you use a drawing program, draw the graphics at the size that is most comfortable for you and most accurate in detail; draw-type graphics can be scaled in PageMaker to any size *after* they are drawn, but the entire drawing is scaled. If you want to maintain type size, but reduce the drawing, use a drawing program (such as MacDraw) to scale the image to final size without reducing the size of type, then place the image in PICT format.

If you want your drawing to be scaled independent of line weights, use Adobe's Illustrator to have the choice of preserving or scaling line weights as you scale the image in Illustrator to final size, then save the image in EPS format for placement on a PageMaker page.

Technical manuals may also need photographs of equipment, which can be scanned into the computer using a desktop scanner. Existing line art can also be scanned to convert drawings on paper into electronic form. Gray scale TIFF images can be created by some scanners (such as ThunderScan and New Image Technology scanners), then edited using a gray-scale paint program (such as Letraset's ImageStudio). When printed on a Linotronic 300 typesetter, or viewed on a Macintosh II's large screen (such as SuperMac Technology's Spectrum display card and 19-inch monitor), these images rival fine-screened conventional halftones in quality. However, scanned images (saved as TIFF files) are large files of paint-type graphics and subject to the same restrictions as paint-type graphics (as described in Chapter 1 and Appendix B). You will get best results from scaling scanned images if you use PageMaker's built-in scaling percentages (holding down the Command key while scaling), or scale the image to final size using a gray-scale paint program, before placing it in PageMaker.

Placing Text and Graphics

The quickest way to place text (and not have to use the text tool to reformat the text) is to place preformatted text. If your text is not preformatted, you can still do some preformatting that will help speed up the process: Use carriage returns (when you type Return in a word processor you generate a carriage return) only at the ends of paragraphs and fixed lines and delete any extra spaces (such as the extra word space following sentences usually inserted by typists). PageMaker automatically converts any instance of a double-hyphen as an em dash (—), and converts quotation marks and single quote marks into the proper open and close quote symbols.

If you are bringing in unformatted text with the Text only option in the Place dialog box, the text will take on the characteristics of the Type specs dialog box (in the Type menu). It makes sense to choose the text style (usually a Times Roman or other serif font, at 10 or 12 points with 12 or 14 points of leading, respectively) in the Type specs menu before placing the text. If you place the text first, choose the text tool, click somewhere

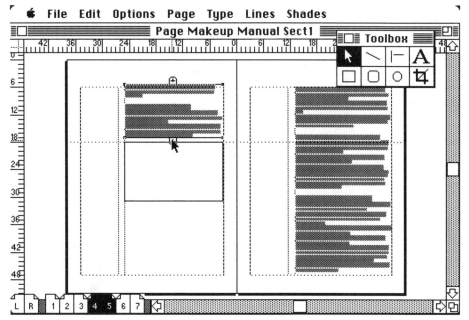

Figure 3-49. Moving text out of the way and placing graphics (or drawing a box), then extending the text.

in the text, and employ the Select all command (Command A) to highlight all of the text; then make changes in the Type specs dialog box (Command T).

It is most practical to start a publication by positioning the graphics and photo boxes, then placing the text around them. However, large publications (such as manuals and books) usually have references to the illustrations and photos, and you want to place them as close to their references as possible. But how do you know where the references will occur without placing all of the text? Although you would start a short publication (such as a newsletter, brochure, or magazine article) by placing the graphics first, you probably won't start a manual or book that way.

The design of this technical manual makes it easy to place all of the text first, and then go back and adjust the text to accommodate illustrations and graphics. To adjust the text, select the column and drag the bottom handle up above the area where graphics will be placed (Figure 3-49). Draw a box (or place a graphics file) to fill the area and click the bottom handle of the

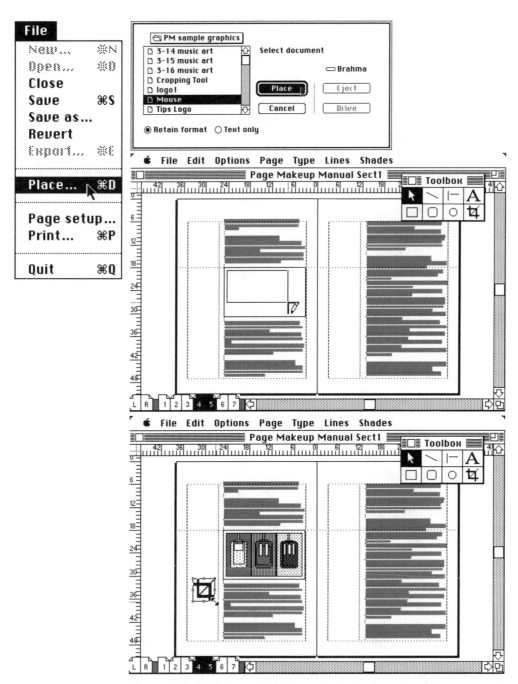

Figure 3-50. Placing and resizing a draw-type graphic by dragging while placing, then placing a paint-type graphic and resizing with the Command and Shift keys.

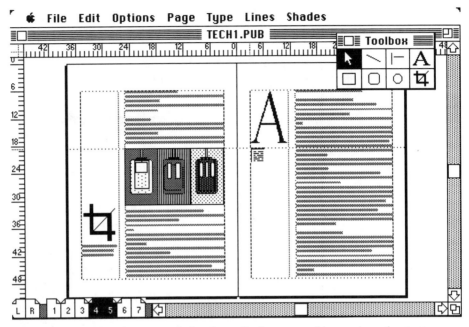

Figure 3-51. Using the narrow left column for icons, graphics, and caption text.

raised column to get the text placement icon, and continue the column below the graphics area.

When positioning draw-type graphics, or if you don't mind distorting paint-type graphics, you can take a shortcut and resize the graphics at the same time, by dragging the placement icon (while placing) across the area that is to be filled by the graphic (Figure 3-50). Dragging while placing is a quick technique for filling an area with text or graphics, but the graphics should be draw-type graphics, since paint-type graphics should be resized by holding down the Command key to get PageMaker's best scale factors, and holding down the Shift key to keep the same proportions and avoid distorting (stretching or compressing) the image. (This technique — dragging while placing — is especially useful if you want to distort a paint-type graphic deliberately.)

Position the graphics and photo boxes and captions, starting at the beginning of the publication and moving through to the end, so that as you adjust the text, references in the text are in a final position when you place the graphics. Use the narrow left column for icons, graphics, and caption text (Figure 3-51).

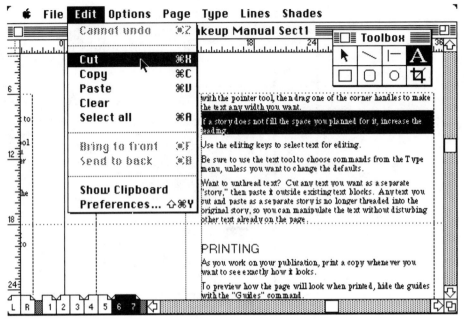

Figure 3-52. Cut text for each column and paste to make separate text blocks.

Constructing a Complex Table

Technical manuals often display charts consisting of boxed tables of words. You can use PageMaker to design such a boxed table with or without placing the text from a file. If the text is in a file, place it first, then use the Cut and Paste commands to separate the text of each column (Figure 3-52). You can stretch or condense each column by dragging its corner (Figure 3-53), then draw a box around the entire table and rules to separate each column (Figure 3-54). For tables that have one line of text in each column, it is much simpler to set tab settings and type or paste tabular text into the column with those settings, or set a column guide, type text for the first column, set a second column next to the first and type text for the second column, and so on for each column.

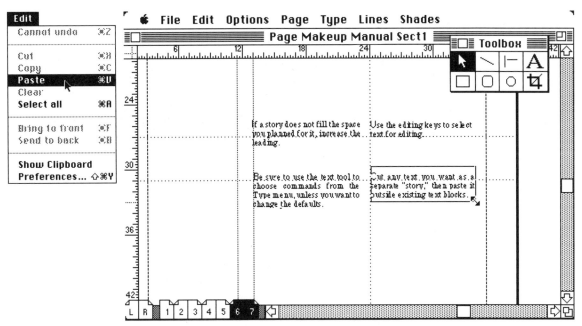

Figure 3-53. Dragging each column's text to make a boxed table.

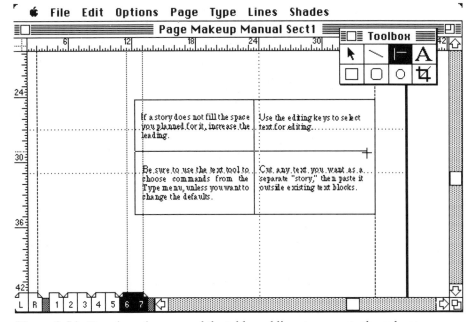

Figure 3-54. Drawing a box around the table and lines to separate the columns.

A Complete Book

It is not only possible to produce a book with PageMaker, it may be the preferred method, so that the book's pages can be flexible in layout. Books can be produced that are visually more interesting and more readable, especially in the case of a book that has a lot of illustrations (as this book does).

Books are like manuals in that they involve the use of long text files, usually separated into chapters, and the use of a single column on each page, although some large books are laid out with two columns. A book is usually completely written before it is produced, and with some books, there is a considerable need to update the pages at the very last minute and save those changes in the text files. For this reason, and since PageMaker has a closer relationship to Microsoft Word than to any other word processor (at the time of this writing), you should consider using Microsoft Word to create the manuscript. When you finally place the text on PageMaker pages, the pages can be edited at the last minute and the text can be exported to a Word file, or as a text only file to MacWrite or another word processing program. (Version 2.0a of PageMaker also includes an export filter for T/Maker's WriteNow.).

PageMaker 2.0 does not have index or table of contents generation, but these can be created using a number of different programs or your word processor. After producing the PageMaker pages, use your word processor to put page breaks in the text files that match the page breaks in PageMaker. You can then use the word processor text file with an indexing program (such as Word's built-in indexer, or Letraset's LetraIndex).

We used Microsoft Word to prepare text files *and* to produce the index for this book. After placing the Word text files onto PageMaker pages, we edited the Word files to include last-minute changes (made in PageMaker) and PageMaker page breaks, as well as index entries. Word lets you create glossary entries (abbreviations you can type that represent index entry markers and delimiters) so that you can move quickly through an electronic manuscript marking index words and phrases. Word then compiles an index from separate chapter files, with page numbers based on the page breaks in those files. The table of contents was created using another code for the table of contents entries in the same text files.

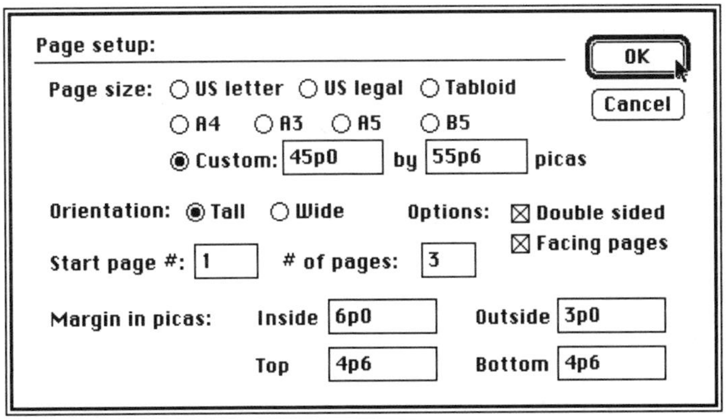

```
┌────────────────────────────────────────────────────┐
│ Page setup:                              ┌─────────┐│
│                                          │   OK    ││
│ Page size:  ○ US letter  ○ US legal  ○ Tabloid      │
│             ○ A4   ○ A3   ○ A5   ○ B5    ┌─────────┐│
│             ● Custom: 45p0   by 55p6   picas Cancel ││
│                                                     │
│ Orientation: ● Tall  ○ Wide   Options: ⊠ Double sided│
│                                        ⊠ Facing pages│
│ Start page #: 1     # of pages: 3                   │
│                                                     │
│ Margin in picas:   Inside 6p0      Outside 3p0      │
│                                                     │
│                    Top  4p6        Bottom 4p6       │
└────────────────────────────────────────────────────┘
```

Figure 3-55. Page setup for this book, which was completely produced using PageMaker.

Designing the Pages

Most books are *not* 8 1/2 by 11 inches, which is a standard page size for letters, newsletters, and some technical manuals. Although you can lay out a smaller book size (such as 6 1/2 by 9 inches) on pages that are standard size (8 1/2 by 11 inches), and you can adjust margin settings to create an image area the size of the book's pages, it is much better to change the page size, so that you can print *crop marks* on the 8 1/2- by 11-inch paper. Crop marks (also called trim marks) are recognized by the volume printer or print shop for defining the edges of the page. They are printed automatically by PageMaker if you select them from the Print dialog box.

Start a new publication for each of the book's chapters, and change the default settings for the page setup menu to have the dimensions of the book pages: a custom page that is 45 picas wide by 55 picas and 6 points high, with tall (portrait) orientation and double-sided pages. The image area is defined by margins that are 6 picas in from the binding, 3 picas in from the edge of the page, 4 picas and 6 points down from the top of the page, and 4 picas and 6 points up from the bottom (Figure 3-55).

On the master pages we placed a horizontal guide for placing text at the top of the page and a different page number header for the left and right pages. We also set up the page layout to be two columns, just like the

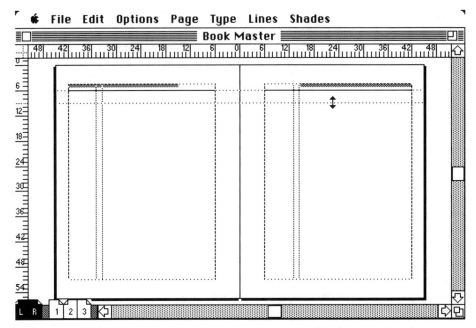

Figure 3-56. The two-column layout for this book (one wide for text, the other narrow for icons and menus).

technical manual in the previous example. First, specify two columns, then drag the right-hand column guide on the left master page over to the left side of the page and line it up with the 35-pica marker. Then, scroll the screen over to the right master page, and line up its right-hand column guide on the 13-pica mark. Both master pages should now have the same column layout (Figure 3-56).

Finally, set the Type specifications for the chapter title (Times Roman bold italic at 36 points with 40 points of leading) and choose Justify from the Type menu. The text will be justified using the minimum and maximum word spacing percentages in the Spacing dialog box, as well as the desired word spacing percentage, which is the only percentage used in ragged-right columns.

Save the publication file as the template (**Book Master**) for use with other chapters of the book, and save it again as the first chapter of the book

(**Chapter 1**). For subsequent chapters, open a copy of the Bookmaster file using the Open copy option, and use it as a template (the publication opens in a new, untitled window, but you can then save the file with a new name (**Chapter 2**, and so on), and the template remains unchanged).

Preparing Text and Graphics

Preformat the manuscript to have italic and bold styles and tabs already set, so that you can use the Retain format option in the Place dialog box to bring formatted text into PageMaker with styles intact. Otherwise you have to reset all instances of italics and bold styles in the text on the PageMaker page, as well as do other formatting. Preformatting minimizes last-minute formatting and allows the author of the book to control the use of type styles as well as contribute significantly to the production effort.

As mentioned previously, PageMaker 2.0 is able to export selected text in Microsoft Word, WriteNow, and text only format, or use the Clipboard to copy and paste selected text into your word processor. This need to make last-minute changes is prevalent in book publishing, since the printing and distribution process takes so long (typically three months) as to make many books out of date before they show up on bookstore shelves. Books can be archived in PageMaker publication files as well as in word processing files.

Refer to the earlier instructions (Preparing Text and Graphics for a technical manual, page 168) for preparing tables of information, tab settings, margin settings, first line indents, and other preformatting suggestions.

Books sometimes require line art (draw-type graphics), as described previously with technical manuals, or paint-type graphics. You may also want to add artistic flourishes or cartoon characters to book pages, either by creating them yourself in a paint program or using (and possibly modifying) electronic clip art from various clip art libraries on disk or CD ROM. You could place clip art such as the samples next to this paragraph (ClickArt images from T/Maker), and resize the images to fit the narrow column next to the text. Remember that with all paint-type graphics you should hold down the Command key while resizing to use PageMaker's built-in optimal sizes (also hold down Shift to remain in the same proportions) for your selected printer.

Placing Text and Graphics

If your text is not preformatted, you can still do some preformatting that will help speed up the process: Use carriage returns only at the ends of paragraphs and fixed lines and delete any extra spaces (such as an extra space between sentences). PageMaker converts any instance of a double-hyphen to an em dash (—) and converts quotation marks and single quote marks into the proper open and close quote symbols.

If you are bringing in unformatted text using the Text only option in the Place dialog box, the text will take on the characteristics of the Type specs dialog box (in the Type menu). We had set up the Type specs for the chapter title, so you must change them after typing the chapter title. For the body of the text, choose Times Roman or other serif font, at 10 or 12 points with 12 or 14 points of leading, respectively. Do this (in the Type specs menu) *before* placing the text. If you place the text first, you can choose the text tool, click somewhere in the text, and employ the Select all command (Command A) to highlight all of the text; then make changes in the Type specs dialog box.

You can place the text of a chapter very quickly, especially using the page layout in this example (since it uses only one column per page for the body of the text). Use the same technique described previously for technical manuals: Place the text first, then start again from the beginning and adjust the text to place graphics or photos that correspond to references in the text.

To avoid having an "orphan" (a single word or very short line by itself at the bottom of the page) or a "widow" (a word or very short line by itself at the top of the page), turn off hyphenation for the appropriate section of the text highlighted with the text tool. You can also change the word spacing used to justify the text (or the hyphenation zone for unjustified text); however, the word spacing (and hyphenation zone) values apply to the entire story or chapter (or text file), not just the area selected with the text tool, and the new setting may cause changes to occur elsewhere in the chapter that are not desired. For optimal spacing for justified text, leave automatic hyphenation on and set the word spacing range at 50% for minimum, 100% for desired, and 200% for maximum. Leave the letter spacing at 0% and 25% for minimum and maximum, respectively. If you need to adjust the automatic hyphenated and justified text to fix a widow

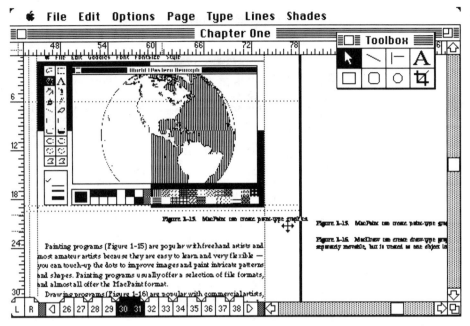

Figure 3-57. Cutting a caption from the caption block to place on the page under an illustration.

or orphan, select an appropriate range of text, and turn automatic hyphenation off and/or turn on prompted hyphenation.

We find it useful to keep captions in a separate file and place that file onto the pasteboard, alongside the page. After positioning an illustration requiring a caption, select the text tool and select and cut (use the Cut command from the Edit menu, or use Command X) the caption from the caption file block (Figure 3-57). Paste it (Command V) onto the pasteboard as a separate block above the caption block by moving the text tool far enough above the caption block, then clicking to create a text insertion point. Select Paste from the Edit menu (Command V) to paste the caption. Select the pointer tool and hold down the mouse button over the new caption block until the double-arrow symbol appears, and then drag the caption to move it into position under the illustration. Drag the corners of the new caption block to stretch or reduce its size, to fit the column margins and place all of the caption.

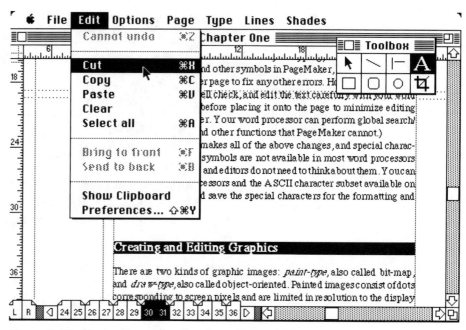

Figure 3-58. Cutting the subheading from the text body.

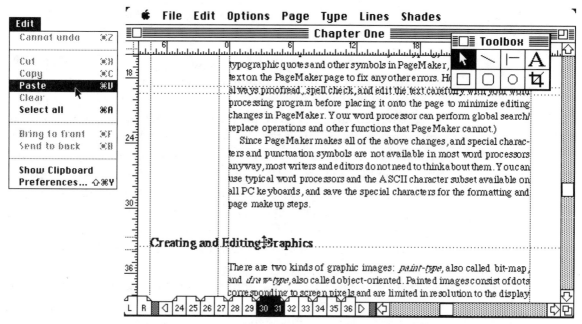

Figure 3-59. Moving the first-level subheadings out into the narrow column.

To make first-level subheadings stick out into the narrow left column, cut the subheading from the body of the text (Figure 3-58) and paste it back in the left column next to the same place, then move it into position (Figure 3-59). Do this operation after you've placed all of the illustrations or photo boxes and made all final adjustments to the text, because if you do any further adjustments, you may also have to move the separated subheadings.

Printing Chapters

Publication files are limited to 128 pages each, so it makes sense to separate a book into chapters and to store each chapter in a separate publication file. You can set the starting page number of a publication file in the Page setup dialog box. PageMaker can automatically number pages up to 9,999 (starting with whatever number you want), using arabic and composite page numbering systems.

If you turn on crop marks in the Print dialog box, you will get crop marks printed at the page boundaries, which are used as trim marks. You can also print the book's pages in reverse order, for use with printers that send pages out face up (and backward in sequence).

Using Masters as Style Sheets

You have already learned that when you first create a set of master pages for a publication, you save it as a template file, then save it as a publication, thus leaving behind a template for use as a starter publication file. This method can be very useful in a work group or in departmental publishing activities, where templates can be easily shared among users. When you select Open from the File menu (or use Command O), and you select a publication file to open, PageMaker gives you a choice of opening the original or opening a copy. A template can be easily shared when other users open a copy of the file. Open the original template file to make any changes to the template.

A template can consist of a set of well-defined master pages; but it might contain a first page with graphics that should appear only on certain pages. An example would be the title page of a manual whose text changes with each new version, but whose format stays the same. The title page may have a corporate logo as well as a design that should be carried over from one publication to another. Rather than having to reposition similar elements on each similar page, simply save the template file with a first page that contains all of the necessary elements, including sample text to be altered for each publication.

Master pages should contain all of the guides, including column guides, that will be used regularly on the pages. They should also contain any headers, footers, or other places where automatic page numbers can be used. Set the paragraph style (justified or ragged right, the tab settings, and the word spacing), the type specifications, and any other options (such as Locked guides, Snap to guides, etc.) you want to have preset for the publication.

Finally, be sure to include any graphics — either on page 1, where they can be used on any page — or on the master pages, to be repeated on every page. Set the printer (and print the file once to set the APD) in the template file to avoid problems, and do not change printer resolution until all of the graphics are placed (Chapter 5 explains how to change the resolution of APD files). Copy large graphics files into the same folder as the publication file they are placed in. Make a copy of that entire folder to use with a different printer.

Make template files available to others in your work group, and make them available on a file server in a network. By using the same template, a large publication staff can produce publications that look alike and are consistent in quality.

Summary

In this chapter, you successfully produced an annual report, a technical manual, and a book, and you learned to do the following with PageMaker:

Produce an Annual Report
Set up master pages, with footers, page numbers (use Command Option P on both left-and right-hand pages as an automatic page number marker), and a logo. Position and resize the logo for master pages, and place it on

page 1 as well (because master items display is turned off for page 1).

Place text on page 1, using a dropped initial for the first letter in the column. Add a headline, remove a footer, draw a rule, and finish placing text.

Subsequent pages get special head and subhead treatments. Check for and fix any widows or orphans by adjusting the word spacing and hyphenation. Cut text blocks to create room to insert graphics.

Add graphics, using the cropping tool, resizing images to fit, incorporating halftones (screened photographs) into the design. Wrap text around images.

Adding spreadsheet data requires special attention to tabs and font compatibility. Use spreadsheet fonts or change fonts for maximum readability and impact. Boxes and drop shadow effects add dimension to charts.

Adding charts and graphs will depend upon what program you used to create the chart or graph, and whether it is a paint (bit-map) or draw (object or vector) type of file. Charts and graphs can be placed, cropped, and resized, and any text they contain can be adjusted or replaced with new text. For bit-map type charts and graphs, typing new labels and text with PageMaker gives best results. A chart can even be extended across a two-page spread, and the pages line up with ease.

Printing the report requires that you check to be sure the fonts you have used are available in your system and printer. For instance, if you used downloadable fonts not available in your system or printer or fonts in your document that are not available in your system or printer, then you need to install those fonts in your system, download them to your printer, change the printer, or print your document with font substitution or bit-map screen fonts. Other printing options include orientation of pages, which paper tray (for printers with more than one tray at a time), number of copies, range of pages, and so on.

Produce a Technical Manual

Design the pages, paying special attention to the title page design. Prepare text and graphics, and position them. Construct a complex table, and place it, then print the manual.

Produce a Book
Design the pages (with crop marks), and create a template file to copy for each chapter. Prepare and place text and graphics, with treatments for captions, headings and subheadings. Print the pages.

Using Masters as Style Sheets
This allows you to share designs in a work group effectively. You can save separate publication files with different master pages and type settings.

4 | Advanced Design

Magazines and coffee table books require pages that have a designed look, and page advertisements and flyers are designed purposely to attract a reader's attention. Magazine pages are designed to be visually exciting, but with a clear hierarchy that starts with the article's title and department heading and extends to the text subheadings and captions for photos or illustrations.

There are only a few clear "right" and "wrong" choices to make — for example, don't mix more than three fonts (not including their italic and bold styles) on a page and don't crowd the page with text and graphics. For the most part design decisions are subjective. There is an art magazine, for example, called *Emigrè*, which has the subtitle "The magazine that ignores boundaries." This magazine, designed on a Macintosh, routinely breaks the so-called design rules to achieve certain artistic effects.

PageMaker excels at providing tools for moving elements on the page and customizing layouts. You can mix two or more column styles on one page (e.g., use a two-column format at the top of the page, and a three-column format at the bottom), wrap text around irregularly shaped objects, put reversed (white) type onto a black background, or even start a paragraph with an enlarged capital letter. You can also move letters

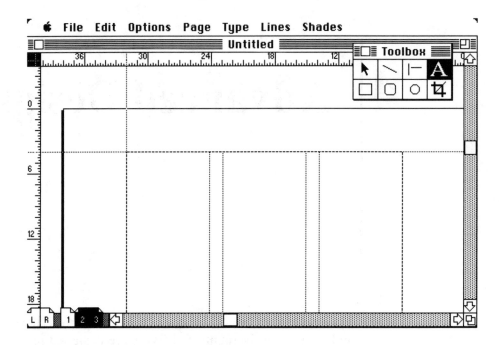

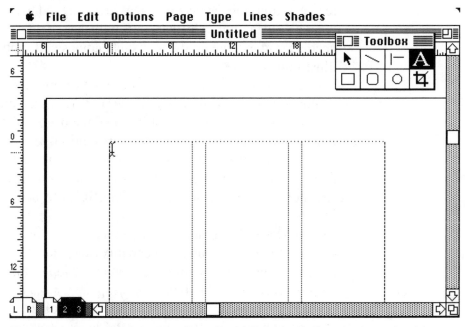

Figure 4-1. Dragging the zero point to the top left margin from its former position on the top left edge of the page.

closer together using a manual kerning function. These kinds of enhancements are necessary if you want your pages to have a designed look.

The trick to producing custom pages is to design the elements first (such as fancy line styles and boxes, or reversed-type-on-black headlines) and copy them for use on different pages. For example, if you design a black panel with reversed (white) text that will be used on many different pages (perhaps with different text), you can copy the panel and text and paste them onto another page, then type new text and resize the panel to fit the new text, without having to reinvent the element. The original elements remain the same so that you can copy and paste them again.

With PageMaker, you can easily print Thumbnails (select this option in the Print dialog box) to see miniature pages to decide if you like the position of elements, then continue to make adjustments to the pages and print thumbnail pages again before printing final pages.

The following special effects and techniques are by no means the only effects you can achieve with PageMaker, but they serve as a representative sample of using PageMaker's tools. Some of the examples in this chapter are from actual publications (where noted), and others are made-up examples. You can use these techniques to design almost anything.

Before proceeding, there is one capability of PageMaker's rulers that has not yet been shown. The rulers start at a zero point corresponding to the top left edge of the page, so that you can measure to the right of the left edge, or down from the top edge. This zero point does not change as you move around the page, so that you can measure distances from a specific point. In a double-page display, the zero point is centered between the pages (between the top right edge of the left-hand page and the top left edge of the right-hand page).

You can move the zero point to be anywhere on the page, for the purpose of measuring distances across or down the page. You can move the zero point at any time, no matter which tool is selected. If you are using the pointer tool, and you have a text or graphics file loaded and ready to place (the pointer is a text icon, a paintbrush, a pencil, a PS, or a box with an X icon), it will still be there after you move the zero point. No matter which tool is selected, the cursor temporarily turns into the arrow pointer when you move it into the rulers.

Many designers prefer to move the zero point to the top left *margin* of the page, rather than the top left edge. To move the zero point, point on the two dotted lines that cross in the upper left corner of the display (Figure 4-1) and drag the two dotted lines diagonally to change both rulers, or horizontally or vertically to change one or the other ruler. The zero point is the base for both rulers.

Once you have the zero point where you want it, you can lock it into place with the Zero lock option in the Options menu, so that you don't accidentally move it. When you start a new publication, the zero point is unlocked so that you can change it or lock it. Once locked, you unlock it to move the zero point again. Change the zero point whenever you want to quickly and easily measure distances.

Wrapping Text Around Graphics

When you place a column of text, the text flows down the page until it bumps up against the margin or against a graphic or line. You can extend

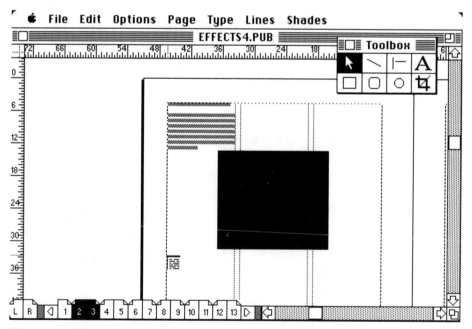

Figure 4-2. Flowing text up to and beyond a rectangular box before wrapping text around the box.

the text by clicking the bottom handle to get the placement icon, and placing that icon below the graphic. You can also flow text through the "alley" created when a graphic extends into a column but does not completely traverse the column.

To wrap text around a rectangular box, which has a straight edge, flow the text to the top of the area or box, then click the + symbol in the bottom handle, and use the text placement icon to continue flowing text below the box (Figure 4-2). Next, drag the text block below the box up to the top of the box, lined up to be just below the preceding text (Figure 4-3) and drag the bottom handle of the same block up to the last line of text next to the box (Figure 4-4). Drag a corner of this short text block diagonally to fit the space between the box and the column margin (Figure 4-5).

Finally, click the + symbol in the bottom handle of the text next to the box and use the text placement icon to continue the full-width text in the column below the box (Figure 4-6). Adjust the text below the box by dragging the top handle up or down, and line up the text with other text

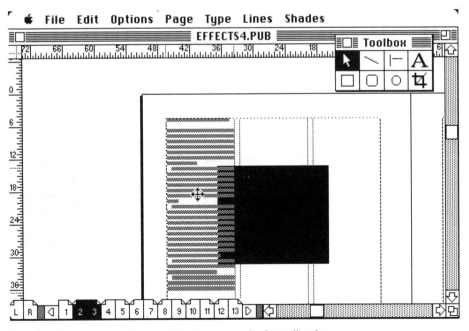

Figure 4-3. Dragging the text block up over the intruding box.

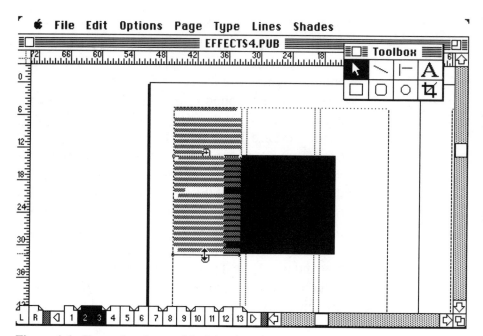

Figure 4-4. Shortening the text block by dragging the bottom of the text up to the bottom of the box.

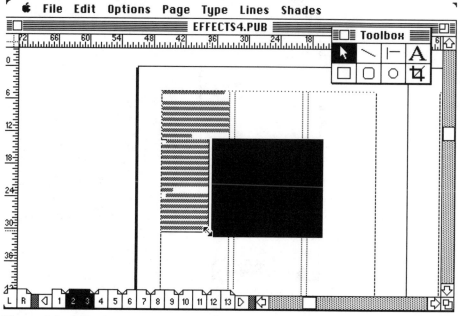

Figure 4-5. Adjusting the column width of the short text block to be next to the box.

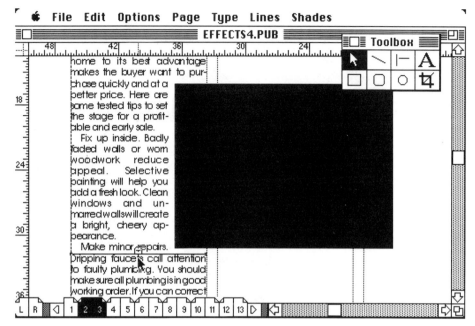

Figure 4-6. Continuing to place the text below the box.

in the next column or with the ruler. You now have text wrapping around the box, and if you later make editing changes, the text will flow naturally around the box.

The box is useful as a placeholder for halftones or four-color separations that are not placed on the electronic page. You can delete the box by selecting it with the pointer tool and choosing Cut from the Edit menu, or by pressing the Backspace key. The blank area could be used for text (e.g., a callout or pull quote) or graphics.

Wrapping around an irregular shape is a little more difficult. If the text is not going to be edited again, you can get away with using the Tab and Enter keys to move words away from the irregular margin, but this is not the preferred method. First, drag the text over the graphic or area, then switch to the text tool and use the Return key to force line endings at the right margin (Figure 4-7). To wrap text around a graphic that intrudes into the middle of the text or at the left margin, use the Tab key to insert tab spaces (Figure 4-8).

If the text may be edited again, the above method would mean you'd have to remove the carriage returns or tabs you had inserted and do the job

Figure 4-7. Wrapping text around an irregular object by inserting carriage returns with the Return key (page from the book, *Whale Song* courtesy of Beyond Words).

over again. Another method, which takes longer at first but only has to be done once, is to create a new text block every time the margin changes, and resize the text blocks individually to fit into the irregular margin (Figure 4-9). If the text changes after editing, it will still flow smoothly through the individual text blocks. If you later decide to delete the image the text flows around, simply cut the image and drag on the corner handles of each selected text block to stretch it to the new margins, and the text within the block automatically reflows, with no extraneous carriage returns or tabs to delete (as you would have to do with the previously described method).

Enlarged Initial Capital

Magazine articles usually start with an enlarged capital letter that kicks off the article's text. Usually the letter is in the same font as the article's title,

Figure 4-8. Creating space in a text block with the Tab key to wrap text around a graphic (page from the book, *Whale Song* courtesy of Beyond Words).

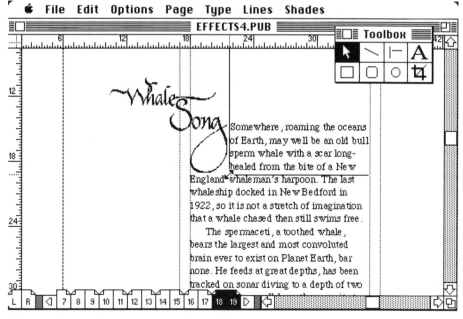

Figure 4-9. Creating text blocks for every change in the margin, and resizing them individually (page from the book, *Whale Song* courtesy of Beyond Words).

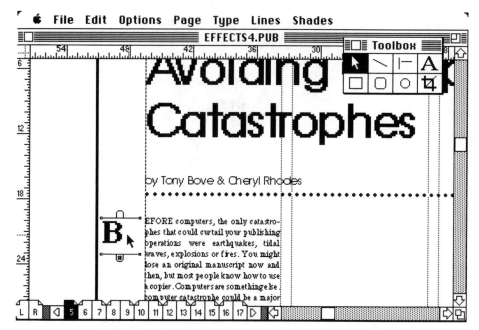

Figure 4-10. The initial capital, cut from the text body and pasted next to the text, or retyped.

but its size is two or three times as large as the rest of the text. Sometimes an enlarged initial capital is used to start a new section of the text as well as at the start of the text.

There are several ways to design a page with an enlarged initial capital, but the most popular ways are to either use a box around the capital letter and wrap the opening text around it, as shown in the first example, or wrap text around the capital letter itself. In both cases the capital letter drops down inside the boundaries of the text and does not stick out of the column at the top or on the side. Or, the capital letter could drop down just a line or two inside the boundaries of the text and stick out of the column at the top. If you choose to use an enlarged capital that is above or outside of the text margin, you don't have to wrap text around it.

Start by typing the letter in an area next to the text body (and deleting that letter from the opening of the article), or by using the Cut command to cut the letter from the opening and the Paste command to paste it in an area next to the text body. Click an insertion point immediately after the

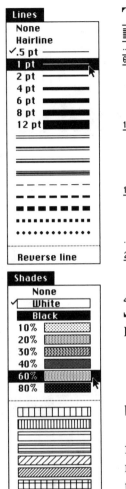

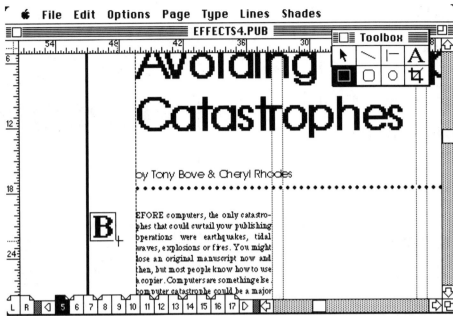

Figure 4-11. Drawing a box and using a pattern to surround the enlarged initial cap.

big letter and press Return to end the line.

Using the text tool, highlight the letter, then set the type specifications for it. The letter should be at least two or three lines deep compared to the regular text, or it will not stand out as it should. However, the letter should not be bigger than the letters used in the article title. If the regular text is 10 points with 12 points of leading (as in the first example), choose a font matching either the text body or the article title (the example uses the text body font, set to bold), and select 36 points or larger for the size.

Figure 4-10 shows the enlarged initial capital, pasted or typed next to the text body across from the actual position it will occupy in the text, and set to the proper point size. You may also want to change the characters in the first word in the text block to be all capital letters, in a smaller point size, as shown.

The first style is to draw a box or other shape around the letter, perhaps with a shadow of the box or shape behind it, and to make the letter appear three-dimensional with the use of a shadow letter behind it. Using the box

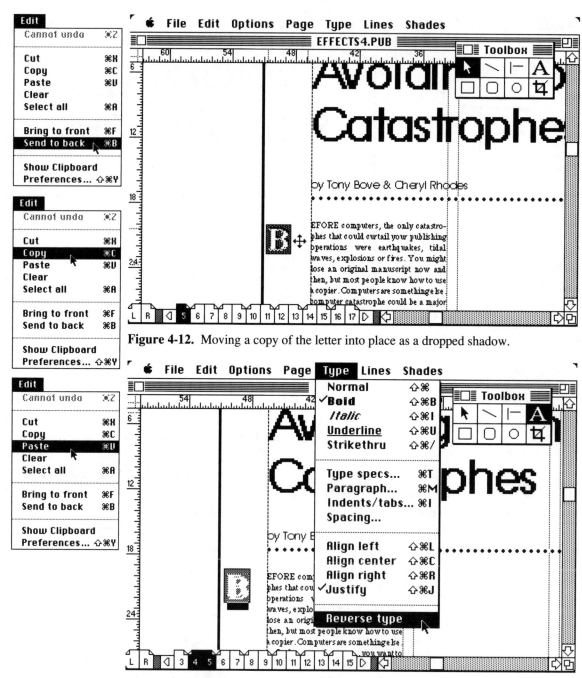

Figure 4-12. Moving a copy of the letter into place as a dropped shadow.

Figure 4-13. Selecting the original letter and changing it to reverse type.

tool, draw a box around the letter so that the letter is centered within the box, then choose the 60% pattern from the Shades menu (Figure 4-11), and choose the Send to back option from the Edit menu (or use Command B) so that the shaded box is behind the letter.

Next, select the letter with the pointing tool, copy it to the Clipboard (Command C), and paste the copy back to the page (Command V). Move the newly pasted letter into position so that it is slightly to the left of and below the original letter (Figure 4-12), then choose the Send to back command from the Edit menu (Command B), so that the copied letter is moved behind the original.

Use the text tool to select the original letter again and choose the Reverse type option in the Type menu (Figure 4-13) to change the original letter into a white (reversed) letter. Select the box with the pointer tool and use the Send to back command again, this time to send the box behind both letters.

Now, while the box is selected, copy it to the Clipboard and paste the copy back to the page. Move the copied box slightly to the left and below

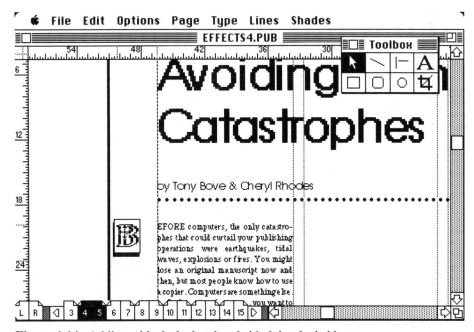

Figure 4-14. Adding a black shadow box behind the shaded box.

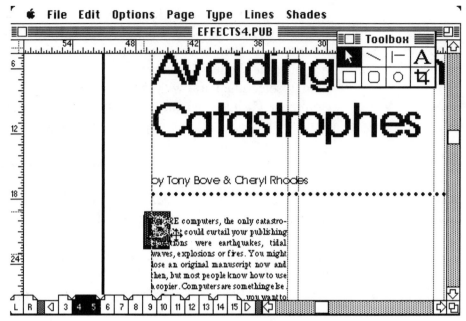

Figure 4-15. Selecting and moving all of the objects into position.

the original box, choose Black from the Shades menu, and then use the Send to back command again, so that the black box becomes a black shadow behind the shaded box (Figure 4-14).

The shadow box should still be selected, and you can select the other objects by holding down the Shift key while clicking the shaded box, the original letter, and the copied letter with the pointer tool. (If you have trouble selecting the shadow letter because it is behind the original letter, hold down the Command key as well as the Shift key while clicking. Depress the Command key and click to select any text block, graphic or rule that is so close to a column guide that you would get the guide if you did not use the Command key.) With all objects selected, point in the middle of them, hold down the mouse button until you see the double-arrow symbol, and drag all of the objects at once into position in the text block (Figure 4-15). If the letters disappear, select the boxes covering them and use the Send to back command in the Edit menu (or select the boxes and use Command B).

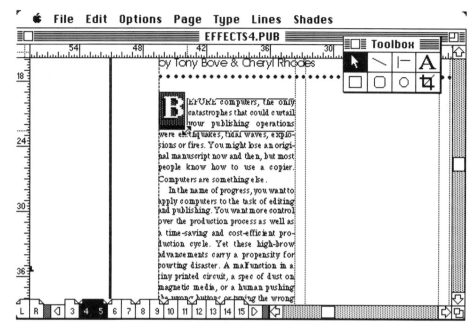

Figure 4-16. Wrapping text around the enlarged initial capital graphic.

Now you can treat the enlarged initial graphic as a box intruding in the column, and you can wrap the text around it (Figure 4-16), just as in the previous example (Figures 4-1 through 4-6).

The second style is to wrap text around the letter itself. Figure 4-17 shows how you would drag the text over the enlarged initial capital letter. (You can also drag the enlarged capital letter over the text, and then use the Send to back command to send the capital letter behind the text.) From that point you can either use the Tab key to insert spaces in the text (Figure 4-18), or you can resize individual text blocks around the irregular edge of the enlarged initial capital (Figure 4-19).

Mixing Column Layouts

You can combine one type of column layout (such as a two-column layout) with any other type of column layout on the same page; however,

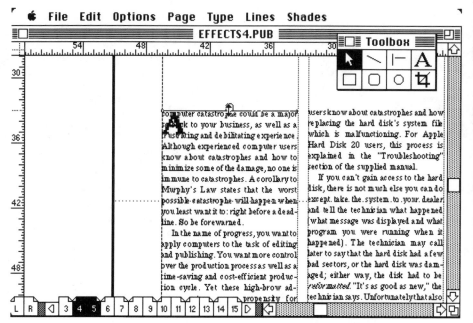

Figure 4-17. Dragging text over the enlarged initial capital before wrapping it around the capital.

it is easier to combine column layouts when you first separate them with a rule or graphic, because text flow will be interrupted by a rule or graphic below. A rule or graphic — or use of white space — to separate different layouts can also make the page more appealing to readers.

A typical combination of layouts may be a two-column layout at the top of a page, and a three- or four-column layout at the bottom. The publication file should have master pages set to the predominant column layout (in this case, the two-column layout). Draw a line to separate the layouts, and (if necessary) change the number of columns with the Column guides option. Start at the top or left-hand section of the page, and place the text in that layout first. Then change the column layout again and continue positioning text in that layout (Figure 4-20). Leave the same spacing between columns or use less spacing if the columns are very narrow. The change in the column layout affects the position of column guides, but does not affect the text you already placed in the two-column layout.

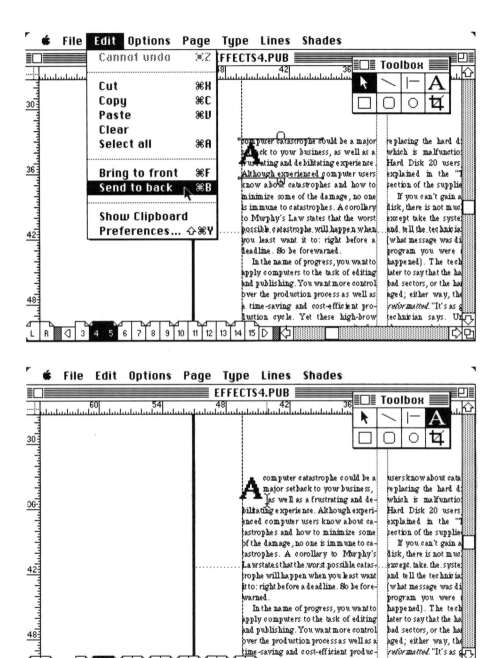

Figure 4-18. Inserting tab spaces to move words around the enlarged initial capital.

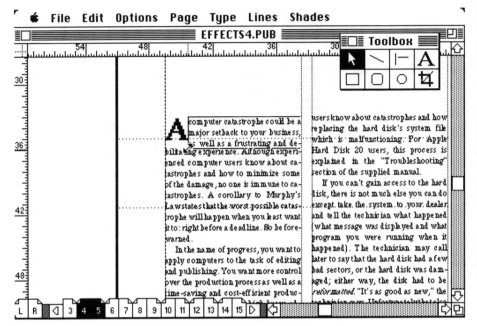

Figure 4-19. Resizing small text blocks to fit around the irregular edge of the enlarged initial capital.

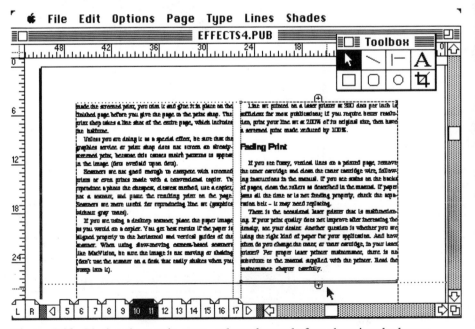

Figure 4-20. Placing the text in a two-column layout before changing the layout.

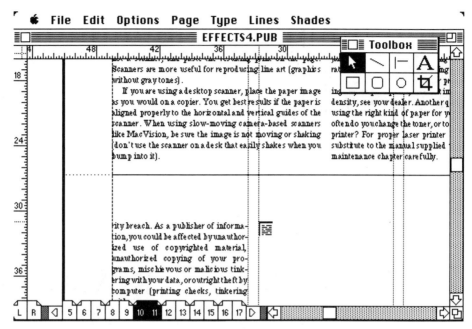

Figure 4-21. Continuing to place the text in the new column layout.

Continue placing the text in the three-column layout (Figure 4-21). When you are finished, you can go back and delete the line and replace it with a stylized border, or draw a box around the new layout to separate it from the two-column layout.

Reverse Type

One popular effect (that has its origins in the design of menus on computer displays) is reverse (white) type on a black or gray background. You have already learned how to set a character in reverse type onto a dark gray background in the first enlarged initial capital example. You should use reverse (white) type in a black background or a background with a 60% or 80% gray shade, because these contrasts give best results, but you can also use a dark-patterned background. You could also print black text over a patterned background (called surprinting), however, be sure the pattern does not affect readability of the text. If you want to surprint type on a

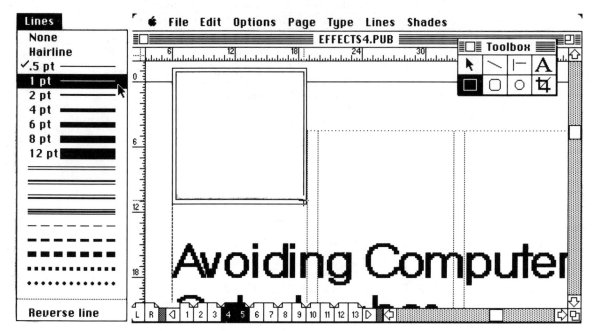

Figure 4-22. Drawing two boxes: the first step toward creating a reversed text panel that will bleed off the top of the page.

patterned or gray-shaded background, or reverse type from a patterned background, experiment to see what pattern or percentage of gray gives you best results. (Ink and paper also affect the results, if your final printed piece includes colored ink or specialty paper, so test print your page on a sample of the stock, if possible, and check that your printer can reproduce your master page for his press without the type breaking or plugging up.)

The example in Figure 4-22 is the first page of a department of a magazine, with a department heading box that is matched with a smaller page number box. First draw the box for the background and another box around it for the outline. The box and outline are drawn to bleed off the top of the page — the part above the page trim mark will not print. Select the outline with the pointer tool and change it to a 1-point line, then select the background box and select Black from the Shades menu (Figure 4-23).

Next, switch to the text tool, select a font, point size, and leading value

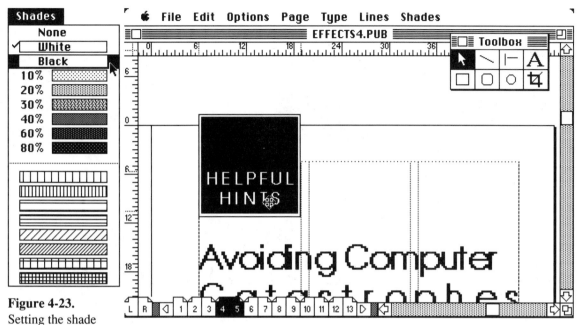

Figure 4-23. Setting the shade of the background for the text panel.

Figure 4-24. Dragging the text into the panel.

in the Type specs dialog box (Command T), and type the text for the panel *outside* of the panel. Note that you will have a crisper white type if you use a sans serif thick font such as Helvetica bold. Although you can use a very light or italic font reversed against a black background, don't use reverse italic type in a gray-shaded box, and always check that your printer can reproduce your master page for his press without the type breaking or plugging up.

After typing, switch to the pointer tool, point in the middle of the text, and drag the text into the black box (Figure 4-24). Finally, switch to the text tool, drag across the area where the text is placed in the panel (you can't see the text until you select to highlight it, since the text is black and fades into the black background), and select Reverse type from the Type menu (Figure 4-25). Now that you can see the white text against the black background, you can switch to the pointer tool, point in the middle of the text, and drag the text to center it properly in the panel.

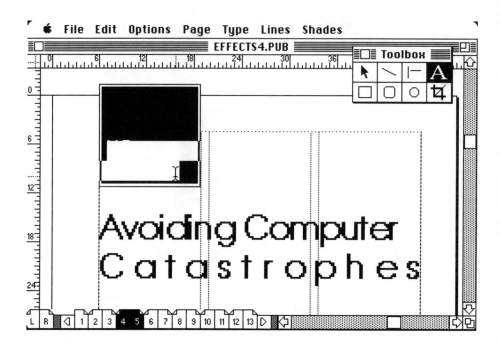

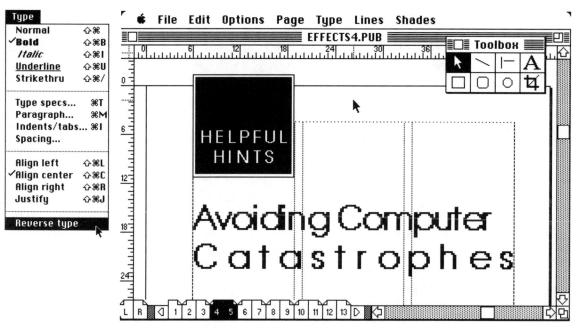

Figure 4-25. Highlighting with the text tool and selecting reversed type.

Fancy Titles and Headlines

Two very common techniques for creating fancy headlines and article titles are spreading a headline (adding space between the letters) or kerning its letters to be closer together (e.g., if the first letter is plain text or bold, and the second letter is italic, or if the title is greater than 18-point type size). PageMaker can handle both effects and many others.

Spreading Text

You can add space to a headline by simply typing a space between each character. Or, you can use nonbreaking spaces, or a mix of nonbreaking spaces and regular spaces typed on the PageMaker page.

A nonbreaking space will never end a line; it glues the characters it separates together (use it between two words you don't want to have separated by a linebreak), and does not get expanded or condensed when

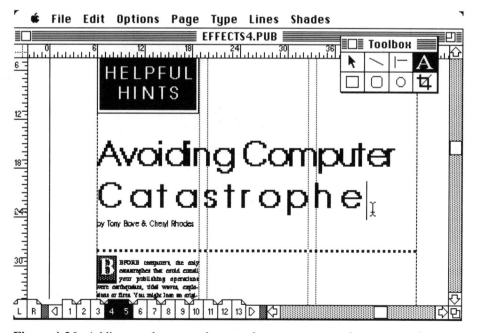

Figure 4-26. Adding regular spaces between letters, two spaces between words, a space at the end, and finally, nonbreaking spaces to fill the line.

you justify lines. PageMaker offers several widths for nonbreaking spaces. These are: em, en, thin, and fixed spaces. Type an em space (dependent on and equal to the current point size) by pressing the Command, Shift, and M keys simultaneously, or type an en space (one half of an em) by holding down the Command, Shift, and N keys simultaneously, or a thin space (one half of an en, and 1/4 of an em, which is also the width of a single number) by pressing Command Shift, and T, and a fixed space (a normal space for the current point size (such as you get when you press the space bar), but invaluable because a fixed space is a nonbreaking space, and also because it is not a variable space, as normal spaces are in justified lines) when you press Option and the space bar simultaneously.

However, to spread a headline so that it fills a specific width, first isolate the headline as a separate text block (cut the headline from the rest of the article text and paste it elsewhere on the page, or simply type the

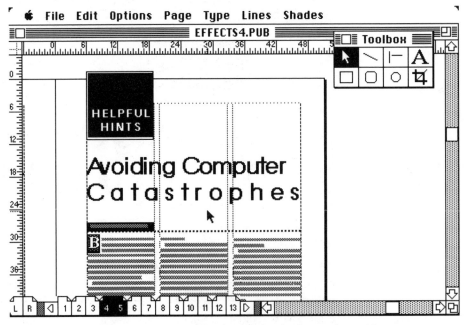

Figure 4-27. An evenly spread headline justified to both margins, with a reverse type panel for the by-line.

headline separately), set its font, size, and leading, select Justified as the paragraph style, and move the headline into place. Then use the space bar to add one regular space between each letter, two spaces between each word, and one regular space at the end of the headline; then hold down the Command key while pressing the space bar to add nonbreaking spaces to fill the line (Figure 4-26) until the cursor jumps to the next line. Select Justify from the Type menu (or Command, Shift, and J), and PageMaker adds an even amount of space between each word, to result in a justified, evenly spread headline (Figure 4-27).

Manual and Automatic Kerning

You can adjust the spacing between letters manually (by kerning) or control the automatic spacing. PageMaker performs automatic kerning with selected pairs of characters, using information supplied by the designer of the printer font (some fonts do not support pair-kerning for particular character pairs). The degree of automatic kerning depends on both the font and size you are using. Pair kerning is usually turned on (defaults to on) for all of the text that is above 12 points in size, but you can change this setting in the Paragraph dialog box (Figure 4-28). Note that automatic kerning, if used for text point sizes under 12 points, slows

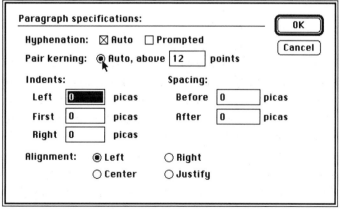

Figure 4-28. Paragraph dialog box, which lets you specify automatic pair kerning settings as well as automatic hyphenation, paragraph indents, alignment, and interparagraph spacing.

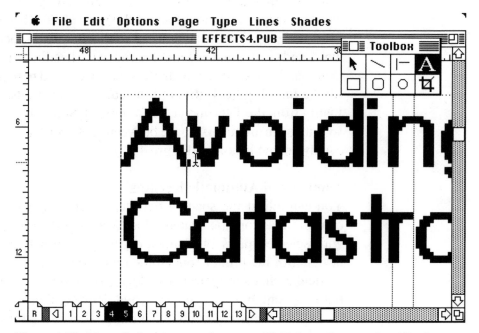

Figure 4-29. Manually kerning two characters: Hold down Command and Backspace to decrease the spacing, or Command, Shift, and Backspace to increase the spacing, in 1/24th increments of the point size of the left character (the first stroke deletes any automatic kern set in the Paragraph dialog box).

down the text flowing and placement functions. You can turn on automatic kerning for selected areas of the text rather than kerning the entire text. For example, it is more important to kern headlines than body type. You might also want to kern paragraphs or blocks of text on certain pages to control widows and orphans.

With headlines you will want to kern the letters manually, decreasing the space to tighten any two letters, or increasing the space to create breathing room between any two letters. Using the text tool, click an insertion point between the two characters, and first type Command Backspace to delete the automatic kern, then press Command Backspace or Command Shift Backspace to begin manual kerning. Hold down the Command key and press Backspace to decrease the spacing, or hold down the Command *and* Shift keys and press Backspace to increase the spacing (Figure 4-29). The amount of spacing is 1/24th of an em space for that font — exactly 1/24th of the point size of the character to the left of the insertion point. For example, if the font size is 24 points, the spacing is increased or decreased by 1 point; for 12-point type, the amount is 1/2 point. You may not notice the space increasing or decreasing on your display — although at 200% viewing size on a large screen, the change is almost always apparent — but the printed page should show properly kerned letters.

Rules, Borders, and Boxes

The judicious use of rules (horizontal and vertical lines on a page), borders, boxes, and line styles for these elements can make your page design more interesting and serve as helpful separators to preserve the hierarchy of headings, subheadings, text body, sidebars, pull quotes, and other elements.

Use a rule to divide one kind of text from another, such as a headline from text, one article from another, or an article from a sidebar. Vertical rules are often used to separate columns of text, especially when the text is aligned on the left margin and ragged on the right margin. Thick rules are often used to identify department headings in a magazine or to create black banners for reversed type. Figure 4-30 shows a thick rule used as a text banner, and a dotted rule to separate articles.

Use the appropriate thickness for the rule — don't use a thick rule to separate text, use a thin one (perhaps a hairline between columns, with a 1-point box surrounding sidebars). To draw attention to a headline, use a thick rule. Double rules tend to look like picture frames, so use them only when they add emphasis to a headline or graphic, or serve as an appropriate frame. Above all, be consistent with the use of rules in a publication. Figure 4-31 shows a sample usage of thin and thick rules to make a pull quote on a magazine page more interesting but not visually distracting (there is plenty of white space to balance the pull quote).

Different line styles can enhance the appearance of the page. The dotted line is used not only for coupons, but also in some popular magazine styles

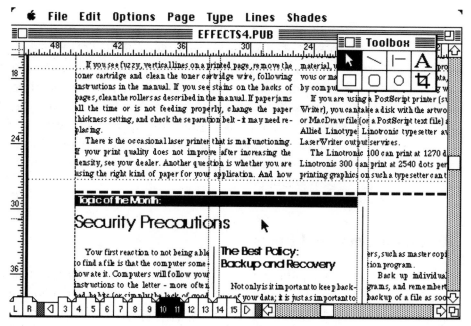

Figure 4-30. A thick rule with reverse type (a banner) and a dotted rule separator.

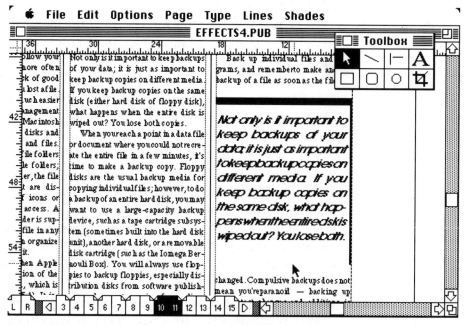

Figure 4-31. Using both thin and thick lines to add visual interest to a pull quote in a magazine article; the combination also makes use of white space.

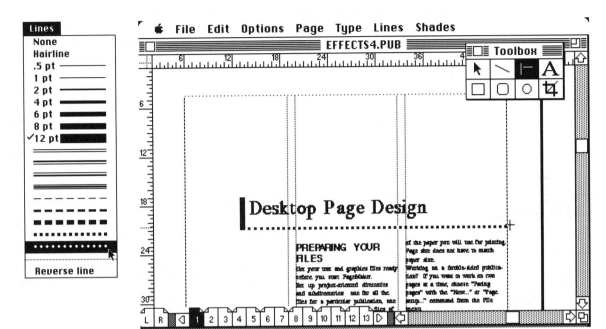

Figure 4-32. Line styles, such as a line of dots, improve the appearance of the page.

(Figure 4-32), as are the lines of dashes. If you want a line style that is not available in the Lines menu, try creating a box that is only one line wide and use an appropriate pattern (select a pattern from the Shades menu, and select None from the Lines menu for the outline of the "box"). For example, you can create a much thinner line of dots by drawing a box the length of the line, overlapping the long edges of the box (Figure 4-33) until they disappear from the display. Then choose the parallel lines pattern from the Shades menu, and PageMaker produces a thin vertical line of dots (Figure 4-34).

Boxes can be useful as borders around text that is separated from the main article (a sidebar), or as a border around an entire page that is different (perhaps using a different column layout). Use thin line styles for borders around text, graphics, or a photo, and an equal amount of white space on all sides from the edge of the graphic or text to the box.

To put a box inside a column, make the box line up with the margins of the column, and resize the text block inside the box to be narrower than the column (Figure 4-35).

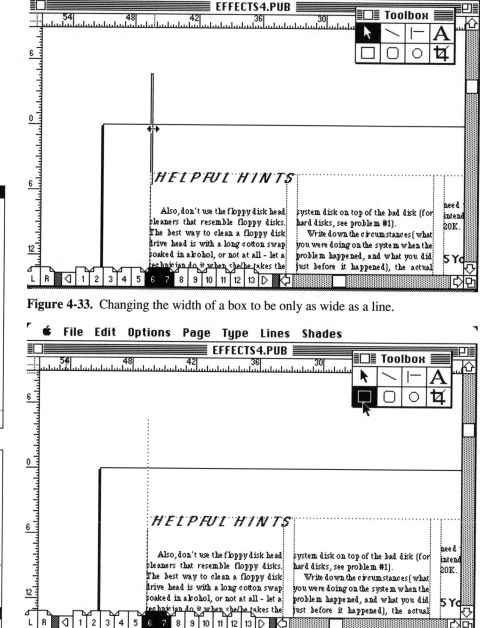

Figure 4-33. Changing the width of a box to be only as wide as a line.

Figure 4-34. By selecting the parallel lines pattern, you change the very thin box into a very thin line of dots.

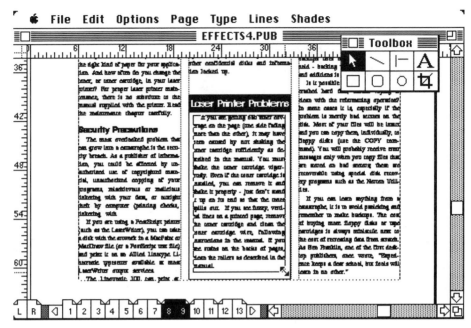

Figure 4-35. Resizing a boxed text block inside a column.

Layouts with Color

PageMaker can place, and even display bit-map color images (providing you have the appropriate hardware; for example, the Spectrum card and 19-inch color monitor from SuperMac Technology for the Mac II) such as those stored in the Scrapbook supplied with the Mac II, or images from color graphics programs. However, when you print the file, colors are converted to shades of gray and black since most laser printers can only print with one color ink at a time (usually black). At this time, the colors red, blue, and yellow on the Mac II print as white areas (unless you mix them with a percentage of black) when you print the page on the LaserWriter Plus. You can use a PostScript film recorder to create a transparency; you can create a color layout on screen, separate the color images into layers for each color (a service bureau may provide this service), and produce color separations from the film.

For color in press runs today, you use a printing press or print shop, providing black-and-white "camera-ready" materials and specifying

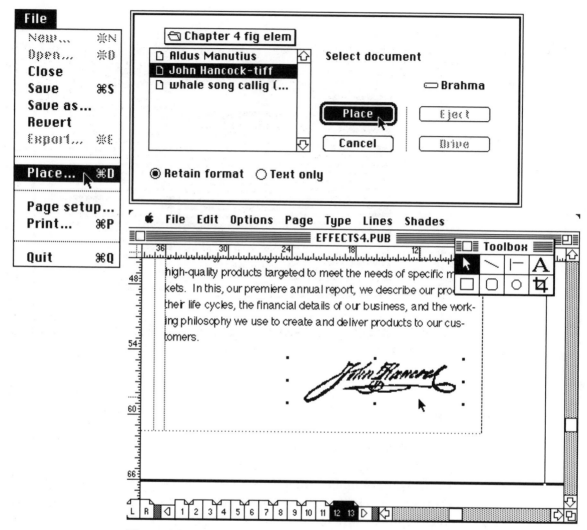

Figure 4-36. A scanned signature is added to a black-and-white page.

colored areas. For spot color (a single color for highlighting text or graphics), color tints (a single color or mix of colors used for a background), and four-color (or full-color) images, you have to separate the color areas from the black-and-white areas by using overlays or masks. PageMaker is very helpful in this task; it can be very easy to "mask"

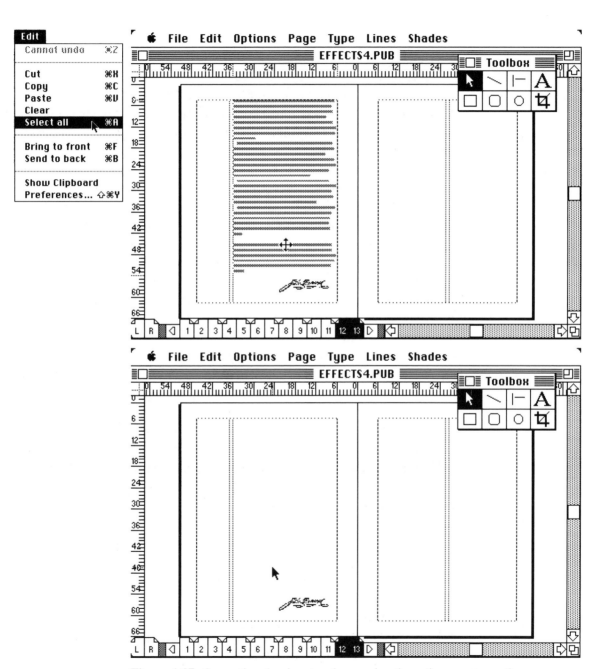

Figure 4-37. Separating the signature by copying the entire page to another page, and removing all elements that will not be printed with red (magenta) ink.

elements, because you can work at a 200% page size for the detail work, and it is easy to delete only those items you don't want to have on the overlay for a specified color.

PageMaker is extremely useful for separating tinted areas of a page or spot-colored elements. For example, a signature could be scanned into a paint program and placed onto a PageMaker page (Figure 4-36), with text above the signature. You want the signature to be in magenta, but the text above to remain black.

First, copy the page to the Clipboard and paste the copy on a separate page. Remove all of the elements from this separate page, except the elements that will be in red — in this case, just the signature (Figure 4-37). This page can now be used as an overlay on the original page if you laser print both this page and the original page with *crop marks* (an option available in the Print dialog box), which your print shop can use as registration marks to register the page and the overlay. (Or, if you are also using Adobe Illustrator to create images for use with PageMaker, and you returned your registration card, you received a set of disks called "Gallery" images from Adobe, which includes a set of registration marks.) Crop marks will only print if the paper size (or film, in the case of typesetters) is larger than the trim size defined in PageMaker. Also, remove the signature element from the original page, which will have all of the black elements but none of the color elements (thereby serving as the black-and-white overlay). Repeat this operation for elements that are in another color, adding another overlay page for each color.

You may want to use copier-certified acetate sheets to print the spot colors, and print the black elements on paper, so that you can easily overlay the paper with the acetate sheets, matching registration marks, and so on. Your printing process will determine this, but check with your printer to see if the final artwork should be printed on separate sheets of paper, or if acetate sheets can be used as final artwork. If your printer can work from both paper and acetate, check the text areas of your pages, looking closely at the type to see whether paper or acetate gives you the crispest characters.

PageMaker is not a painting or drawing program, and the separation of four-color images must be precise. Programs such as Adobe Illustrator, and others described in Chapter 1 can separate an image into overlays for specifying colors. You can then use PageMaker to draw a placeholder box for the separated image. In fact, you can combine spot color with four-color images on a page by isolating the spot color elements as described above, and providing a black-filled box as a placeholder on the black-and-white page. The print shop can then drop the four-color separation (prepared photographically or digitally) onto the page before printing.

Special Layouts

The role of PageMaker, when designing special layouts for publications, is to provide boilerplate graphics, design elements (such as rules, boxes, and reverse text panels), and repeatable formats (such as indented paragraphs, dot leaders, and stretched headline or title blocks). Save all of the designed elements in a separate publication file that can be opened whenever you need them. You can copy the elements to your publication via the Clipboard and the Copy and Paste commands, and save some of them on master pages to be repeated as necessary. Save also the column layout of each page without text and graphics, so that you can place new text and graphics without redrawing the column rules and reinventing other design elements.

Magazine Page

Figure 4-38 shows a magazine page with a three-column layout customized to include four-color photographs and stylized captions. To prepare this page, place the left column of text first, then the top of the middle and right columns. Then change the column layout by unlocking the guides and dragging the right column guide farther to the right to accommodate the photos (Figure 4-39). Draw separate boxes around the caption and the photo area, with the boxes overlapping on one edge (using a 1-point line for the box). To overlap an edge, draw the box over the other box so that the edge disappears in your display.

Next, place the caption text in the narrow right column next to the photo areas. For each caption, draw a circle and wrap the text around it by inserting tab spaces (Figure 4-40). Finally, complete the caption's circled numbers by selecting a black shade for the circle and dragging a number

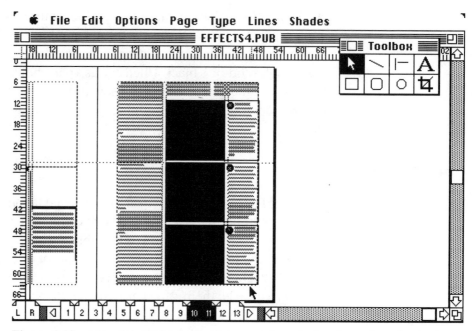

Figure 4-38. A layout with four-color images and captions, using a tint color in the caption background, and reverse type within spot-colored circles.

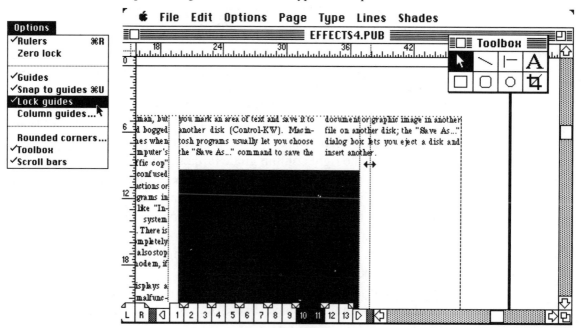

Figure 4-39. Changing the column layout after placing the text.

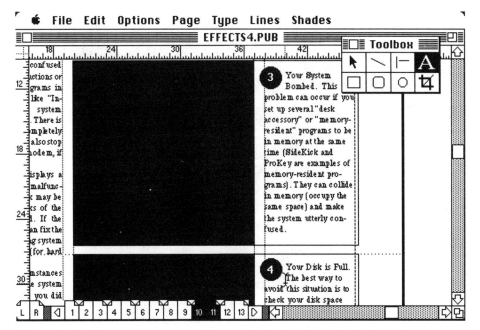

Figure 4-40. Wrapping text around the caption's circled number by inserting tab spaces.

you typed in a sans serif bold font (to adjust the letter properly, you may want to turn off the Snap to guides option). Then select Reverse type (Figure 4-41).

To specify the tint color in the caption background, this page can be copied to another page, and all of the elements can be deleted except the boxes around the captions (delete the caption text also). Print both pages with crop marks, and show the print shop what the page should look like (the original page with the box). Since the background on the original is white, you don't have to delete the box from the original.

Magazine or Newsletter News Section

The news pages of magazines usually have narrow type columns mixed with photos. The example in Figure 4-42 shows a four-column layout with photos that intrude slightly out of their frames and into the adjacent text columns. To make the photo intrude accurately, scan the image with any desktop scanner, place the scanned image onto the page, and then resize

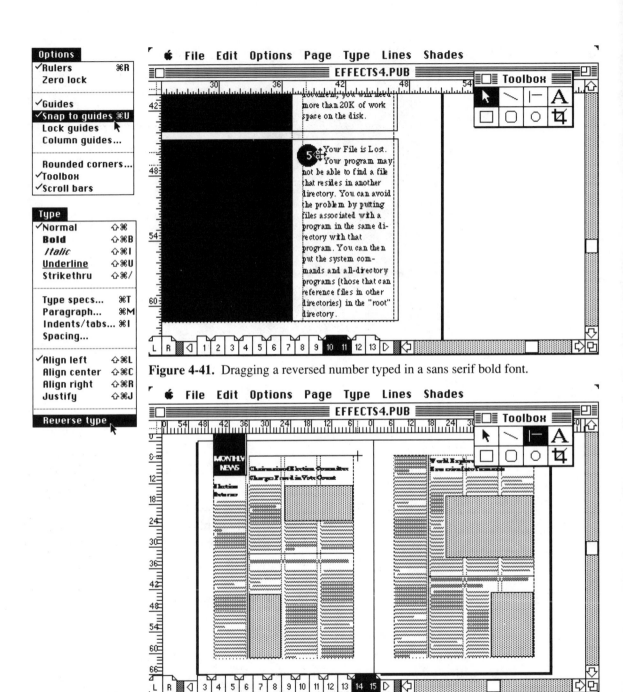

Figure 4-41. Dragging a reversed number typed in a sans serif bold font.

Figure 4-42. Layout of a news section of a magazine, with a photo object that intrudes into a column.

and crop it to fit properly (or use a reducing/enlarging copier to resize the photo, and then draw crop marks on the photocopy to get the proper dimensions). Adjust the text around the intruding scanned image by resizing a separated text block, then delete the scanned image leaving only the frame. The photographic halftone or four-color separation can be added to the film negative of the page by your print shop, so that the intruding portion of the image overlaps the frame.

Table of Contents

Publications usually have special pages, such as a table of contents or index page, that require a special layout and elements not used in other pages. Catalogs and data base listings may also require the use of special page elements and very narrow columns.

Design a table of contents page so that you can indent the subheadings under the chapter headings or the descriptive text under the article titles. You can use PageMaker's tab settings and leaders in the Indents/tabs

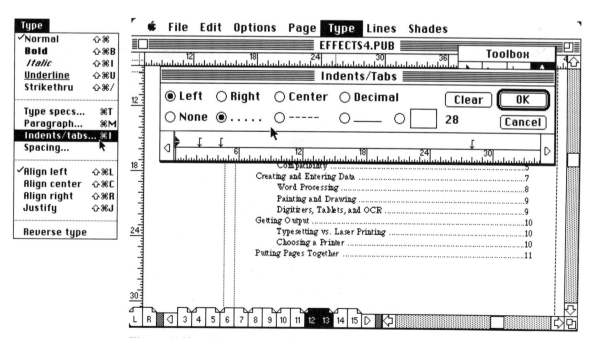

Figure 4-43. After setting the tab space, choose dot leading to typeset a horizontal line of very small dots in the tab space.

dialog box. First move the dialog box so that the ruler lines up with the text, then point on the ruler for each tab setting to mark the end of each tab space (Figure 4-43). The first two tab settings mark the tab spaces for indenting subheadings. For the tab space between the text and the page number, select a leader pattern to fill the tab space (Figure 4-44). You can specify a different character to use for a leader or use the dotted or dashed line leaders. You can also control the alignment of the characters within a tab space (the arrows in the ruler define the endpoint of a tab space). The tab spaces in the table of contents example are all left-justified.

Catalog Page

A catalog page may have many small items and one large item, or a mix of sizes. Figure 4-45 shows a page from a publisher's catalog, using the Bookman font (supplied with LaserWriter Plus printers, and available from Adobe Systems for other PostScript printers). To prepare this page, first change the column layout to have two columns (leave the space

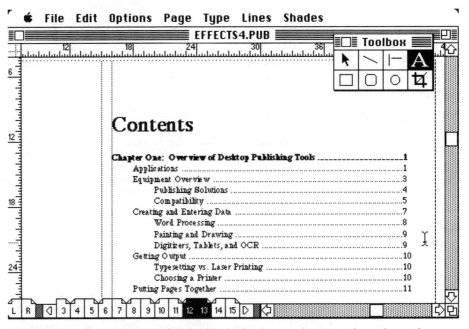

Figure 4-44. The tab space is filled with dot leaders, and paragraphs under each article title are indented.

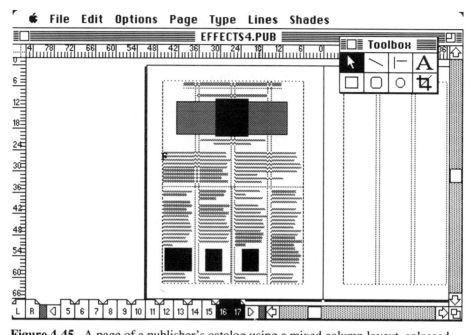

Figure 4-45. A page of a publisher's catalog using a mixed column layout, enlarged initial capital, dotted rules, and placeholders for four-color images.

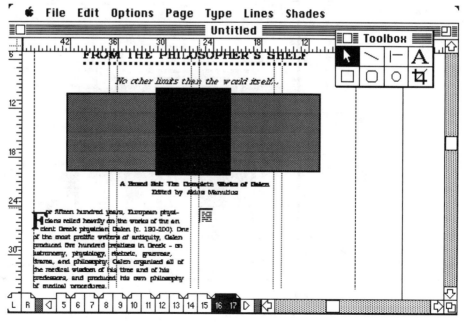

Figure 4-46. Placing and customizing text in the two column layout first.

between columns unchanged), then place the headings, photo placeholders and text in the two columns at the top of the page. Add the enlarged initial capital, then balance the two columns (Figure 4-46).

Change the column layout to four columns, then place the other text and graphic items in the four-column layout, customize the text with enlarged initial capitals, and draw column rules with the dotted line style (Figure 4-47).

Advertisements, Flyers, and Brochures

A flyer or handout is usually a standard 8 1/2 inches by 11 inches and is designed to look like a one-page advertisement. Brochures can be almost any size and shape, depending on how they are folded. The simplest folding methods are done with standard 8 1/2-inch wide by 11- or 14-inch-long paper.

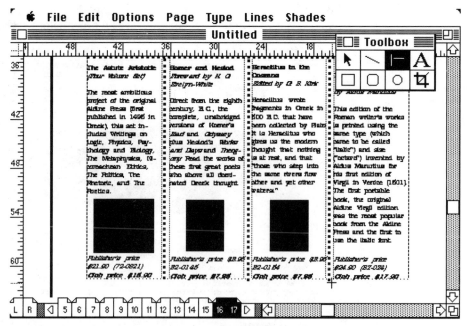

Figure 4-47. Placing and customizing the text and graphics in the four-column layout, and adding column rules using the dotted line style.

A helpful way to decide what size to use is to get samples from a printer. The type of fold you choose should be one that can be handled by the printer's machines, because hand folding is expensive.

There are many different ways to lay out information for a brochure or flyer, but it is most helpful to first define the page setup to reflect the measurements of a folded and trimmed page of the brochure. Figure 4-48 shows the page setup dialog box for a typical gate-folded brochure using standard 8 1/2- by 11-inch paper, printed in landscape mode (using the 11-inch dimension as the width). The margins are reduced from the default sizes (to avoid wide edges on the front panels when folded), and the selection is for two-sided facing pages in order to display both sides of the brochure.

Figure 4-49 shows how two pages in a publication file can produce a gate-folded brochure, so that the panels are ready for folding. Graphics and text bleed across the middle panels on the front and back of the brochure. (Experiment with page mockups on your printer before doing real production work, because laser printers differ, and most laser printers

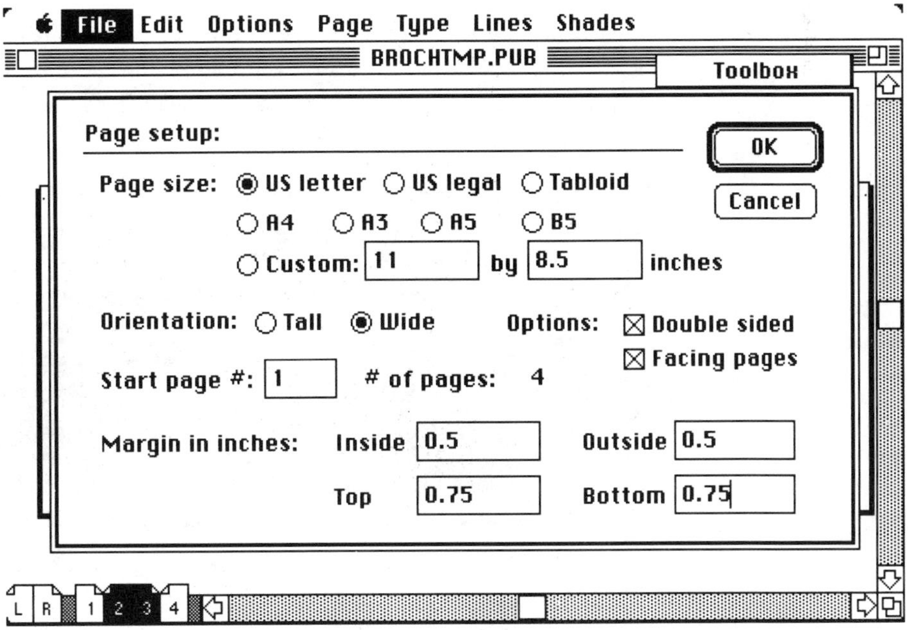

Figure 4-48. Page setup for a gate-folded brochure.

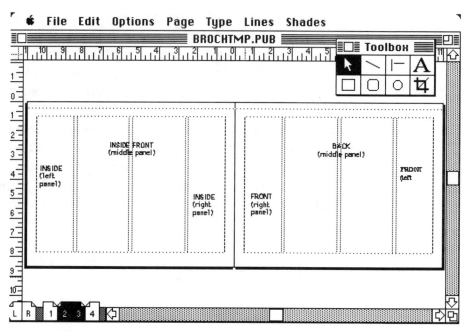

Figure 4-49. Pages 2 and 3 show the layout of pages in landscape mode.

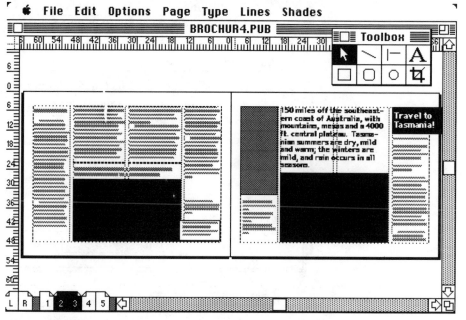

Figure 4-50. The layout of a brochure that uses black boxes as placeholders for four-color separations.

can't print to the very edge of standard-sized paper, leaving about 1/8 inch or so of blank paper at the margins.)

Use special graphic effects on brochures and advertisements to attract the reader's attention. Enlarged initial capitals, dotted line styles for rules, and four-color photos or other colored images can enrich the information in your brochure. Use a small font size for charts and diagrams and a larger size for headlines and attention grabbers. Banners with white or black type (with black or a specified background tint, as described previously with color layouts) are especially useful as attention grabbers. Figure 4-50 shows the layout of the black-and-white elements and placeholders for four-color separations, and Figure 4-51 shows an overlay created for the background tint in an attention-grabbing banner headline.

There are few rules for designing effective advertisements, but there are plenty of guidelines published in magazines and newsletters on advertising and design. These publications have regular feature columns

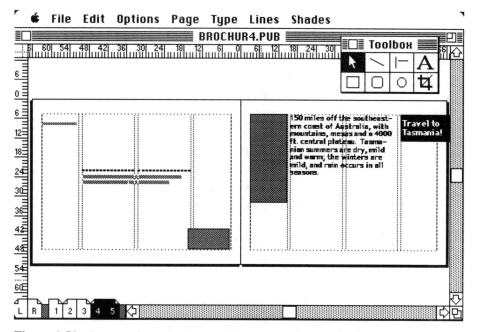

Figure 4-51. A spot color or background tint overlay is made by first copying the two pages, then removing black and other colored elements (make a separate overlay for each color).

by the design experts that critique advertising. It helps a great deal to read about actual ads that worked or flopped. Advertisements take up costly space in magazines, and direct-mail promotions are expensive to create, mail, and manage.

Promotions and advertisements should directly generate income for your business. Therefore, consult with a communications or design expert before finalizing your ad or brochure design to make sure your ad or brochure looks as good as it possibly can.

Summary

In this chapter, you learned a few design rules, and techniques for achieving various special effects with PageMaker, as follows:

Wrapping Text Around Graphics
Text can wrap around a rectangular shape, such as a box, or around an irregular shape. Although there is more than one way to wrap text around an object, the best method to use if you want to be able to reflow the text later will take a little extra time at first, as you create a new text block each time the margin changes, and then resize text blocks individually to fit the margin. Once you have done this, text can reflow properly, without requiring you to add extra linebreaks or tabs.

Enlarged Initial Capital
Several treatments of enlarged capital letters at the start of a text block are possible. You have learned how to wrap text around a single letter, as well as a letter enclosed in a box (with or without a pattern or shadow).

Mixing Column Layouts
You can combine articles with both two- and three-column layouts on the same page. First set the page to have two columns (either directly on the page or in the master pages), position all two-column text, then change the number of columns to three, and position the three-column text, which won't disturb the two-column layout.

Reverse Type

Reverse letters, lines, and shapes for special effects. Although you usually set black type on a white background, you can reverse white type or rules out of a black box or band.

Fancy Titles and Headlines

You can spread titles to fit a particular width, do manual kerning, and control automatic kerning. To do manual kerning, click an insertion point with the text tool and use Command Backspace to delete the automatic kern, then use Command Backspace to decrease the space, or Command Shift Backspace to increase the space (manual kerning).

Rules, Borders, and Boxes

This chapter showed some techniques for effective use of rules, borders, and boxes. Custom rules can be designed by using very thin, shade-filled boxes with no lines (a box can be as thin as one line).

Layouts with Color

PageMaker does not automatically create four-color separations (though it might in a future release), but preparing your art for spot color printing is possible by separating the black elements and the elements of each color into overlays of paper or acetate, with crop marks (trim marks, to be used as registration marks) printed on each page, which are acceptable by most printers. The crop marks are available in the Print dialog box, but will only print if the paper (or film, in the case of typesetters) size is larger than the trim size defined in PageMaker.

Special Layouts

Using publication files to hold design elements and boilerplate graphics, you can manage production of magazine pages (such as a news section), create a catalog page, and a table of contents. Advertisements, flyers, and brochures can also be created from a boilerplate file of master pages. Use techniques learned in this chapter to enhance page designs. Consult a design expert before you mass produce your masterpiece, or get feedback on the design from the intended audience to get the best possible result.

5 | Tips and Techniques

This chapter contains the most important tips, tricks, and techniques for working with PageMaker. Tips have been organized by topic, and the topics are listed in the same logical order that you are likely to encounter them. This simple organization should provide easy access to the information without having to search through previous chapters. Should you want more information about a topic, or for topics not covered here, refer to the index of this book and the PageMaker manuals.

Very Important!

Before starting a publication, select a final printer. You can change the printer for a publication anytime; however, when you change your printer, the composition can be altered, because different printers could have different downloaded fonts and options for resolution of images. If you specify a font not available on your target printer, and font substitution is turned on, PageMaker substitutes its default font, 12-point Times, but remembers the fonts you specified. Resolution of images can be a problem, if you set your printer to be a Linotronic typesetter, and then size some of your images, using Command Shift to get sizes optimized for the

Linotronic 100 or 300. If you print such images on a lower-resolution LaserWriter Plus, you could get muddy areas (or resize the images after changing printers).

PageMaker does a mini-save whenever you turn the page. You can revert back to the way the publication file was at the last full save operation, or you can revert back to the last mini-save operation by holding down the Shift key when selecting Revert.

Preparation

PageMaker allows you to type and edit words on the page; but use a word processor if you are writing more than a page of text or writing text that will be used with different programs or in other publications.

Although you can change typefaces, styles, and sizes for the text in PageMaker, select typefaces (if possible), styles, and sizes in the word processor (if it is one supported by PageMaker) while you write and edit the text to save time. The text is then formatted for placing onto a PageMaker page, and you will be able to place text on many pages at once in the PageMaker publication file without stopping to select fonts. If your word processor is not listed in the PageMaker reference manual, then your file should be saved and placed with the Text only option.

PageMaker recognizes tabs in a word processor file and uses them to align text or numbers in tables. You can change tab settings in PageMaker to fit the column width. The word processor file should already have the tab characters, and each line of a table should end with a carriage return.

Typeset copy should not have two spaces following sentences. One formatting step you should perform with your word processor, before placing files in PageMaker, is to search for and replace all instances of two consecutive spaces following a period with one space. (You could also search for unwanted extraneous spaces between words, replacing two spaces with one space.)

Captions, footnotes, graphics, and other independent elements should be placed into a file separate from the text.

If you want text to run vertically alongside a vertical axis, or in any other orientation besides the usual horizontal orientation, use a graphics program (such as Adobe Illustrator or Cricket Draw) to define it, since PageMaker does not offer the ability to rotate text.

Break up very large text files into smaller files of less than 64K each, so that PageMaker can respond quickly when you adjust text.

Design

You can print "thumbnail" sketches of the pages, using gray boxes to represent text, black boxes to represent images, and white boxes for line art. For paper sizes other than 8 1/2 by 11 inches, select the Page Setup command from the File menu, and uncheck the Facing pages box before printing thumbnails.

You can bypass image area specifications either by choosing the default specs (click OK) or by starting with a template — a predesigned publication file empty of text and graphics, but ready for use in page makeup.

Use about 1/4 inch (0.25) for the column gap (space between columns) to open up more space, or use the PageMaker default of .167 inch (1 pica).

Don't mix more than three fonts (not including their italic and bold styles) on a page, and use white space so that the page is not overcrowded with text and graphics.

You can use reverse (white) type in a black background or a background with a 60% or 80% gray shade, but check that your paper and ink choices and method of printing will be able to reproduce the result without type plugging up or breaking.

Don't use a thick rule to separate text, use a thin one (perhaps a hairline). To draw attention to a headline, use a thick rule. Double rules tend to look like picture frames, so use them only when they add emphasis to a headline, graphic, or serve as an appropriate frame. Above all, be consistent with the use of rules in a publication.

Use thin line styles for borders around text, graphics, or a photo, with an equal amount of white space on all sides from the edge of the graphic or text to the box.

To put boxed text inside a column, make the box line up with the margins/column guides of the column, and resize the text block inside the box to be narrower than the column.

Placing Text

PageMaker does not use the footnotes, page numbers, headers, footers, or special formatting features created by word processors. The program breaks lines to fit its columns and treats carriage returns as paragraph endings. PageMaker recognizes most fonts, type styles and sizes, line spacing (leading), upper- and lowercase letters, left and right indents, first line indents, tab settings, and the right margin setting for most word processors. See the PageMaker reference manual and Appendix A of this book for the specifics for your word processor. If your word processor is not one PageMaker can import directly, or to ignore text file formatting, place your file using the Text only setting, and PageMaker will apply default type specifications.

If you have a 1-inch indent from the left or right margin in a word processor file and you place the file retaining its formatting, PageMaker measures 1-inch from the left or right edge of the column.

PageMaker recognizes (and retains) first-line indents in a word processor file that are either indented to the right (regular) or to the left of the left margin (a hanging indent). See Appendix A for more information on how PageMaker treats text files from popular word processing programs.

Tabs, carriage returns, and spaces are recognized in text-only files; but no formatting settings from the word processor are used. You can bring tables (with tabs) and paragraphs of text into PageMaker with the Text only option (without formatting) and still retain paragraph endings and table column positions in most cases. See Appendix A for more information.

PageMaker automatically changes a double quote (") with a preceding space into an open quote ("), and a double quote (") with a following space into a closed quote ("). The program also changes a single quote (') in the same manner, so that contractions, possessives, and quotes-within-quotes have the properly slanted punctuation symbols. PageMaker changes a double hyphen (- -) into an em dash (—), and a series of hyphens into half as many em dashes (creating a solid line). (Carefully proofread your layout after placing the text to look for any instances of an incorrect substitution, as PageMaker wouldn't know it if you had accidentally inserted a space before an intended apostrophe — the program could have substituted a single open quote. See Appendix C for a list of these special punctuation symbols and other special characters, and how to type them.)

PageMaker 2.0a offers a "drag-place" feature that allows you to drag while placing text (especially useful for headlines you want to place across more than one column on a page). Instead of simply clicking the mouse button to place text, you can press down on the mouse button, and drag diagonally to establish a bottom right corner point, before releasing the mouse button.

After you have placed text by simply clicking the mouse button, you can resize the text block at any time by using the pointer tool to select the block, then click and drag any corner to make the text block wider or more narrow. Use this technique for text you want to have span more than one column boundary (such as a headline or title), or for text you want to enclose in a box.

Placing Graphics

When you place a bit-mapped image (from a paint program, or a scanned image) larger then 64K in size onto a page, PageMaker creates a lower-resolution display version and stores it in the publication file. However, it establishes a link to the original, higher-resolution version so that the program can use the higher-resolution version when printing. PageMaker uses the lower-resolution image for display purposes in order to increase the speed of the program. You can move, resize, and crop the image and PageMaker will apply those changes to the original when printing. However, when you print the publication PageMaker first looks in the folder containing your publication to find the image, so you should place the image in the same folder as your publication. If PageMaker doesn't find the original image file in the publication's folder, it will display a dialog box asking for the image file. You can, at that time, ignore the original higher-resolution version and print using the lower-resolution version, but for best results, locate the original version in the dialog box and click OK to use the higher resolution version.

You can continue to work on an image file with your painting or drawing program after placing it, and if it is larger than 64K, PageMaker will substitute the final edited image file at print time. Or, to print the newer version if the image is less then 64K in size, you can replace the image by cutting the older version from the publication file and pasting the newer version in before printing.

PageMaker 2.0a offers a "drag-place" feature that allows you to drag while placing an image (especially useful for images you want to place across more than one column on a page). Instead of simply clicking the mouse button to place the image, you can press down on the mouse button, and drag diagonally to establish a bottom right corner point, before releasing the mouse button. This is similar to the "drag-place" text feature.

As with text, after you have placed an image by simply clicking the mouse button, you can resize it at any time by using the pointer tool to select it, then click and drag any corner to make the image wider or more narrow.

If the graphic is a line drawing (without patterns and a lot of details), you can resize it by dragging a handle until the graphic is the right size for your layout. If, however, the graphic has a pattern or has fine detail, you should hold down the Command key to display a selection of the optimal sizes for your printer's resolution automatically. In addition, hold down the Shift key while resizing, in order to keep the same proportions; otherwise you can distort the image by stretching or compressing from any side of the image.

By holding down the Shift key you constrain the scaling to be in the same ratio, and by holding down the Command key, you select only those sizes that work well with your printer. Without holding the Shift key you can stretch or compress an image or graphic as well as change its size; without the Command key you can scale to any size, even those that are not optimal for your printer's resolution. Remember to release the mouse button before you release the Shift and/or Command keys to achieve the desired result.

For faster placement, segment large graphics files (such as scanned images) into smaller files less than 64K each, then connect the pieces on the PageMaker page. (However, PageMaker can place an image as large as 2MB in size, because it uses a lower resolution version of the image for display, linked to the original file for printing.) Alternatively, to reduce the size of a graphics file with text that doesn't print well (especially graphics with small text to be scaled smaller on the PageMaker page), first use the graphics program to delete the text. Place just the graphics and then add text with PageMaker for more control over text size and styles within a text block.

Spreadsheet and business graphics programs can do the calculations to produce a bar or pie chart or an x–y graph that is accurate in proportion to the calculations. If you can copy these charts and graphs to the Clipboard or Scrapbook, you can use your drawing program to edit them and save them in the PICT format, before placing them in PageMaker. Some business graphics programs (such as Cricket Graph) also offer the option to save a PICT format file.

When a PICT image is resized on the PageMaker page, the fonts are also reduced in size. Object-drawing programs use PostScript fonts for text, and these fonts are carried over into PageMaker, but they are scaled along with the rest of the drawing, and you can't change their point sizes or styles. For this reason, you may prefer to use the drawing program to scale the image (and finalize type sizes and styles) before placing it in PageMaker.

You can change a chart or graph at the last minute before publication. If the chart is from a graphics file larger than 64K in size, PageMaker will use the original file when it prints the report, so update the original file first. Then, if you have time, place it in PageMaker, replacing the older image; if you don't have time, simply update the original and try printing the report.

Viewing Pages

You can switch back and forth from Fit in window (full page) size to actual size by holding down Command and Option and clicking the mouse while pointing to a spot on the page that you want to look at. (This is a very powerful and convenient way to move quickly to any spot on the page, without having to use the slower method of moving the scroll bars.) You can change the display quickly from any size to a full-page (Fit in window) view by typing Command W (or pick the Fit in Window option from the Page menu).

When you hold down Command and Option and click the mouse while pointing to a spot on the page that you want to look at, PageMaker jumps into actual size. Do it again and PageMaker jumps to full-page view (Fit in window); the command toggles the displays.

When you hold down Shift, Command and Option and click the mouse while pointing to a spot on the page at 200% size, PageMaker jumps into actual size. Do it again and PageMaker jumps to 200% view; the command toggles the displays.

Actual size approximates the printed page size, and has the most accurately calibrated rulers, but 200% size (Command 2) gives the most accurate display for positioning text and images.

Hold down Command Shift W to see the full-page view (Fit in window) and the entire pasteboard, or Command W to center all of the page or spread you are working on and see some of the pasteboard (Fit in window).

Another alternative to using the scroll bars is the grabber hand, available at all times, no matter which tool you are using. Hold down the Option key, then press down on the mouse button, and the pointer changes to the grabber hand. Drag the grabber hand, and the page moves in the window. Release the mouse button when the portion of the page you want is in view, and the pointer reverts to the tool you were using. If you hold down the Shift key as well as the Option key, and drag the grabber hand up/down or left/right, the scrolling is constrained to vertical or horizontal movement.

Necessary Skills

To move several objects selected in a row (by holding down Shift while clicking to select each object with the pointer tool, or by clicking and dragging to surround the desired items with the pointer tool), point in the middle of them, hold down the mouse button until you see the double-arrow symbol, and drag all of the objects at once into position. If a text block, graphic, or box disappears, select whatever is covering them and use the Send to back command in the Edit menu.

By holding down the Shift key while dragging a graphic or text block, you can drag evenly, without moving up or down if you first drag left or right, or without moving left or right if you first drag up or down (constrain the text or graphic to horizontal or vertical movement).

You can drag text over a graphic or drag a graphic over text, but if you want the text to appear (since text blocks are transparent), select the text and choose the Bring to front command in the Edit menu.

If you want a line style that is not available in the Lines menu, try creating a box that is only one line wide by overlapping the edges until they disappear from the display, and while the box is still selected, choose a pattern from the Shades menu, and change the outline of the box to None in the Lines menu.

When you delete the text in a text block, you also delete the text block. Do not delete the only text block of a story, or you will delete the story. (If you did not want to delete it, use Undo from the Edit menu).

You can delete a text block without deleting its text by clicking and dragging the block's bottom handle up until the line at the top of the block and the line at the bottom of the block form a single line with upper and lower handles. Then click the + symbol of the block's bottom handle to regain the text placement icon, and click at a new point on the page (or go to another page and click) to continue flowing the text, which will be threaded to the first text block.

There are several different ways to select text with the text tool (see text tool and text insertion pointer in margin). Select a single word and the space after it by double-clicking the word; you can then drag in any direction to select a group of words. To select a single paragraph, triple-click anywhere in the middle of it. You can extend a selection from an existing selection by holding down the Shift key and clicking a new ending point (you can also use the cursor movement keys rather than the mouse to extend a selection). Another way to select a large area of text is to click a starting (or ending) point at one end, then Shift-click the ending point (or starting point) at the other end. The easiest way to select all of the text in an article that extends over several blocks is to click anywhere in the text once, then choose the Select all command from the Edit menu (or type Command A).

Changing a Layout

Although the text wraps within the column width, you can change the text block's width by switching to the pointer tool and dragging the top or bottom right corner of the block of text to be wider or thinner, and longer or shorter. You can also drag the top or bottom left corner in the same manner.

To make the text block wider than a column (e.g., for positioning a headline across text that spans two columns), use the pointer tool to click the bottom right corner of the new text block formed by the Paste command, and drag it to be a wider but shorter text block, until the headline fits on one line.

PageMaker calculates leading for a line of mixed type sizes based on 120% of the largest point size specified. To adjust leading of such a line, you can separate the text into more than one block as you do for dropped caps (also called dropped initial caps).

Move a text block the same way you move a graphic — point in the middle, hold down the mouse button until you see the double-arrow icon, and drag the block into position. With Snap to guides on, you can attach a text block or graphic to a column guide or ruler guide.

To mix column layouts on one page, draw a line to separate the layouts, and (if necessary) change the number of columns with the Column guides option, but leave the same spacing between columns (or use less spacing if the columns are very narrow). Start at the top or left-hand section of the page and position the text in that layout first. Then change the column layout again and continue placing text in that layout. The change does not affect the text you already placed in the first layout.

To combine multiple text blocks into one block (effectively deleting a layout so that you can start fresh and place the text again), delete the text blocks but not the text inside them. (See detailed steps under the heading "Necessary Skills," above.) Start with the last text block of the story and work backward to the first; however, don't delete the first block. Reflow the text by clicking the + symbol of the first block's bottom handle.

Master Pages and Stylesheets

Put a page header and footer on the master page so that they are repeated on each page. Such headers and footers can accommodate a page number that changes for each page (use Option Command P on the master pages, and set a Starting page number in the Page setup dialog box). Turn off the display of master items (in the Page menu) for those pages you don't want the header or footer to repeat on.

Save all designed elements in a separate publication file — you can copy them to another publication via the Clipboard and the Copy and Paste commands, or open a copy of that publication file to use as a template. Save elements on master pages to be repeated on almost every page (except those for which you have selected to Remove master items). Save also the column layout of each page without text and graphics, but with design elements (including rules, and ruler and column guides), so that you can place new text and graphics without reinventing and repositioning the elements.

The Display master items option in the Page menu, which is usually turned on (a check mark is displayed next to it), means that PageMaker copies text and graphic items from the master pages to the selected page for displaying and printing. To turn off the display and printing of master items for a selected page, choose the option again (the check mark disappears).

Typographic Controls

Em spaces (Command Shift M for each space) are fixed spaces that are roughly the width of a capital "M" in the font chosen (the width of an em space or em dash is equal to the point size of characters), and unlike regular spaces between words, they are not changed by PageMaker. En spaces (Command Shift N for each space) are fixed spaces that are one half of an em — roughly the width of a capital "N" — in the font chosen.

Thin spaces (Command Shift T) are one half of an en space, and fixed spaces (Command and space bar) — the width of a space at the current point size, such as you get when you press the space bar, except a fixed space's width does not change if the line is justified — can also be typed in PageMaker. Em, en, thin, and fixed spaces are all nonbreaking spaces. Connecting the characters (or words) to their left and right sides, they never fall at the end of a line.

Automatic kerning, if used for text point sizes under 12 points, slows down text placement and flow over pages. You can turn on automatic kerning for selected areas of the text rather than kerning the entire text. The degree of automatic kerning depends on the font and point size you are using; kerning occurs for all those pairs of letters specified by the font designer for that particular font (some fonts have more pairs than others). Pair kerning is usually turned on (default value) for all of the text that is above 12 points in size, but you can change this setting in the Paragraph dialog box, in the Type menu (Command M).

To kern characters manually, use the text tool to click an insertion point between the two characters, then use Command Backspace to decrease the spacing, or Command Shift Backspace to increase the spacing. The first Command Backspace (or Command Shift Backspace) deletes the automatic kerning (if it was turned on), and the second begins the manual kerning. The amount of spacing is 1/24th of the point size of the character to the left of the insertion point. You may not see the characters move on your display with each kern, because of the display's lower resolution, but if you perform the manual kerning operation at 200% view on a large screen, you will see a more accurate display.

Justified text is automatically aligned to the left and right margins of a column. You can control justification by decreasing or increasing the space between words (word spacing) and the space between characters (letter spacing). First use the text tool to select the desired text, then choose Spacing from the Type menu to specify new settings for word and letter spacing. PageMaker will reform the entire text file — not just the selected block — using the new settings.

To justify text, PageMaker first adds spaces between words (within the specified word-spacing ranges), then it adds spaces between characters (within the specified letter-spacing ranges), and if it still can't justify the line, then it expands word spacing as necessary to justify the line. If your justified text contains more hyphens than you want, change the settings for word and letter spacing — Aldus recommends a word-spacing range of 50 to 200%, and a letter-spacing range of 0 to 25%. The narrower the range between minimum and maximum spacing, the more PageMaker will hyphenate; the greater the range, the less it will hyphenate, but you will have more space between words (looser lines).

Auto hyphenation is also recommended for justified text. The hyphenation zone setting in the Spacing dialog box in the Type menu is not applied to justified text — it works with ragged text. To control hyphenation of justified text, use the text tool to select the text, then choose Paragraph from the Type menu to turn on auto hyphenation. PageMaker uses a 110,000 word built-in dictionary, plus your supplementary dictionary to place discretionary hyphens in words that don't fit at the end of lines.

To control hyphenation of words that are not in PageMaker's built-in hyphenation dictionary, turn on prompted hyphenation as well as auto hyphenation. When PageMaker encounters a word not in its dictionaries that doesn't fit at the end of a line, it prompts you to click an insertion point for each place you want a discretionary hyphen in the word. You can also add the new word to PageMaker's supplementary dictionary, so that the word is automatically hyphenated the next time it is encountered. Adding the word to the dictionary saves time later if the text block is reformatted to be wider or narrower, and line endings change. If you choose not to hyphenate the word, then PageMaker will increase word and letter spacing for that line until the line is justified, and move the word that was too long to the following line.

If you are prompted to hyphenate a word that you never want to break, add it to the supplementary dictionary without any hyphens, and Page-Maker will never hyphenate it.

To break lines only at hyphens, spaces between words, and discretionary hyphens, and to be prompted for hyphenation of all words that do not fit at the ends of lines, turn on prompted hyphenation, but do not turn on automatic hyphenation. You will then have full control of hyphenation. PageMaker will prompt you to click an insertion point at each spot where you want it to insert a discretionary hyphen, each time it encounters a word that doesn't fit at the end of a line. When prompted to hyphenate an unknown word, you should add the word to PageMaker's supplementary dictionary so that you won't have to hyphenate the same word if it is encountered again, or if PageMaker later has to reflow the text, and the line endings change.

If you turn on prompted hyphenation, it is only in effect for the selected text, and it automatically switches off after your text file has been recomposed. Automatic hyphenation is one of PageMaker's default settings, and is always on until you turn it off.

For non-justified text you can adjust the word spacing, but not the letter spacing — the built-in letter spacing is used. In addition to word spacing, you can specify a width for the hyphenation zone, which is in effect when automatic or prompted hyphenation is turned on. The smaller the zone, the more PageMaker will hyphenate words. The larger the zone, the less PageMaker will hyphenate words at the ends of lines, but the right margin will be more ragged (greater contrast in line lengths).

When PageMaker encounters a word that falls into the hyphenation zone that is too long to fit on that line, it looks at the preceding word to see if it also falls into the hyphenation zone. If both words are in the hyphenation zone, PageMaker breaks the line after the first word and moves the second word to the next line. (In other words, a smaller zone will allow more type to fit on the line.) If the first word is not in the hyphenation zone, then PageMaker tries to hyphenate the second word. If auto hyphenation is not on, or if the word can't be hyphenated to fit the line, then the line is broken after the first word and the second word moves to the next line. Turn on prompted hyphenation only, for full control.

If you turn hyphenation off for non-justified text, and if the column width is narrow in relation to the font used, or if hyphenation is on but the hyphenation zone is large in relation to the column width, then text will be more ragged than usual.

To quickly change leading, style, and other font attributes such as point size, first select the text tool, then double-click on a word (to select a word), triple-click to select a paragraph, or click an insertion point and use Command A (Select All from the Edit menu) to select the entire text block.

To select a range of text, first click an insertion point at the start of the range, then either drag until you have selected the desired area, or hold down the Shift key and click a second insertion point at the end of the range. After selecting your text, use Command T to display and change the type specs (font name, size, leading, style, position, and case) quickly, or use other shortcuts listed in the type menu to change alignment or justify text, control indents and tabs, or change the style — normal (Shift Command), bold (Shift Command B), italic (Shift Command I), Strikethrough (Shift Command /), and underline (Shift Command U) — of the selected range of type.

Font Issues

PageMaker will remember the font you've chosen, even if your final printer does not print that font. PageMaker substitutes its default font, Times 12 point, but remembers and uses the actual font (such as a downloadable font) when you switch to a printer that can print it.

Some bit-map painting programs, or drawing programs, let you select fonts or graphics fonts for text, and these fonts are carried over into PageMaker when you place the image. These graphics fonts are reduced or enlarged with the image as you resize it, so you might prefer to delete them from the image file before placing the image, and then retype the text in PageMaker for more control.

If the publication file was previously printed at a different resolution, changing printers could cause problems if you have already placed some images using the Command key, or Command and Shift keys, before changing printers, and then you try to place more. PageMaker sizes such images based on the resolution of the printer, so the same size choices might not be available after you switch printers.

You would especially notice this problem if your original printer was set to be a high-resolution printer such as the Linotronic 100/300, then you switched to a LaserWriter, perhaps to print test pages, and you then continued placing bit-map MacPaint Macintosh screen shots (capture a Macintosh screen as a MacPaint file — provided the mouse button is not depressed — with Command Shift 3), because you would not get as many choices of image sizes, after selecting the LaserWriter. Switch your printer back, modify the LaserWriter resolution setting in its APD file (using a word processor to edit and save the text only APD file), or resize all placed images for the new printer, for best results.

Keyboard Controls

Any international character can be typed, but may not display. To see the character, change the page view to another size. You can then change it back to the previous size view, and the character will be displayed correctly.

The left/right cursor movement keys move the insertion point by a single character or space, and the up/down keys move the point by a single line. Holding down Command when pressing a left or right key moves the insertion point to the beginning of the next or previous word; when pressing an up or down key, Command moves the point to the beginning of the next or previous paragraph.

Special Effects

To type a bullet, hold down the Option and 8 keys. (See Appendix C for additional special characters you can type in PageMaker.)

To draw a drop shadow of a frame, copy the frame to the Clipboard, paste the copy back to the page, move it to a shadow position, and change its shade to black. To move all of the elements at once, hold down Shift to select the frame and the text without deselecting the already-selected black shadow, then release Shift and click in the center of the group until you see the double-arrow symbol, then drag the entire group. Finally, to move the black shadow behind the frame and text, deselect all by clicking the pointer tool, then select only the shadow and use Send to back.

To wrap text around a box, flow the text to the top of the box, click the + symbol in the bottom handle, and continue flowing text below the box. Drag the text block up to the top of the box, lined up below the preceding text, and drag the bottom handle up to the bottom of the box. Resize this short text block diagonally to fit the space between the box and the column margin by dragging a corner of the block. Finally, click the + symbol in the bottom handle of the resized block, to continue placing full-width text.

To wrap text around an irregular right margin, first drag the text over the graphic or area, then switch to the text tool and use the Return key to force a line ending at the right margin. To wrap text around a graphic that intrudes into the middle of the text or at the left margin, use the Tab key to insert tab spaces. However, if you change the text, you must remove the carriage returns or tabs and do the job over again. A better method, which takes longer at first but only has to be done once, is to create a new text block every time the margin changes, and resize the text blocks individually to fit into the irregular margin, just as you resize a text block to wrap text around a box. If the text changes after editing, it will still flow smoothly through the individual text blocks.

To spread a headline to fill a specific width, first isolate the headline as a separate text block, select Justified as the paragraph style, and move the headline into place. Add one regular space between each letter, two spaces between each word, and one regular space at the end of the headline; then hold down Command while pressing the space bar to add nonbreaking spaces to fill the line until the cursor jumps to the next line. The result will be a justified, evenly spread headline.

Box and Line Tools

You can draw an entire chart or graph using PageMaker's line drawing, box drawing, and circle drawing tools and gray shades. PageMaker's Snap to guides feature makes it easy to line up several distinct boxes to form a bar chart, and you can draw perfect circles by holding down the Shift key while dragging with the oval/circle tool, or perfect squares by holding down Shift while dragging with the box tool.

Printing

Since PostScript devices can vary in resolution, resizing bit-mapped images that contain simulated gray shades with dot patterns can cause unwanted patterns at different resolutions (for example, a LaserWriter prints at 300 dpi, and the Linotype 100 can print at 1270 dpi). If you do not use the same resolution for final output of pages, you should resize the images once with the Command key held down to use built-in sizes and avoid unwanted moirè patterns. You can set up a publication file with built-in sizes for the final output device by first printing a page to that device; from that point on, the file remembers the device resolution.

To prepare your files to print at final resolution without a printer available at that resolution, you can use any word processor to edit an APD (Adobe Printer Description) file to change the resolution setting for the printer. For example, if a LaserWriter is available, but your final printer will be a Linotronic typesetter available at a service bureau, (you could transmit the prepared publication file via modem to a service bureau's Linotronic typesetter), you can use your word processor to change the resolution in the LaserWriter APD file in your System folder to be 635 or 1270, then save the file using the word processor's Text only option (use the Save as option to save the modified LaserWriter APD with a new name, such as LaserWriter635, to preserve the original LaserWriter APD file without changes), then select the new APD file from the list of Printer APDs available, using the Change printer option in the Print dialog box, and print proof pages using the modified LaserWriter APD.

You can also cause PageMaker to create a "PostScript file" of the pages, to be transmitted to another computer over a modem and telephone line or transferred by disk. The receiving computer does not have to run PageMaker to send the file to the printer, but it must have the same fonts, or PageMaker will substitute either a bit-map or Courier font.

To separate elements for spot color from the black-and-white page elements, copy the entire page to the Clipboard (switch to the pointer tool and choose the Select all command from the Edit menu), and paste it on a separate page. Remove all of the elements from this separate page except the elements that will be in a specific color. Use this page as an overlay on the original page by printing both pages with crop marks (an option available in the Print dialog box), which the print shop can use as registration marks. Remove color elements from the original page, which serves as the overlay for black-and-white elements. Repeat this operation for elements using another color, adding another overlay for each color.

You can choose Page setup from the File menu to change the margin settings, but that will affect your layout and make changes you may not want. To print the completed pages at a smaller size without changing the layout, scale the publication to less than 100% in the Print dialog box, selected from the File menu at print time (and allow extra printing time for reduced and enlarged pages).

APPENDIX A
Word Processing Programs

PageMaker 2.0a imports text and some formatting from these word processor files:

Word Processor Files

ASCII files (all)	Aldus supplied with 2.0
MacWrite	Aldus supplied with 2.0
Microsoft Windows Write	Query Microsoft about status
Microsoft Word 1.05 & 3.0 (Mac)	Aldus supplied with 2.0
Microsoft Word (PC)	Query Microsoft about status
Microsoft Works (Mac)	Aldus supplied with 2.0
MultiMate	Query Ashton-Tate about status
WordPerfect	Query Aldus about status
WordStar 3.3	Query Aldus about status
WriteNow	Aldus supplied with 2.0a
XyWrite III	Query Aldus about status
Text-only files	Aldus supplied with 2.0
DCA files	Aldus supplied with 2.0

(from PCs — includes IBM Displaywrite, Lotus Manuscript, Office Writer, MicroPro WordStar 2000, Samna Word, and Volkswriter 3)

Microsoft Word, MacWrite, Microsoft Works, and WriteNow are fully supported — PageMaker recognizes character formats and fonts, indents, justification styles, and tab settings.

Microsoft Word 3.01 has the closest relationship to PageMaker 2.0a, and allows you to paste graphics within the text, but you should remove the graphics into a separate file for faster and easier PageMaker placement. Also, use Word's Save As command to turn off Fast Save, or PageMaker may require a long time to place the file. Word 3.01 lets you specify half-point type sizes, but you should only use whole-point sizes in Word, because PageMaker converts Word's half-point sizes down to the next whole point size. Additionally, all of Word's various underline styles are converted to a single unbroken underline. PageMaker strips Word 3.0's hidden text (it becomes regular text), and converts Bar tabs to left aligned tabs. Style sheets are not transferred, but the text that was formatted using a stylesheet retains its style sheet assigned formatting. Word's nested indents and bulleted nested hanging indents become regular paragraphs; however, they still look nested, and retain other formatting. Word's footnotes carry over, and are grouped at the end of the file (because we use Word's footnote facility to create and number captions, we prefer to copy all footnotes into a separate Word file for additional formatting, and delete them from our text file, before placing the text file).

PageMaker can also export text from the publication file back to Word's format, with some formatting not transferred. For example, PageMaker imports Word's graphics (although we don't advise doing it this way), but does not export them back to Word again. Style sheet formatted text is carried over to PageMaker, and exported back to Word, but the style sheets are not transferred.

For all the details and latest information on how your word processor works with PageMaker, read the PageMaker manuals, and the Read Me Now notes supplied on the PageMaker disks.

Version 2.0a exports text to Word 3.0 and 3.01, T/Maker's WriteNow, or export text as a text-only (ASCII) file. Export filters for the word processing programs listed on page 253 are in development at Aldus and other companies. Inquire about availability.

ASCII: The Standard Character Set for Text

PageMaker reads text-only files, thanks to ASCII. ANSI (American National Standards Institute), the US version of the ISO (International Standards Organization), its European counterpart, has developed ASCII (American Standard Code for Information Interchange), a character code for representing a character set (text and symbols) that has been adopted by the ISO, and is known in Europe as the ISO character set.

IBM uses EBCDIC (Extended Binary Coded Decimal Interchange Code) for their character set, which represents most ASCII characters, but the 8-bit numerical values assigned by EBCDIC differ from the 8-bit numerical ASCII values. You can translate ASCII to EBCDIC, and vice versa, with the appropriate software. IBM's PC uses an ASCII character set, rather than the EBCDIC used on their large computers.

Text-only Files

Macintosh word processed text files can usually be saved with a text-only option for use with PageMaker. Use the text-only format whenever PageMaker can't recognize the word processor's formatting. Use your word processor's text-only option to save text from communications programs (use text from mainframes, electronic mail services, and bulletin boards). Be sure that line-feed characters are stripped from the text file (the communications program should offer a strip line-feeds option), or you may see boxes at the beginning of each line. You can strip these boxes using your word processing program (select the first column to cut these characters), before you place the file with PageMaker.

APPENDIX B
Graphics Programs

PageMaker accepts paint-type graphics files (MacPaint format), draw-type graphics files (PICT format), and EPSF (for Encapsulated PostScript Format, also known as EPS) and TIFF (Tag Image File Format) graphics files. Paint-type graphics can be produced by almost all painting programs, and print with coarse edges because they are tied to 72 dpi resolution (e.g., an angled line is made up of linked squares called pixels). TIFF files created by scanners can also be paint-type graphics, but resolution depends on how they were scanned (There are two kinds of TIFF; bi-level, tied to the scanned resolution, and gray scale, tied to the print resolution). EPSF files and draw-type graphics are preferred for their high quality printed result (they print at the highest resolution of the printer).

Graphics files larger than 64K in size should be stored in the same folder as the publication file (for faster printing), and can be placed on PageMaker pages, where they can be stretched, reduced, and cropped (and restored to the size you first placed them at if you don't like the cropped result).

Paint-type and scanned images can be resized (using the Command key, or Command and Shift keys) to give optimal results for your printer (choose a printer using the Print dialog box in the File menu *before* placing such images). Draw-type images can be resized to any size, and print without mottling or muddiness. You can pull on any handle to distort the image's height or width without affecting the final resolution.

Restore any graphic to the size you first placed it at by using the pointer tool to select the image (its handles appear), then hold down the Shift key and click any handle. Placed graphics can also be trimmed (cropped), resized, and can even be repositioned within their frames (you can restore cropped portions, yet retain the sized window).

Painting Programs

With paint-type graphics (also called bit-map graphics) larger than 64K in size, PageMaker creates a low-resolution display version and establishes a link to the original graphics file. Graphics placed and resized with the Command key are adjusted to the best resolution of the printer.

To use the built-in resizing feature that automatically selects the best sizes for printing with your target printer, hold down the Command key while resizing (dragging a corner of the image). Hold down the Shift key as well if you want to resize the graphic proportionately.

TIFF (tag image file format) files can be produced by a variety of graphics programs. Scanner manufacturers bundle software with the scanner that produces TIFF files. Scanned images are paint-type graphics, displayed with less resolution than when they are printed. PageMaker prints scanned images at actual size and at reduced or expanded sizes very well if you use the automatic resizing. Because scanners usually create files larger than 64K in size, PageMaker uses a lower-resolution version of the image for display, and creates a link to and prints the larger original image stored in its separate image file. If the image file is moved after placing it in a PageMaker publication file, when you print the publication, PageMaker asks you to supply its new location in another folder, or disk (or specify a new file name to be substituted for the missing image), or you can print the lower-resolution screen version.

Scanners create image files at various resolutions (from 72-75, to 150, to 300 dpi), and may save in various levels of gray (from 16, to 64, or 256 levels of gray), and typesetters and laser printers don't need all of that information. With gray scale TIFF, printing resolutions vary from the equivalent of a 53-line screen with 25 shades of gray on a 300 dpi laser printer (or change the default values to produce a 100 line-screen, with only 9 shades of gray), to the equivalent of a 90-line screen with 200 shades of gray on the Linotronic 100 typesetter at 1270 dpi (or change the default values to produce a 150-line screen with 70 shades of gray). For the best results with photographs, and to reproduce them at higher resolutions than your laser printer or typesetter offers, you might prefer to scan photos only for placement, sizing, and cropping in the PageMaker publication file. Line art should be scanned in bi-level TIFF (also called black-and-white TIFF). If you scan the image at 300 dpi using bi-level TIFF, the results may be better than if you scanned the image using gray scale TIFF at 300 dpi on the same scanner, when the image is printed at 300 dpi. If you intend to print the image on a higher resolution device, such as a typesetter, scan it at 150 dpi, using gray scale TIFF, for better results than using bi-level TIFF and scanning at 300 dpi. Type at 300 dpi is often more pleasing than images at 300 dpi, but using even the lowest resolution scanned images ensures that the proper image, at the proper size and crop will appear in your final printed publication. Printing gray scale TIFF can take from one minute to one hour, depending on the size of the image, how many shades of gray it uses, and printer speed.

You can save lots of disk space and time by scanning images at the lowest resolution of your scanner if you plan to use the scanned images only for placement, sizing, and cropping, and then have your printing shop create photographic halftone negatives from the original photos to substitute for the scanned images in your camera ready art. (Camera ready art is your printer's term for the printed publication file, either laser printed or typeset on paper. You can also create final film — negatives or positives, emulsion side up or down — with a Linotype 100 or 300 and PageMaker. The printer uses your camera ready art or film to create printing plates for the presses.)

You can edit a TIFF file (or paint-type file larger than 64K in size) after placing it, and PageMaker will simply use the latest version at print time. This is a great time-saving feature for two reasons. First, because the lower-resolution display version is placed, layout is faster and the size of the publication is smaller than if the complete image is placed. Second, you can create a fast and rough scan and place the image, then continue to work on the scanned image file to clean it up and modify it with a graphics program, and only the final edited version will be printed in the publication. See Bibliography (Appendix E) for technical reference materials on TIFF.

Future Developments
Both color and black-and-white paint-type graphics are placed (and displayed on a color screen, such as the Spectrum card and 19-inch color screen from SuperMac Technology), but at this time PageMaker converts color paint-type images to black-and-white for printing (for example, yellow, red and blue print as white, and gray shades and black print as black). It is best to convert all color images to black-and-white with a painting program before placing them in PageMaker publications. Black-and-white Adobe Illustrator files place beautifully in PageMaker 2.0, and Illustrator will use color in a future release, so the use and treatment of color is a field still under development at this time.

Drawing Programs

Draw-type graphics (also called object-oriented and vector graphics) can be placed, resized, and cropped. You can use Cut or Copy and Paste, or use Place to transfer images in the PICT format from the Scrapbook and Clipboard onto the PageMaker page. Text is transferred to PageMaker but remains part of the graphic; therefore if you reduce the image, you also reduce the size of the type. If type is not readable at the final size, remove the text from the graphic and then add the text separately with PageMaker, for more control.

PostScript and PageMaker

EPS-formatted graphics files can be used if your printer is a PostScript device, such as an Apple LaserWriter or Allied Linotype typesetter (EPS files cannot be printed on an ImageWriter). These files contain PostScript code, and the format is useful for transferring descriptions of very complex line art graphics (such as technical illustrations and logos) to and from different types of computers. EPS files can carry information for displaying the graphic as well as printing it, so you may see an image on the screen; if the EPS file does not contain that information, you will see a text header describing the image, and a bounding box marking the boundaries of the image. You can crop and resize the image freely, even though you may not be able to see it.

Scanned images can also be used as templates (use a 72 dpi image, either from a paint-type program or from a scanner), and traced over with Adobe Illustrator to create an EPSF file to place in a PageMaker publication. An EPSF file prints at the highest resolution of your laser printer or typesetter. EPSF files created with Illustrator and some other painting and drawing programs include a 72 dpi version of the image to display on screen in the PageMaker publication file (as well as the PostScript code to produce a higher-resolution printed version). EPSF files created with some other drawing programs will appear in a PageMaker publication as a gray shaded box when you place them, with text describing the image (such as the date and time it was created, the name of the program that created it, and the name of the image file). Print using the PostScript code to produce a higher resolution version of the image for printers.

If you are a PostScript programmer, you can create your own EPSF files for use with PageMaker; otherwise, use a painting or drawing program that saves an EPS file. PageMaker requires that the PostScript code in EPS files be "well-behaved" in the use of certain operators, stacks, global dictionaries, and the "graphics state." PageMaker will not recognize ill-behaved PostScript code, and you will have to strip out the bad operators. The manual clearly states which operators and conventions to use and how to use them, but this information is only of use to PostScript programmers. For such tasks we recommend that you read Appendix C of the *PostScript Language Reference Manual*. (See Bibliography, Appendix E, which contains the address for EPSF technical specifications, written for PostScript programmers.)

APPENDIX C
Special Characters

Bullet	Command-Shift-**8**
Close double quote	Option-Shift-[
Close single quote	Option-Shift-]
Copyright symbol	Option-**g**
Discretionary hyphen	Command—
Em dash	Option-Shift-=
Em space (nonbreaking space)	Command-Shift-**M**
En dash	Option--
En space (nonbreaking space)	Command-Shift-**N**
Fixed space (nonbreaking space)	Option-Spacebar
Open double quote	Option-[
Open single quote	Option-]
Page number marker	Command-Option-**P**
Paragraph marker	Option-**7**
Registered trademark symbol	Option-**r**
Section marker	Option-**6**
Thin space (nonbreaking space)	Command-Shift-**T**
Trademark symbol	Option-**2**

Use the above special character codes in your text file (if your word processor can produce them), or you can add the special characters after you have placed the text in the PageMaker publication file. (You have to do the latter if your word processor won't let you create or export the special characters; however, you have to read your word processor manual to determine this.) If quotation marks and apostrophes are substituted by PageMaker while the file is being placed, the placed text should then be proofread and edited for incorrect substitutions.

A nonbreaking space should be inserted when you do not want a line to break between two words. The size of the spaces range from an em space (equal to the point size), to a fixed space (a normal space, except at a fixed length that is not changed when the line is justified), to an en space (1/2 the point size), and a thin space (1/4 the point size, or the width of a number).

APPENDIX D
Transferring Publication Files

One reason PageMaker is attractive to service bureaus is because it can save a publication file that can be used on either a Macintosh or a PC-compatible computer. Another feature attractive to almost any user is its ability to import files from a variety of word processors (as described in Appendix A) and graphics programs (as described in Appendix B). You can therefore use either the Macintosh 2.0a version or the PC 1.0a version of PageMaker to publish information derived from Macintosh or PC files.

You can also transfer PageMaker publication files to remote computers for further production work or for printing or typesetting. You can recompose the publication for the system and printer at the remote site. When screen fonts are available for the fonts you've chosen, PageMaker uses them; otherwise, PageMaker substitutes its default fonts: Times 12 point. If PageMaker uses a screen font for printing, your document will take longer to print, because your laser printer must find the largest installed version of that bit-map (72 dpi) font in your Macintosh system, then scale it to a final printed size. Such screen fonts may also give you jagged results. If there is some reason why PageMaker can't convert the bit-map screen font to a printable version, a Courier font will be substituted. No matter which font PageMaker chooses, and no matter if screen versions of bold and italic fonts appear too wide on screen, the line endings on screen will match the line length of the printed version.

PageMaker can remember printer font selection information, and uses those fonts if they are available in the system folder or in the printer you use to print the file. If you print a publication on a printer that has different fonts than those specified in the publication, PageMaker will try to print the best possible matching font and size. For best results, use a printer with the same fonts, or change the printer using PageMaker's Change printer dialog box, available from the Print command dialog box (the Print command is in the File menu).

PageMaker 2.0a supplied APD files include Apple LaserWriter, LaserWriter Plus, Dataproducts LZR 2665, and Linotronic 100/300. All are PostScript printers. For a different PostScript printer, you could try to use a supplied driver that matches it most closely, modify the PostScript commands (such as the resolution setting) in one of the supplied APD (Adobe Printer Description) files, or contact Aldus or Adobe to create an APD file for a new printer. (Contact Adobe Systems Inc. to get the Adobe APD specifications before modifying an APD file, other than to change the resolution setting.)

If you placed and then resized bit-map graphics using the Command key, and you have switched to a printer with a different resolution, you may want to resize all previously resized bit-map graphics if they look muddy or mottled after printing a few test pages.

Converting Graphics

PageMaker publication files can be transferred to a Macintosh and used with the Macintosh version of PageMaker, and vice-versa, using version 2.0a of PageMaker for the Macintosh and version 1.0a of PageMaker for the PC. Use MacLink Plus (DataViz, Inc.) RS-232 cable and file transfer software, or TOPS (Centram, Inc.) or PC MacBridge (Tangent Technologies, Ltd.) AppleTalk boards for the PC with AppleTalk cabling between the Mac and PC, plus file transfer software. To open a PC PageMaker publication for use with the Macintosh version of PageMaker, after transferring the file to the Macintosh, the PC publication file must have an eight character name with the three letter extension PUB. Rename the publication to have a PUB extension if it has a different or no extension, before you open it with the Macintosh 2.0a version of PageMaker. The first time you open the PC publication, start up PageMaker and use the Open command in the File menu to select the filename. (After the first time, you can simply click the publication icon to both start PageMaker and open the file in one step.)

All text and font information is preserved when you transfer the publication to the Macintosh version or to the PC version, and use the same type of printer, but you may not get the results you expected if you specified half-point font sizes in the PC publication. PageMaker 2.0a (on the Macintosh) initially displays, for example, 12.5 point type specified in the PC publication file, but when you print that file with 2.0a, all half-point sizes are changed to the next lowest whole point size (12.5 point type becomes 12 point type), and printed at the new whole point size. Leading can be specified and printed in half-point increments in both the PC 1.0 and Macintosh 2.0a versions of PageMaker.

Draw-type graphics, however, are best handled by first converting and transferring the graphics files separately, then using the Place command in PageMaker to reposition the converted graphics back on the page at the receiving computer end of the transfer. Do it this way because when PageMaker 2.0a converts your PC publication for use with the Macintosh, all draw-type graphics display on the Macintosh screen as a box with an X, and they do not print.

For example, if your graphics came from PC programs such as Lotus 1-2-3 (PIC files), Windows "Draw!," Windows "Graph!," In*a*Vision, or AutoCAD, you have to transfer these graphics separately and convert them to the Macintosh PICT file format, or use the Encapsulated Post-Script Format (EPSF) as described in Appendix B. You can place Macintosh graphics (PICT files) directly into the PC version of Page-Maker, or you can first save the graphics as EPSF files and transfer them separately. You should store the graphics files in the same folder as your publication file so PageMaker can find them quickly at print time.

Once you have the graphics files transferred and converted into the appropriate format, use the PageMaker Place command to position the graphics in the receiving computer's publication file. By replacing the appropriately converted graphics you gain the benefit of being able to use PageMaker's automatic scaling to resize paint-type graphics, with a selection of optimal printing sizes that will depend upon the resolution of the printer (also called the destination or target printer) connected to the receiving computer.

To convert paint-type graphics you can use various public domain programs, such as MACTOWIN (MacPaint-to-Windows Paint), which converts MacPaint or PICT graphics to Windows Paint files for use with the PC version of PageMaker. The Missing Link ($99, PC Quik-Art, Inc.) handles a variety of paint-type graphic file formats including MacPaint, Windows Paint, GEM Paint, PC Paint, PC Paintbrush, BLOAD (PIC files), Dr. Halo, EGA Paint, and Publisher's Paintbrush.

A final alternative, if there is no way to convert a graphic from its native format to the Macintosh or PC format, is to scan the graphic and save it as a TIFF (Tag Image File Format) file, or as an EPSF (Encapsulated PostScript Format) file. TIFF and EPSF files can be imported into any version of PageMaker. You can also create an EPSF file by tracing over a MacPaint or PICT image using the Adobe Illustrator program for the Macintosh, which creates a PostScript representation of the artwork.

Transferring By Disk

You can use a variety of methods to transfer data to and from various PC-compatible computers. The easiest method is by exchanging floppy disks, and many vendors offer disk drives that accept PC-formatted 5 1/4-inch disks that hold 360 kilobytes (roughly 360,000 characters). You can transfer information by copying files from one disk to another. You may be able to transfer files on PC AT-compatible disks which can hold up to 1.2 megabytes (roughly 1.2 million characters). Another method is to use portable hard disk cartridges, portable hard disks, or magnetic tape cartridges for larger files.

For Macintosh computers you can purchase an optional 5 1/4-inch disk drive for reading and writing PC-formatted 5 1/4-inch disks (360 kilobytes each), from Apple, Abaton, AST, or Dayna.

When using MS-DOS add-in cards with the Macintosh SE and Macintosh II, such as the AST Mac86 (for the SE) or Mac286 (for the II) packages, your Macintosh is turned into a PC-compatible computer.

Drives C, A, and B are simulated by Macintosh disks or folders. DOS applications run in a window on the Macintosh screen which can be scrolled and resized so that other windows also appear on the screen. The Mac86 add-in card for the Macintosh SE provides PC XT performance; the Mac286 add-in card for the Macintosh II provides PC AT performance. Both cards let the Macintosh keyboard, mouse, display, hard disk, and printer emulate MS-DOS counterparts (the mouse emulates a Microsoft Mouse). The display can emulate the IBM Monochrome and IBM Color Graphics Adaptors (color on the II, black and white on the SE), and the Hercules monochrome adaptor. Your ImageWriter or LaserWriter (or LaserWriter Plus) can emulate an Epson FX-80 printer, and DOS applications that output PostScript for printing can use the LaserWriter's native PostScript features.

You can even run copy-protected PC software on the simulated drive C, although applications that use a parallel port for copy protection can't run because the Macintosh does not provide a parallel port. You can transfer files to and from a Macintosh folder using the simulated drive D and the MS-DOS COPY command. Files stored on the simulated D drive can be accessed by the Macintosh Finder and System.

We do not have the space to describe MS-DOS operations, but there is one very important feature relating to communications: the ability to copy or cut data from one window, such as the Macintosh version of Page-Maker, and paste the data into another window running a DOS application. Also you can copy or cut data from a DOS window and paste it into the Macintosh PageMaker publication.

Mac86 uses an Intel 8086 processor for compatibility with PC XT computers, and Mac286 uses an Intel 80286 processor for compatibility with PC AT computers. The add-in cards will not run software that requires any special PC Bus hardware, except floppy disk drives and the display adaptors mentioned above.

Transferring By Network

A popular method for managing the sharing of information among different types of computers is a *local area network*: computers linked by twisted-pair or wide-band cable, with files available to some or all computers through the use of a file server — a computer with a hard disk containing the files that are shared. Some networks are controlled by the file server computer; others allow any computer on the network to act as a file server.

PageMaker publication files can be shared over these networks just as easily as other files, but you may not receive high-quality output if you use a printer that is substantially different from the target printer. In addition, PageMaker prefers that you leave graphics files in the directories (or folders) they were in when you placed them. For faster operation, first copy the graphics files to the same directory or folder as the publication, and then place the graphics. The recommended method for organizing files on a network for production and printing is to copy any shared files into a local disk storage device for use with PageMaker, and then to print the publication from the same computer with which you placed those files onto PageMaker pages.

The AppleTalk network from Apple Computer can connect several Macintosh computers to each other, to one or more LaserWriters, and to PCs and Personal Systems that are IBM-compatible. Other choices include interface boxes, called "gateways," that connect PC networks and other networks to AppleTalk (available from third-party vendors). Or, you can link PCs and Macintosh computers in an Ethernet network from 3Com Corporation, which can also be used to link PCs and Macintosh computers to minicomputers and mainframes.

AppleTalk is a good choice for sharing a LaserWriter between Macintosh computers and PCs, or if you want to have several PC users sharing one LaserWriter. You can choose from the AppleTalk PC Card ($399 for each PC, Apple Computer), the PC MacBridge board ($650 for each PC, Tangent Technologies), or the TOPS network board ($349 for each PC, $149 for each Mac, Centram).

The software supplied with these products allows the transfer of PageMaker publication files (and other types of files) simply and easily from Macintosh computers to PCs and vice-versa. The PC MacBridge product, for example, lets you copy files by choosing that function from a menu. Another method is to use electronic mail software such as InBox (Think Technologies) to send publication files, text files, and graphics files as part of electronic mail messages to a user at another computer linked with AppleTalk (using TOPS, PC MacBridge, or AppleTalk PC).

The TOPS network lets you designate a disk drive as "published" — you can access the drive as if it were attached to your system. With TOPS, you "publish" a disk or folder from the Macintosh over AppleTalk, and treat it as a separate disk on the PC (such as drive E), then use the COPY command on the PC to copy files from the Macintosh to the PC, or vice-versa. You can also "publish" a PC disk or directory and treat it as a separate disk on the Macintosh, represented by a special icon; you can then drag a file from that disk to a Macintosh disk.

There are many features in TOPS that make it a superb network, including access modes that can restrict access, the ability to browse volumes and list a volume's *clients* (users sharing that volume), and many shortcuts. However, one feature of TOPS to mention in this appendix is the "quick copy conversion" feature and the full conversion utility offered with TOPS. The "quick conversion" feature copies only ASCII text when transferring a file from one TOPS volume to another, leaving out any unrecognized characters (such as formatting and control characters). You can see what characters TOPS will recognize by first clicking the Help button for the selected file and looking at the "sample" or "filtered sample" window.

For full conversion between file formats such as MultiMate to MacWrite, or MacWrite to WordStar, or Lotus 1-2-3 to Excel, Centram provides a version of the MacLink Plus program with settings documents (files you can use to launch an application program with appropriate settings already set), called TOPS Translator. (The MacLink Plus program is described in the next section.)

Another program that offers file transfer over a network is the electronic mail package InBox ($350 starter kit, $125 per connection for the Macintosh, $195 per connection for the PC, Think Technologies). InBox lets you establish electronic mail across an entire AppleTalk network with gateways to other networks. You can use InBox with most AppleTalk cards for the PC, including the AppleTalk PC Card from Apple, PC MacBridge from Tangent, and TOPS from Centram. Any type of PC or Macintosh file can be sent "clipped" to an electronic mail message, and InBox can run simultaneously with Centram's TOPS and with both

Apple's and Tangent's LaserWriter spooling programs for the PC.

With InBox, you use one Macintosh on the network as the Message Center. This Macintosh should have a hard disk to be able to handle a lot of message traffic. Every user on the network can have an electronic mailbox in the Message Center. When you send a message to someone, the message is stored in this mailbox at the Message Center. The receiver can read the message and save it on his or her disk.

The benefit of this arrangement is that a Macintosh user can send or receive messages and transfer files with a PC user at any time, even when the PC user has turned off the machine. The PC user, of course, has the same benefit. Neither party has to leave the machine on to keep available a published directory or folder, as with TOPS file transfer (but InBox can run simultaneously with TOPS). Nor do the people have to be actively involved at both ends of the transfer, as with MacLink Plus and other communications programs (however, MacLink Plus is useful for format conversion in addition to using InBox).

Transferring By Serial Cable or Modem

Direct connection over serial (RS-232C) cable, or modem link through a telephone line, is the least expensive way to connect a PC-compatible computer to a Macintosh. It is also the only way to transfer files to and from a computer other than a PC (such as a mainframe, a Kaypro, Osborne, other CP/M-based machines, Atari, and Commodore computers).

With a serial cable connection or a modem-to-modem connection you can use a communications or transfer program, such as MacLink Plus ($195, Dataviz). The MacLink Plus package includes a cable that plugs into an asynchronous port on the PC-compatible computer and into the modem port on the Macintosh, and PC and Macintosh software to enable the machines to communicate.

MacLink Plus provides a table of file formats on the PC and a matching table of Macintosh formats, so that you can transfer Lotus 1-2-3 files to Microsoft Excel or vice-versa. You can translate nearly every popular PC word processing file format into the Macintosh version of Microsoft

Word, or MacWrite, file formats. You can also translate data from dBASE II and other data base structures to Macintosh data base structures.

Essential to any file transfer method is the use of communication *protocols*. Protocols let you transfer information with the secure feeling that there will be no errors placed in the data from noisy telephone lines or other electromagnetic interference. MacLink Plus provides a protocol for transfer, and communication programs usually offer one or more protocols. The best protocols for transferring PageMaker files from one computer to another are Xmodem, Kermit, X.PC, or MNP. In every case you need to use the same protocol in the programs running on both computers.

You can use the Xmodem protocol to transfer files to PCs from Macintosh computers, and to Macs from PCs, and from both types of computers to CP/M, Apple //, and other computers — and back again — without loss of data integrity. Almost every communication program for PC-compatible computers offers the Xmodem protocol, including PC Talk III (Headlands Press), Crosstalk Mk.4 (Digital Communications Associates, Inc.), Relay (VMPC), ProComm (PIL Software Systems), MaxiMITE (Mycroft Labs), and public domain programs such as QMODEM.

Transferring to a Typesetting Service

You can send PageMaker publication files to a typesetting service that uses PostScript typesetters and film recorders, or PostScript converters for other typesetters and devices. Many services use PageMaker. You must supply the publication file on disk, or transfer the publication file using a modem as described above.

Other services require a downloadable PostScript file. You can create one quickly by selecting Print from the File menu, then hold down the Option key while clicking the Print button to display a PostScript options dialog box. Click the Print PostScript to disk option, and click the Normal button to save a normal PostScript file that can be sent to a service bureau, or to a remote printer. You can then transfer that file using a modem, a direct cable (such as MacLink Plus), or a disk.

Use the EPS button instead of the Normal button to save a single page (including a display version of the page) in an EPS format (EPSF) file, for use with other programs that assemble PostScript programs. Use this option to save a page to place into anotherpublication file, or to save a file that can be imported into another PostScript application program.

PostScript options in this dialog box are set to default values, until you click their boxes to change them. PageMaker assumes your file will be sent to a printer that does not have Aldus Prep, but if the destination printer already has Aldus Prep, you must click this box (the X will disappear) to not include Aldus Prep. Also, uncheck the Make Aldus Prep permanent box, unless the destination printer does not have Aldus Prep, and this is the first of two or more files you will transfer: turn off the Make Aldus Prep permanent option for all subsequent files after the first file.

You also need to download bit-map and PostScript fonts, unless they are already downloaded or resident in the destination printer. Both of these options are checked unless you uncheck them, because PageMaker assumes the destination printer does not have the same fonts you use in your document. Uncheck the Download bit-map fonts option, unless you want to print a bit map version of the font (such as for a special effect in a headline) instead of a PostScript version of the font. You must uncheck the Download PostScript fonts option if the destination printer already has the downloadable fonts you need, or the file might not print.

If you turn off both bit-map and PostScript font download options, Courier may be substituted for any fonts you use in your document that are not available in the destination printer.

After selecting PostScript print options, you might want to save this version of the file as a new, separate file, or save it in a different folder, or on a different disk than the original. Click the Set file name button to save the file with another name, on another disk, or in another folder, so that the new file does not overwrite the current file. To print the file to disk after setting desired options, click the Print buttons in the PostScript Options and Print dialog boxes.

Printing to Spoolers

Even one user with a LaserWriter can derive benefit by using network products such as a print spooler, which greatly reduces the waiting time for printing operations by letting you go back to work on your computer while printing takes place. You share printers simply by connecting them to the network and, when you are ready to print, choosing which printer you want with the Chooser.

Spoolers are programs that intercept data on its way to the printer and store the data in a disk file called a *spool file*. The disk accepts the data faster than the printer, so the Macintosh issuing the print command thinks that printing has finished and returns control to you. The spooler then initiates printing (*despooling*) and queues other print requests.

Print spooling can be complicated on the Macintosh, especially if you are using downloadable fonts, or a special printer preparation file such as PageMaker's AldusPrep rather than Apple's LaserPrep. The spooler intercepts the data in either of two places: right after the Macintosh constructs QuickDraw commands to describe the page to be printed, or right after the Macintosh translates the QuickDraw commands to Post-Script instructions for the printer. Usually a spooler that intercepts at the QuickDraw stage is faster at freeing the Macintosh than a spooler that waits until after PostScript conversion.

Other differences between spoolers, besides speed, is how much disk space and memory space is taken up by the spooler and spool files, whether the spooler can handle downloadable fonts and programs such as PageMaker, and how the spooler lets you manage the queue.

Finally, there are spoolers that operate on each Macintosh that needs one (client spooling), and a spooler from Apple that operates on a Macintosh that is dedicated to both file serving and spooling (server spooling). Both types of spoolers can manage the sharing of a PostScript printer with multiple users on a network.

The most popular spoolers for the Macintosh are LaserSpeed ($99 single user, $495 Office Pak/5 users, Think Technologies), LaserServe ($95 per user, Infosphere), and SuperLaserSpool ($395 multiuser version, $149.95 single user version, SuperMac Software).

All of the above spoolers are client-type spoolers that run on individual Macintosh computers. Of the above spoolers, SuperLaserSpool offers the most features and the best overall performance. The spooler works with the ImageWriter as well as LaserWriter and other PostScript devices (such as the Linotronic typesetters), and intercepts data at the QuickDraw level, saving compact QuickDraw code to the spool file. SuperLaser-Spool uses less disk space than other spoolers that store PostScript (which takes up more space), and offers a Preview function that lets you display pages while they are in the print queue.

Another great feature of SuperLaserSpool is the ability to take spool files and despool them on another Macintosh running SuperLaserSpool. For example, you could take spool files to your typesetting service and despool them without running the application program (however, you may need the downloadable font files and prep files associated with the application). You can also designate a folder on a published TOPS volume that resides on another Macintosh, then ship spool files to that volume for spooling from that Macintosh.

APPENDIX E
Bibliography

Books

Adobe Systems, Inc., *PostScript Language Reference Manual* and *Post-Script Language Tutorial and Cookbook* (2 volume set), Addison-Wesley Publishing Co., Reading, MA. 1985.

Baxter, John, *Macintosh Desktop Typography*, *Macintosh Desktop Design*, and *Macintosh Desktop Production*, The Baxter Group, PO Box 61672, Sunnyvale, CA 94086. 1986.

Berryman, Greg, *Notes on Graphic Design and Visual Communication*, William Kaufmann, Inc., Los Altos, CA. 1984.

Bove, Tony, Rhodes, Cheryl, and Thomas, Wes, *The Art of Desktop Publishing 2nd Ed.*, Bantam Computer Books, New York, NY. 1987.

Felici, James, and Nace, Ted, *Desktop Publishing Skills*, Addison-Wesley Publishing Company, Inc., Reading, MA. 1987.

Garcia, Mario R., *Contemporary Newspaper Design 2nd Ed.*, Prentice-Hall, Inc., Englewood Cliffs, NJ. 1987.

Green, Michael, *Zen and the Art of the Macintosh, Discoveries on the Path to Computer Enlightenment*, Running Press Book Publishers, Philadelphia, PA. 1986.

Holt, Robert Lawrence, *How to Publish, Promote, and Sell Your Own Book*, St. Martin's Press, New York, NY. 1985.

International Paper Company, *Pocket Pal, A graphics arts production handbook*, International Paper Company, New York, NY. 1983. (Includes extensive Glossary of graphic arts terms.)

Laing, John, *Do-It-Yourself Graphic Design*, Macmillan Publishing, New York, NY. 1984.

Lem, Dean Phillip, *Graphics Master 3*, Dean Lem Associates, Inc., Los Angeles, CA. 1985.

Parker, Roger C., *The Aldus Guide to Basic Design*, Aldus Corp., Seattle, WA. 1987

Poynter, Dan, *The Self-Publishing Manual*, Para Publishing, Santa Barbara, CA. 1984.

Poynter, Dan, *Publishing Short-Run Books 4th Ed.*, Para Publishing, Santa Barbara, CA. 1987.

Seybold, John, and Dressler, Fritz, *Publishing From the Desktop*, Bantam Computer Books, New York, NY. 1987.

Solomon, Martin, *The Art of Typography*, Watson-Guptill Publications, a division of Billboard Publications, Inc., New York, NY. 1986.

Shibukawa, Ikuyoshi and Takahashi, Yumi, *Designer's Guide to Color*, *Designer's Guide to Color 2* and *Designer's Guide to Color 3*, Chronicle Books, San Francisco, CA. 1983, 1984, and 1986.

Simpson, MacKinnon, and Goodman, Robert B., *WhaleSong, A Pictorial History of Whaling and Hawai'i*, Beyond Words Publishing Company, Honolulu, HI. (808) 595-8166. 1986.

Strunk, William and White, E. B., *The Elements of Style*, Macmillan Publishing Co., New York, NY. 1972.

University of Chicago Press, *A Manual of Style*, University of Chicago Press, Chicago, IL. 1979.

Venolia, Jan, *Write Right!*, Ten Speed Press, Berkeley, CA. 1982.

White, Jan V., *Designing for Magazines* and*Editing by Design*, R.R. Bowker, New York, NY. 1982.

White, Jan V., *Graphic Idea Notebook*, R.R. Bowker, New York, NY. 1981.

White, Jan V., *Mastering Graphics*, R.R. Bowker, New York, NY. 1983.

White, Jan V., *Using Charts and Graphs*, R.R. Bowker, New York, NY. 1984.

Wilson, Adrian, *The Design of Books*, Gibbs M. Smith, Inc., Peregrine Smith Books, Salt Lake City, UT. 1974.

Magazines, Journals, Newspapers

American Printer, 300 West Adams Street, Chicago IL 60606. $35 per year.

Desktop Graphics, Dynamic Graphics, 6000 N Forest Pk Dr., PO Box 1901, Peoria, IL 61656-1901. (800) 255-8800. First issue free with software purchase.

Folio, the Magazine for Magazine Management, P. O. Box 4006, 125 Elm Street, New Canaan CT 06840. (203) 972-0761. $58 per year.

The Futurist, World Future Society, 4916 St. Elmo Avenue, Bethesda MD 20814. (301) 656-8274. $25 per year.

Graphic Perspective, Ashley House, 176 Wicksteed Avenue, Toronto, Ontario, M4G 2B6 Canada. (416) 422-1446. $40 per year.

Graphics Arts Monthly and The Printing Industry, Technical Publishing, 875 Third Avenue, New York NY 10022. (212) 605-9548. $50 per year.

Inside Print (formerly *Magazine Age*), MPE Inc., 125 Elm Street, New Canaan CT 06840. (203) 972-0761. $36 per year.

Magazine Design and Production, Globecom Publishing Ltd., 4551 West 107th Street #343, Overland KS 66207. $36 per year.

Personal Publishing, Renegade Publications, Box 390, Itasca IL 60143. $36 per year.

Printing Impressions, 401 North Broad Street, Philadelphia PA 19108. $50 per year.

Printing Journal, 2401 Charleston Road, Mountain View CA 94943. $16 per year.

Processed World, 41 Sutter Street #1829, San Francisco, CA 94104. (415) 495-6823. $10 per year.

Publish!, PC World Communications, 501 Second Street, #600, San Francisco, CA 94107. (415) 546-7722. $29.95 per year.

Publisher's Weekly, R. R. Bowker, 205 East 42nd Street, New York NY 10017. $89 per year.

Showpage, 1044 Howard Street, San Francisco, CA 94103. (415) 621-8808. $20 per year.

Small Press, the Magazine of Independent Publishing, R. R. Bowker, 205 East 42nd Street, New York NY 10017. $18 per year.

TypeWorld, 15 Oakridge Circle, Wilmington MA 01887. $20 per year.

VERBUM, Journal of Personal Computer Aesthetics, P.O. Box 15439, San Diego, CA 92115. (619) 463-9977. MCI Mail: VERBUM. $28 per year.

Newsletters

Brilliant Ideas for Publishers, Creative Brilliance Associates, 4709 Sherwood Road, Box 4237, Madison WI 53711. (608) 271-6867. Free to publishers.

CAP (Computer Aided Publishing) Report, InfoVision Inc., 52 Dragon Court, Woburn MA 01801. (617) 935-5186. $195 per year.

The Desktop Publisher, Aldus Corp., 616 First Avenue, Suite 400, Seattle WA 98104. (206) 441-8666. Free to registered users of Aldus software.

Desktop Publishing: Bove and Rhodes Inside Report, PC World Communications, 501 Second Street, #600, San Francisco, CA 94107. (415) 546-7722. $195 per year.

microPublishing Report, 2004 Curtis Avenue #A, Redondo Beach CA 90278. (213) 376-5724. $175 per year.

Quick Printer's Guide, Lambda Company, 3655 Frontier Avenue, Boulder CO 80301. (303) 449-4827. $75 per year.

ReCAP, Boston Computer Society, Desktop Publishing User Group, One Center Plaza, Boston, MA 02108. (617) 367-8080. $28 per year.

Seybold Report on Publishing Systems, Seybold Publications, Box 644, Media PA 19063. (215) 565-2480. $240 per year. *Seybold Report on Desktop Publishing*, $150 per year.

SWADTP, Southwest Association of Desktop Publishers, 1208 West Brooks, Norman, OK 73069. (405) 360-5554.

Writers Connection, Writers Connection, 1601 Saratoga-Sunnyvale Road, Suite 180, Cupertino, CA 95014. (408) 973-0227. $12 per year.

WYSIWYG, Ramos Publishing Company, 127 Columbia Avenue, Redwood City CA 94063. (415) 364-4867. $195 per year.

User Groups

Boston Computer Society, One Center Plaza, Boston, MA 02108. (617) 367-8080. $35 per year membership includes publications: *Boston Computer Society Update*, *re:CAP*, *the publishing/computer-aided publishing newsletter*, and *Graphics News*, plus other newsletters available to members at $4 each per year.

National Association of Desktop Publishers, PO Box 508, Boston, MA 02215-9998. (617) 437-6472. $95 per year.

New England PageMaker Users Group, c/o WordWorks, 222 Richmond Street, Providence, RI 02903. (401) 274-0033. Also represented by MCM Associates, 22 1/2 Lee Street, Marblehead, MA 01945. (617) 639-1548.

SouthWest Association of DeskTop Publishers, 1208 West Brooks, Norman, OK 73069. (405) 360-5554, 682-8541, and 364-2751.

Technical References

Encapsulated PostScript (EPS) format was developed and placed in the public domain and is maintained by Altsys Corporation. It was originally designed as a standard for mixed PostScript and QuickDraw files. A copy of the specification is available for $1 postage from Altsys Corp., Atth: Jim Von Ehr, 720 Avenue F, Suite 108, Plano TX 75074. (214) 424-4888. MCI Mail: ALTSYS

Tag Image File Format (TIFF) was originally developed and placed in the public domain by Aldus Corporation, in cooperation with several scanner and printer manufacturers. It was designed as a format for digital data interchange, and is independent of specific operating systems, filing systems, compilers and processors. For a copy of the latest description of TIFF, and further information, contact Aldus or Microsoft. Address queries to: Tim Davenport, Aldus Corp., 411 First Avenue South, Seattle WA 98104. (206) 622-5500, or Manny Vellon, Microsoft Corp., 16011 NE 36th Way, Box 97017. (206) 882-8080.

Index